THE SUEZ CANAL IN PEACE AND WAR

Ferdinand de Lesseps

THE SUEZ CANAL

in

PEACE AND WAR

1869-1969

by

HUGH J. SCHONFIELD

UNIVERSITY OF MIAMI PRESS
CORAL GABLES, FLORIDA

First published in Great Britain 1952 under the title
THE SUEZ CANAL IN WORLD AFFAIRS

This revised edition © 1969 by Hugh J. Schonfield

Library of Congress Catalog Card Number: 70-86500
SBN 87024-126-5

Manufactured in Great Britain

CONTENTS

ILLUSTRATIONS

ACKNOWLEDGMENTS

The author wishes to thank Mr. John Gilbert for his invaluable assistance in the preparation of the new edition of this book and the proprietors of *Punch* for the cartoon "Mose in Egitto".

Grateful acknowledgment is made for the use of the following pictures:

Radio Times Hulton Picture Library for:
Cutting the Sweet Water Canal at Nefriche.
Cutting the Canal near Chalouf.
The Isthmus of Suez Maritime Canal near Kantara.
The Prince of Wales letting the waters of the Mediterranean into the Bitter Lakes.
Opening of the Suez Canal.
Bird's eye view of Suez Canal, 1869.
An aerial view of the ships sunk by Nasser to block the Canal, 1956.

Camera Press Limited for:
The Suez Canal Company offices at Port Said.
An aerial view of the Canal, prior to the British evacuation of the Canal base.
Contrasts—a passenger liner and an Arab craft laden with cotton.
Widening the Canal. Egyptian labourers moving soil.
An Israeli soldier stands guard at Kantara after the Six-Day War.
The ruins of the Nasr Oil Refinery at Suez after shelling by Israeli guns.

Paul Popper Ltd. for:
British troops outside wrecked police headquarters in Port Said.
A British soldier watches a minesweeper at work in the Canal after the cease fire.

United Press International for:
The Statue of de Lesseps at Port Said after being dynamited.
Israeli soldiers alongside the Canal at Kantara.
Two small vessels stranded in the Canal after the Six-Day War.

Newsphot, Tel Aviv for:
Smoke pours from the Nasr Oil Refinery at Suez after shelling by Israeli guns.
The burning Nasr Oil Refinery at Suez after shelling by Israeli guns.

PREFACE

WHATEVER may be thought of the conclusions reached by certain geopoliticians, no one can gainsay that physical geography has exerted a profound influence on ethnical and political history. From the most ancient times man moved in quest of better pasture lands and hunting grounds. Settled life and civilisation sprang up along the line of the great river valleys and on fertile plains. Rising ground was chosen for tribal security. Kingdoms and empires flourished through favourable geographical conditions, and embarked on conquest and exploration to procure more of natural riches and resources. National territories were largely defined by natural boundaries, and the character of their climate and products determined their degree of potency and self-sufficiency. With the coming of sea and ocean-going vessels States with seaboards provided with good harbours quickly forged ahead of those which were land-locked.

Our modern age is no less affected than the past by geographical features and considerations, and in some ways to an even greater and more terrifying extent. Scientific discovery and technological development have created a vast demand for raw materials which previously were utilised on a small scale or for other purposes or not at all: timber, coal, iron, oil, rubber, and a variety of ores and deposits. Possession of these has not only made countries rich and powerful: it has led to the exploitation of more backward peoples by the mechanically skilled in lands where such resources exist and can be secured by concession, domination, or conquest. In the manœuvring of Great Powers for political and material advantage in a world where distance is being largely annihilated by jet-propelled planes flying faster than sound it is still geography that substantially dictates policy. The configurations of the Earth are minutely studied for what they can offer by way of naval base or air strip, defensive line or concentration area. Alliances are sought or demanded, revolutions are staged, to check or hold, contain or outflank. Lands and seas are estimated at their strategic worth.

It has been the fortune and misfortune of Egypt that she lies between the Mediterranean and the Indian Ocean, herself the gateway between East and West. For here is a natural bridge, which he who takes and holds may use to bestride the world like a colossus. And here is a people, dependent on a river, fenced in by deserts, which can never—even if so minded—become a colossus. The greatness which is Egypt can never be an expanding, materialistic greatness. Her grandeur and influence, and better so, must be of a spiritual order.

Inevitably Egypt has been coveted by a succession of Great Powers; and since the narrow neck of land separating the Mediterranean from the Red Sea was finally pierced by the persistent efforts of De Lesseps, and the Suez Canal became part of the world's geography, control of this vital artery has made her even more desirable. It is one of the great tragedies of history that a work designed in the interests of peaceful commerce and closer relations between East and West should have become so involved in international rivalry and strife.

The Canal belongs to Egypt; but it also belongs to Mankind. How can it effectively serve these two masters? That is the modern riddle of the sphinx which has to be solved. Perhaps the true answer to the riddle is: when the two shall be one, and under an enlightened world government all geography and all humanity shall be unified. Meanwhile, much depends on Egypt herself, and as much, if not more, on the Great Powers who have it within their capacity to turn conflict into co-operation, and so to remove the fears which madden men and nations.

HUGH J. SCHONFIELD.

CHAPTER I

THE CANAL OF THE PHARAOHS

ONE of the oldest engineering enterprises considered by civilised man was the linking of the Mediterranean with the Red Sea by a waterway. Its advantages were recognised in the twentieth century B.C., though of course to a much less extent than in the twentieth century A.D. If an Egyptian merchant of the reign of Pharaoh Sesostris could converse with his modern brother of the reign of King Farouk, it would be found that they were in substantial agreement on the commercial importance of such a speedy, safe, and economical means of transport.

Geographically, Egypt is the natural gateway between East and West, and when once intercontinental trade routes were opened up it was inevitable that through her should pass the wealth and produce of the nations. In her prosperous cities were sold and exchanged the goods of the Far East, of Persia, Babylon, and Arabia, of Somaliland, and the Sudan, of Greece and Rome, of the southern French seaboard, of northern Africa, Spain, and the Isles of the Sea. The possessor of Egypt held the mart of the world. No wonder then that successive empires have cast envious eyes upon this favoured land, and have sought by conquest to secure by her peculiar strategic and commercial position the fulfilment of their dreams of domination.

On the east of Egypt a comparatively narrow neck of land, narrower still in ancient times—the Isthmus of Suez—joined Africa to Asia. The tongue of the Red Sea, since somewhat receded, licked up close to Mediterranean waters, and seemed as if it would willingly dart across the intervening stretch of country. Not so far to the west, and almost parallel, the River Nile flowed, and did indeed reach the middle sea through its seven or eight original Delta channels, one of which—the Pelusiac—so enticingly crossed the edge of the Isthmus. It would have been surprising if acute minds of the progressive world of four thousand years ago had not

1

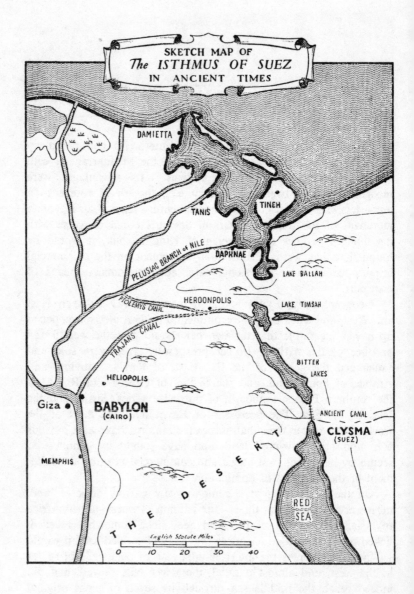

SKETCH MAP OF
The ISTHMUS OF SUEZ
IN ANCIENT TIMES

DAMIETTA

TANIS

TINEH

PELUSIAC BRANCH of NILE

DAPHNAE

LAKE BALLAH

PTOLEMYS CANAL

HEROONPOLIS

LAKE TIMSAH

TRAJANS CANAL

HELIOPOLIS

BITTER
LAKES

Giza

BABYLON
(CAIRO)

ANCIENT CANAL

CLYSMA
(SUEZ)

MEMPHIS

T H E   D E S E R T

RED
SEA

English Statute Miles

0   10   20   30   40

associated these circumstances, and envisaged the possibility of providing the Nile with an additional artificial mouth opening into the Red Sea, and connected with the Mediterranean through the Pelusiac branch.

Before the growth of the central empires of Greece and Rome, and the commercial development of Europe, access by shipping from the Red Sea to western waters could not perhaps be regarded as a vital necessity, though it had its obvious uses. The earliest Egyptian canal builders were immediately concerned with providing a passage for vessels from the Red Sea to the great interior cities along the Nile. From the dawn of Egyptian civilisation a profitable trade had been carried on with the Land of Punt (Somaliland ?), and the country had been enriched with the gold, ivory, and spices brought back from the East African coast. A wealth of merchandise also passed to and fro between Egypt and the lands bordering on the Persian Gulf.

Details of the construction of the first navigable canal linking the Nile with the Red Sea are lost in the mists of antiquity. Tradition claims that it was Sesostris, a Pharaoh of the Twelfth Dynasty (*circa* 2000 B.C.), who first set his hand to this enterprise. At intervals, certainly, during the next thousand years such a canal was available to shipping : it is remembered as the Canal of the Pharaohs. Issuing from the Pelusiac branch of the Nile at a point north of the city of Bubastis, it followed the green belt of the Wadi Tumilat—the Land of Goshen—eastward, and then turned south and reached the Red Sea through the Bitter Lakes at the port of Clysma.

Political changes caused the maintenance of this canal to be abandoned at some time before the beginning of the seventh century B.C., when it had almost completely silted up. The famous Pharaoh Necho (612 B.C.), who defeated Josiah, King cf Judah, at the Battle of Megiddo, undertook to recut it. He employed 120,000 slaves on the labour ; but finally desisted from his attempt when he was warned by an oracle that he was preparing the way for the barbarian invader. This oracle was thought afterwards to refer to the Persians, who, less than a century later, conquered Egypt under Cambyses. It was a Persian ruler, Darius Hystaspes (521 B.C.), who restored and enlarged the Canal of the Pharaohs.

There is all the arrogance of the Oriental despot in the language of the monumental record of his achievement, which has been recovered :

" I am a Persian : with the power of Persia I conquered Egypt. I ordered this canal to be dug from the river called Pirava (the Nile) which flows in Egypt, to the sea which comes out of Persia (the Red Sea). This canal was afterwards dug as I had commanded. . . ."

Subsequently Darius, for a reason unknown, destroyed the last section of the canal ; but it was re-excavated by his successor Xerxes. Herodotus* mentions that the transit occupied four days and that it could be navigated by two triremes abreast.

Under the Ptolemies, Philadelphus (286 B.C.) and Euergetes (246 B.C.), the Canal of the Pharaohs was reconditioned, and in part carried along a new course. Its terminus was now at Arsinoë, near the modern Suez, and a lock with a double gate was built from fear of inundation. Ptolemy Philadelphus had proposed to cut a canal direct through the Isthmus, thus joining sea to sea ; but he abandoned the project in the belief that the level of the Red Sea was so much higher than that of the Mediterranean that it would flood the country†—a belief that persisted down to the early part of the nineteenth century. It has been suggested that the inspirers of the scheme for a direct canal were the Greeks, who were fully alive to the commercial advantages of the undertaking. The port of Pelusium on the Mediterranean seaboard of the Isthmus was at this time a flourishing rival to the new city of Alexandria, and but for the error in calculating the levels a true Suez Canal from sea to sea might have been an accomplished fact more than two thousand years ago.

The Roman occupation of Egypt saw the Canal of the Pharaohs converted in due course into the River of Trajan. The Emperor Trajan (98 A.D.) cleaned out the old canal, which had passed through so many vicissitudes, and gave it a better water supply by uniting it with the main stream of the Nile at Babylon (near Cairo). As now constructed the canal described an arc, and remained navigable until some time in the third century A.D. By the reign of Constantine it was once again out of commission.

With the Arab conquest of Egypt in the seventh century the Nile-Red Sea canal entered on the last phase of its history. By permission of the Caliph Omar, Amru, Governor of Egypt, reopened

---

*Euterpe, 158-9.
†See Diodorus, Bk. I, i ; Strabo, Bk. XVII ; and Pliny, Bk. XVI, c, 29.

the waterway in the winter of 641-642, and until the end of the eighth century it rendered useful service under the name of the Canal of the Prince of the Faithful. It was finally closed in 776 A.D. by order of the second Abbassid Caliph, Aben-Jafar-Al Mansour, as a blockading measure against the revolted holy cities of Mecca and Medina. In Amru's time again the project was mooted of cutting a canal from Lake Timsah in the middle of the Isthmus to the Mediterranean ; but it was not proceeded with on the ground that it would confer advantage on the shipping of Christian countries.

From this period commerce between East and West *via* Egypt steadily declined. Through the journeys of Marco Polo and other travellers the northern overland route to India and China was developed in the thirteenth and fourteenth centuries, until the growth and aggressive power of Turkey robbed the merchants of this avenue for their profitable traffic, and brought to an end the commercial supremacy in Europe of the Venetians and Genoese which depended so largely on the Levant.

A new means of access to the East became a crying need in face of the Turkish barrier. While Christopher Columbus sought for this in the West, another intrepid voyager sailed to the South down the western coast of Africa and succeeded in rounding the Cape of Good Hope. His expedition reached India on May 20, 1498, and after remaining six months, was able to return to Lisbon—the port of embarkation—by the same route. He brought back a letter from the Zamorin of Malabar to the King of Portugal :

" Vasco da Gama, a nobleman of your household, has visited my kingdom and has given me great pleasure. In my kingdom there is abundance of cinnamon, cloves, ginger, pepper, and precious stones. What I seek from thy country is gold, silver, coral, and scarlet."

Thus was opened up the long but effective ocean route to India and the Far East, which prevailed for more than four hundred years, and gave successively to the Atlantic maritime Powers, the Portuguese, Dutch, French, and British, a virtual monopoly of the Oriental trade.

The Venetians took very hardly the loss of their lucrative commerce, and as early as 1504 the Council of Ten seriously discussed the possibility of suggesting to the Sultan of Egypt the cutting of a Suez Canal. The idea, however, was not proceeded with, and we hear nothing further of such a proposal until nearly the close of the century. Then it was put forward, not by any of the European Powers but by the Turkish Pasha of Egypt, El-Eudj-Ali. He suggested to his suzerain what was virtually the reopening of the old Nile-Red Sea canal, with access to the Mediterranean, which would not only facilitate the transport of materials across the Isthmus but by providing a waterway between the two seas would give a great advantage to the Turkish fleet. The details were duly reported to Henry III of France by his Ambassador at Constantinople, Savary de Lancosme. " This wonderful scheme," he wrote, " has so greatly inflated their usual vanity and has so stirred their ambition and avarice that they already believe they have the treasures and gems of India." Though the Sultan might be enamoured of the project he was eventually deterred from sanctioning it owing to the difficulties and the heavy cost.

Among the European States France now held a leading position in the eastern Mediterranean, and for geographical reasons her interest in the ancient commercial route through Egypt was bound to be greater than that of any other country. While England and Holland could be content with the Cape route as an avenue for trade with the Far East, France had the needs of her southern seaboard to consider, especially of her important port of Marseilles. Importation on competitive terms was impossible so long as goods shipped from India to Suez had to be carried by camel to Cairo, then conveyed by canal to Alexandria, and finally trans-shipped to Europe. The only solution, an anonymous writer represented to Richelieu, would be " a canal cut from Suez to Cairo, such as was effected under the ancient Egyptian kings, and perhaps under Solomon." In this way, continued the writer, warming to his theme, " the Turk will expect to enrich his country ; Venice will recover ; Marseilles will become powerful ; the ancient commerce with Abyssinia will revive. By this junction of the seas, the Spaniards will be weakened in the Mediterranean, and all other princes strengthened."

The political difficulties, however, quite apart from the practical ones, were at this time insurmountable. Leibnitz, the German philosopher, proposed at least to remove the former by recommending to Louis XIV in an enthusiastic memoir that France should

The Stone of Darius recording the cutting of the Nile-Red Sea Canal

Mose in Egitto. Cartoon published in *Punch*, December 11th, 1875, illustrating Disraeli's action in buying, on behalf of the British Government, the Khedive's shares in the Suez Canal Company

seize Egypt, and with it secure all the prizes of the eastern traffic. His sentiments were addressed to " The Most Christian Monarch," but Louis' Minister for Foreign Affairs intervened with the acid reminder that these were not the days of St. Louis the Crusader, and that Holy Wars were out of fashion. Nevertheless a forward move was made by Colbert's formation of a Company of the Levant, which obtained a concession from the Sultan giving its merchants a transport monopoly and a right of navigation in the Red Sea, hitherto barred to Christian vessels. This effected a substantial reduction in transit dues and costs.

In the literature of the seventeenth century the most outstanding contribution to the discussion of a Suez Canal was undoubtedly that of Jacques Savary in his work *The Complete Merchant,* which passed through a number of editions. The attitude of Savary was that of a patriotic business man who sees fully the advantages that will accrue to his country's trade from the control and development of the Egyptian route. He was a firm believer in the possibility of competing successfully with the Cape route through the saving in time and risk. He strongly advocated the cutting of a canal direct through the Isthmus, having its Mediterranean outlet in the neighbourhood of Damietta. He was aware of the difficulties which faced the Ptolemies and others in studying this plan, occasioned by the supposed higher level of the Red Sea over the Mediterranean, to which he added the Red Sea tides ; but he was convinced that the Grand Monarch would be able to overcome every technical obstacle.

From Savary's time the project for constructing a Suez Canal became of keen interest to the merchant and engineer, and ceased to be limited to the consideration of diplomats.

The India trade so much increased during the eighteenth century that to the popular mind in Europe this source of wealth acquired an almost fabulous character. Despite the wars and political upheavals which more frequently engaged the attention of governments elsewhere, the several India companies, and particularly those of England and France, developed their activities to such an extent, and with such strong rivalry, as to make it impossible to dissociate commercial from political imperialism. The loss of Canada by France and of the American Colonies by England contributed towards the transfer of the struggle for power to the

B

Asiatic theatre. Already as a result of the Seven Years' War, and the victories of Clive, France had been forced to relinquish her ambitions of an Indian empire. But the magnitude of the Far Eastern traffic seaborne over thousands of leagues assured that the conflict would continue, not for the territorial prize but for control of the cheapest, safest, and most expeditious trade route.

No triumph in Europe, however spectacular, could be anything but barren if it did not carry with it the exploitation of the riches of the Orient.

It was with this knowledge that Britain strove to be Mistress of the Seas, so that the Cape route might be ever free for her merchantmen. It was with this knowledge that France was concerned to reopen the old route through Egypt, and so to deal a heavy blow at the Cape commerce.

British traders seem to have been aware of the designs of France long before the British Government took any serious cognisance of them ; and the French representatives kept a watchful eye on the efforts of the East India Company and the Levant Company to secure even innocent privileges in Egypt, and especially on the illicit use by English vessels of the port of Suez, barred to the shipping of Christian Powers.

But even France was slow to take any official action to serve her own ends, though her agents and merchants in Egypt ceaselessly requested that she should possess herself of that country. Among others, Mure, the French Consul-General in Egypt, wrote :

" The proximity of India, the activity that would result from the communications of this part of the world (with the East) by the Red Sea, the facilities for transporting merchandise from Suez to the Nile by a canal which needs only to be recut in part ... will infinitely lessen the time, expense, and loss of seamen which voyages by the Cape of Good Hope occasion, and will assure preference to merchandise employing the ancient route."

In spite of this and similar communications, France did not immediately contemplate the annexation of Egypt ; her Government contented itself with negotiating treaties with the Beys which would have the effect of giving her merchants transport facilities through the country. Nevertheless the tendency of these treaties was sufficiently plain to such men as George Baldwin of the British Levant Company, who warned England :

"France, in possession of Egypt, would possess the master-key to all the trading stations of the earth. Enlightened, as the times are, in the general arts of navigation and commerce, she might make it the emporium of the world: she might make it the *awe* of the Eastern world, by the facility she would command of transporting her forces thither, by surprise, in any number, and at any time ; and England would hold her possessions in India at the mercy of France."

The British Government so far responded to this warning as to decide to re-establish her Consulate in Egypt and to assure English merchants of an equal share in any rights of transit which Murad Bey might be prevailed upon to grant ; but it was not for one moment considered that French activities offered any real threat to Anglo-Indian communications. Control of the Cape route was deemed adequate to meet any challenge.

It was almost in vain that Mr. (afterwards Colonel) James Capper, in his book *Observations on the Passage to India through Egypt* (1785), pointed out the folly of depending on a route which at some time might be superseded by the discovery of a better. It was just in this way that former Powers had been deprived of their supremacy.

"When the Venetians lost the India trade." he wrote, "no violence, no finesse was used to deprive them of it ; the trade died away of itself, because the Portuguese and other European nations, passing round the Cape of Good Hope, could by means of the shortness and safety of the voyage, afford to under-sell them in those articles of India commerce which they received only by the more tedious, dangerous, and expensive channel of the Red Sea. But the probability of the danger of the trade by this route becoming prejudicial to ours by the Cape of Good Hope, being admitted in its fullest extent ; are we to suppose that other European nations are so blind to their own interest, so strangely ignorant, or so absurdly indolent, as not to discover it, and immediately avail themselves of their knowledge ? If goods can really be brought cheaper from India to Europe that way, in vain shall we attempt to oppose the general interests of Europe and Asia ; the Indian trade must in the course of a few years unavoidably find its way to the easiest and most profitable channel. He who thinks otherwise, knows but little of human nature, and still less of the principles of politics and trade."

Those who, at this time, were anxious to develop the Egypt-Red Sea route saw clearly that it could never be prejudicial to the

Cape route so long as Turkey continued her obstructive attitude in Egypt, and so long as the complicated system of transport from the Red Sea to the Mediterranean prevailed.

It was evident, however, that the power of Turkey in Egypt was weakening, and it only required that the Government of that country be replaced by one more amenable, or controlled by one of the Western Powers, to make immediately practicable the construction of a Suez Canal, either by cutting through the Isthmus or restoring the ancient indirect Nile-Red Sea system.

The advocacy of a Suez Canal, mainly and naturally by the French, had been going on continuously. The alternative schemes had been propounded with much erudition and attention to detail, and it was a foregone conclusion that if ever France should establish herself in Egypt the Suez Canal would be one of the first great works with which she would occupy herself. Apparently the credit should go to Baron de Waldner for asserting that the major obstacle to the cutting of a direct canal—the difference in the levels between the Mediterranean and the Red Sea—was wholly legendary, "a phantom of ignorance," and a "vulgar fear." But proof, which should banish the bogy which had intimidated the monarchs of the ancient world, was still lacking.

So matters stood at the beginning of the last decade of the eighteenth century, when the political situation suddenly took a turn which brought the Egyptian question right to the front. War broke out between England and Republican France in 1793. Four years later the young General Bonaparte was writing to Talleyrand: "The time is not far distant when we shall feel that in order to destroy England it is necessary for us to possess Egypt."

Talleyrand had already been deeply impressed by the dispatches of Charles Magallon, French Consul-General in Egypt, who, from the commercial angle, had for many years been stressing this very thing, and who was now summoned to Paris by the Directorate to set forth his suggestions. Largely using Magallon's material, Talleyrand informed the Directorate in March, 1798:

" The event of establishing the French in Egypt will bring about a revolution in European commerce which will strike particularly at England. It will destroy her power in India, the only basis for her grandeur in Europe. The revival of the Suez route will have an effect upon her . . . as fatal as the discovery of the Cape of Good Hope was to the Genoese and Venetians in the sixteenth century. The result of this revolution will be wholly to the advantage of the Republic, because it is by its geographical position, population, genius and activity . . . the one of all Powers which can derive most from it. Let us never forget that the ancient and modern nations which have controlled the trade with India have always reached a high degree of wealth. When the French Republic becomes master of Cairo and consequently of Suez, it will make little difference in whose hands the Cape of Good Hope happens to be. . . ."

An expedition to Egypt commanded by Napoleon was forthwith decided upon. The instructions signed by the Directorate on April 12, 1798, were explicit.

" The Army of the East shall take possession of Egypt. The Commander-in-Chief . . . shall have the Isthmus of Suez cut through, and he shall take the necessary steps to assure the free and exclusive possession of the Red Sea to the French Republic. . . ."

England was taken completely by surprise when Napoleon landed his forces at Alexandria and occupied the country. No more time than was made essential by military measures was lost in carrying out the preliminaries to cutting the canal which was one of the major objects of the expedition. For this very purpose a number of engineers and scientists had been sent out with the troops, and these became the foundation members of the newly established Institute of Egypt. Among them was the famous engineer J. M. Lepère.

Napoleon took a keen personal interest in the project, and led the party of technicians who from Suez traced out the remains of the former Nile-Red Sea canal. There was something infinitely appealing in the grandiose scheme of restoring a waterway of such remarkable antiquity in the history of which the mighty dead of so many nations had played a part. For a thousand years the waters had ceased to flow, and the prosperity of Egypt had dried up with their departure. Now all this was to be changed, and it was to be the pride of France and of Napoleon to revive and to enhance the ancient glories.

A survey was duly instituted and completed under the circumstances of the greatest difficulty. As a result Lepère reported against the cutting of a direct Suez Canal, convinced that the Red Sea was more than thirty feet higher than the level of the Mediterranean, and in favour of reopening the Canal of the Pharaohs. He estimated that the task would occupy ten thousand workmen for four years, and that the cost would be in the neighbourhood of £1,500,000.

There were those who dissented from the findings of Lepère about the levels, but the error persisted another half century. The cutting of the canal had also to be postponed, and for an even longer period ; for the fortune of war turned against Napoleon, and as a result of the Battle of the Nile in August, 1798, when the French fleet was destroyed by Nelson in Aboukir Bay, he was forced to abandon his designs in Egypt. " The work is great," he told his engineer, " and though I shall not now be able to accomplish it, the Turkish Government will some day, perhaps, reap the glory of the enterprise."

The Peace of Amiens in 1802 put an end to French territorial ambitions in Egypt, though France never lost her interest in that country or in the Suez Canal project. Indeed her technicians, scholars, and statesmen were chiefly to be instrumental in restoring to Egypt a fertility and prosperity which she had not enjoyed since the days of the Pharaohs. No longer, however, was French interest narrowed by selfish ambition to strike a blow at England by dominating the India trade. That chapter was virtually closed with the death of her first emperor. In the years to come she would shape her policy to serve nobler ends, inclusive and humanitarian, to be exemplified in the work of one of her greatest sons, Ferdinand de Lesseps, the man who was finally to achieve the cutting of the Suez Canal.

CHAPTER II

THE POSTAL ROUTE:
RAILWAY *versus* CANAL

AFTER the French occupation of Egypt it was obvious that the affairs of this strategically important country could no longer be a matter of unconcern to European governments. Turkey, it is true, had had her sovereign rights there restored and guaranteed ; but Egypt was ripe for development : her position as the commercial gateway between East and West had been recognised— belatedly by England—and she would not be suffered through Turkish apathy or misrule, and still less religious bigotry, to slide back into a position of neglect and *laissez faire*. This was the nineteenth century, the opening of the era of industrial and technological progress. Barriers were beginning to be broken down, and distance increasingly to be annihilated.

Whatever intentions the Powers might have for the future of Egypt, the event which brought about the most radical and far-reaching changes in her internal administration was the rise to power of Mohammed Ali. By a succession of sharp and decisive actions this former Colonel of Albanian Irregulars made himself undisputed master of the country, and proclaimed himself Viceroy. Nominally he was serving the Sultan of Turkey, and in due course was invested with the hereditary pashalik of Egypt ; but for all practical purposes he was an independent sovereign, and Egypt under him became very largely an autonomous State. Only in external affairs, and after a prolonged struggle with the Porte in which England, France, and Russia were involved, was there any real restriction of the Viceroy's powers, and mainly to this extent was it possible to recognise that Egypt was still a part of the dwindling Ottoman Empire.

Mohammed Ali was in certain respects an enlightened ruler, with great force of character and strong personal ambition. He readily perceived the benefits to be derived from the introduction of European capital and methods, and determined to avail himself of these to the full in his plans for economic development and public works. In his political sympathies he on the whole favoured

13

the French, and every opportunity was afforded to French experts to come in and assist him in his schemes of construction and organisation.

Under Mohammed Ali Egypt awakened from her long sleep and became a factor to be reckoned with in world affairs. Cairo became a hotbed of European intrigue, with the Viceroy trying to play off one Power against another to his own and his country's advantage. At the same time, by the Treaty of Adrianople in 1829, Greece won her independence from Turkey, and with Russia scheming for dominance over the Sultan, the combination of circumstances was swiftly shaping into the Near-Eastern problem, which has been a fruitful source of conflict ever since.

Certainly England now became really anxious about the Egyptian route to India, and concerned to maintain the existence of the Ottoman Empire as a bulwark against the intentions of any other European Power to deprive her of the use of this route. The Tsar Nicholas I of Russia warned M. Barante, the French Ambassador, in February, 1839: " The English have their eyes on Egypt. The country is necessary to them on account of the new line of communication they seek to open with India. They are establishing themselves in the Red Sea and the Persian Gulf. You will have trouble with them over Egypt."

At long last England had come to realise the necessity for more speedy communication with India than was afforded by the Cape route, and was exploring the possibilities of the Euphrates Valley line as well as that through Egypt and the Red Sea. Already in the eighteenth century, for a time, dispatches had been sent *via* Egypt by agreement with the Bey ; but it had not been possible in those days to obtain permission for a regular service, or for European vessels to unload or embark goods at Suez. Now that these prohibitions had ceased to apply and steam navigation had been introduced, nothing stood in the way of the full employment of this valuable alternative and shorter route, at least for travel and postal dispatch.

It was Lieutenant Thomas Waghorn who was the first to demonstrate practically the advantages of the route to India through Egypt. In 1837 he wrote:

" I doubt not that, by some, my opinions may be called enthusiastic ; and, as such, subject me to attack ; however, they led me to

14

Egypt eight years ago. I felt convinced that that country ought to be the road to India ; and I maintained my principle in three-quarters of the globe. I have travelled, since then, some hundreds of thousands of miles to disseminate my opinions, and I will never content myself till I *find it* the high road to India."

Waghorn's individual enterprise had been initiated in January, 1835, when he had sent out his historical circular letter.

" I write to inform you, and other business men having relations with India, that I am leaving England the 5th and Falmouth the 8th of February, by the Postal Steamer for Malta. On arriving there I shall leave for Alexandria, thence by land to Suez, thence down the Red Sea and hope to arrive at Bombay seventy days after leaving England. On this occasion I shall take charge of any letters given me at five shillings each. I shall be happy to accept all letters which your company or your friends wish to send by this rapid route. I shall return to England in November and in all probability I shall travel this route each year in February so that once a year you can count on rapid communication with India, on condition, however, that a postal steamer service is not established."

Previously, in 1829-1830, Waghorn had tested this route by journeying from London to Bombay in the then record period of $40\frac{1}{2}$ travelling days ; but his feat had failed to receive adequate recognition. As a direct result of his later travels, however, the British Government, in August, 1837, entered into an agreement with the Peninsular and Oriental Company for the regular carriage of mails to Alexandria, and thence *via* the Nile and overland to Suez, where the ships of the East India Company would convey them to Bombay. Arrangements for the Egyptian section of the journey were in Waghorn's hands, and from 1838 for some years the outward mails bore the cachet, " Care of Mr. Waghorn, Alexandria," and the inward mails, "Care of Mr. Waghorn, Suez."

With the establishment of the P. & O. Line passengers as well as mails could travel by the speedier route to India, saving some 60 days compared with the Cape route. Waghorn's company provided hotels at Alexandria, Cairo, and Suez, and attended to all arrangements for the conveyance of travellers across Egypt, first by canal from Alexandria to the Nile at Atfé, then by steamer to Cairo, and finally by the alternatives of carriage, donkey chairs, camels, or horses to Suez.

The work of Thomas Waghorn was one of the major contributions towards the advancement of the cause of a Suez Canal. No one appreciated this more than De Lesseps, who, when his own task was eventually completed, had the following inscription placed below a bust of Waghorn at the canal's entrance:

" In homage to the memory of the generous though unfortunate man, who alone, without any help, by a long series of labours and heroic efforts, practically demonstrated and determined the adoption of the postal route through Egypt, and the communication between the East and the West of the world ; and this was the originator and pioneer of the great Egyptian maritime commerce completed by the canal of the two seas."*

Waghorn and his one-time associate, Lieutenant-Colonel (afterwards General) F. R. Chesney, studied the question of the difference in the levels of the Red Sea and the Mediterranean, but the British survey was indecisive in its results.

Afterwards other engineers in the service of Mohammed Ali worked on the practical issues involved in cutting both a direct and an indirect canal. Notable among these was Linant Bey, in charge of Egyptian canal construction, who, before 1841, prepared a detailed scheme for a direct canal between Suez and Pelusium, which later became the basis of the studies and achievement of De Lesseps. Gallice Bey, director of the Alexandria fortifications, and Mougel Bey, director of the Nile dam undertaking, also worked on the project. All three were Frenchmen. Early British investigators included Maclaren and Captain James Vetch, R.E., the latter basing his plans on the assumed drop in levels.

At this stage the Saint-Simonians came on the scene. They were a French semi-religious sect founded by Count Henri de Saint-Simon, who believed in " the redemption of human society through the dignity of labour." Among projects in the programme of this society was the cutting of a Suez Canal. Saint-Simon himself died in 1825 without having taken any definite steps to accomplish this object ; but his successor, Father Enfantin, set about the task with faith and energy. The Saint-Simonians duly set forth from Marseilles in 1833, after narrowly escaping a ducking by the scoffing dockers, and spent four years in Egypt. In the end they had to abandon their attempt after losing several of their number through disease and having failed to obtain a concession from the Viceroy.

*In England Lt. Waghorn's pioneer work is commemorated by a statue with map and inscription at Chatham.

Despite this setback the Saint-Simonians clung to their convictions, and carried on a zealous propaganda in favour of cutting the canal. In 1846 they were instrumental in forming an international organisation, the *Société d'Etudes du Canal de Suez*, first, as the title implies, to make a complete study of the whole question financially and technically, using Linant Bey's plans as a basis, and then to enlist the support of European capitalists in the enterprise. The headquarters of the Society was in Paris, and it had a fund of 150,000 francs divided into three equal parts. Three experts were further appointed with distinct functions. Negrelli, an Austrian, was to find a suitable site for the Mediterranean entrance to the proposed canal. Robert Stephenson, an Englishman—son of the inventor of the steam engine—was to study the port of Suez. Paulin Talabot, a Frenchman, was to cover the intermediate ground.

In entrusting the execution of the project to an international company, backed by the private enterprise of capitalists, the Saint-Simonians undoubtedly paved the way for De Lesseps' *Compagnie Universelle du Canal Maritime de Suez*, but Prince Metternich rightly saw at the time that " a private company will not be allowed to bring the project into life without the assistance of the governments whose harmony is indispensable for its promotion."

One of the major obstacles continued to be failure to obtain a concession for the enterprise. The Viceroy was not unfavourable to granting one provided that he had certain guarantees from the Powers ; but he held back because the rivalry of the European Governments seemed to make such guarantees unobtainable.

Metternich had been entirely right. The Society was quite unable to proceed further than its preliminary investigations because England, France, and Austria were each trying to gain the ascendancy over the other in securing Egypt as a sphere of influence. Badgered and beset by consuls and agents the Viceroy continually put off the hour of decision until it was evident that nothing would be done in his lifetime. He was now nearing his 80th year, degenerating mentally, and steadily less inclined to place himself and his country under the domination of foreigners whose intentions and opposing interests he had every reason to fear. Moreover, an alternative scheme not so costly or politically complicated was now being vigorously pressed, which designed to link Alexandria with Suez by railroad. This project had the support of Stephenson, one of the

Saint-Simonian engineers, greatly to the distress of Father Enfantin, who did all he could to block it.

As a result, the railway in turn was made an issue between the contending Powers. A survey of the route between Cairo and Suez had been made in 1834 on the Viceroy's orders. Writing of this, the head of the engineering firm of Galloway, the company concerned, afterwards stated :

" His Highness, foreseeing the probable increase in the intercourse that would take place with India, via the Red Sea, by the introduction of steam navigation, decided upon forming a railroad across the desert of Suez to Cairo, and for that purpose instructed my late brother, Galloway Bey, to make the necessary surveys and estimates, and our establishment was directed to carry out the work, in furtherance of which all the preliminary arrangements were made, and a large portion of the rails and machinery supplied. Unfortunately the agents of foreign powers, who were opposed to this work in a political point of view, used every possible exertion and means to dissuade His Highness from proceeding with it, alleging, among other reasons, that the traffic, the extent of which was then doubtful, would not repay so large an outlay, and the necessary expenditure for working the line."

Championed by England, the project was attacked by France and Austria, who continued to agitate in favour of a canal. Diplomatic documents of the period fully reveal how each side suspected the motives of the other. Mr. Murray, the British Consul-General in Egypt, was instructed by Lord Palmerston to " lose no opportunity of enforcing upon the Pasha and his ministers the costliness, if not the impracticability of such a project (as the Suez Canal)," and " that the persons who press upon the Pasha such a chimerical scheme do so evidently for the purpose of diverting him from the railway which would be perfectly practicable and comparatively cheap." " The persons " included M. Barrot, the French Consul-General, who is found reporting to M. Guizot, the head of his own Government, that he had told Mohammed Ali, " that if Egypt should one day become a great route toward Europe and India, it would be better that it should be open by means of a canal to the passage of all European nations who would naturally control it, than the construction of a railway which would make the passage through Egypt the monopoly of England, that is to say, the nation which most ardently covets the possession of this country, and which would not be slow to make this concession . . . a pretext and a means of arriving at her ends."

The Viceroy's attitude differently expressed, amounted to " a plague on both your houses." " He is happy," wrote Barrot, " to be able to count upon the support of England to refuse the canal and on France and Austria to oppose the railway." Mohammed Ali died in 1849 without having finally committed himself to either scheme.

Immediately the European agents fastened on to his successor, Abbas. The British, however, had stolen a march on their rivals by cultivating and paying court to the new Viceroy before his accession, with evident effect. Abbas speedily exhibited himself as an anglophile, which meant in the result that the railway would be built and the canal project shelved. The contract for the first stretch of the railway from Alexandria to Cairo was signed in due course, and construction entrusted to Stephenson was completed in 1854, when Abbas died.

It may be imagined that the French were deeply chagrined by the British victory, and the relations between the respective Consuls-General in Egypt were somewhat strained. Fortunately for both countries they were now so closely allied, and at the time pressingly engaged in the prosecution of the Crimean campaign against Russia, that what might easily have become a dangerous difference between the two Powers was never allowed to develop. As it transpired the tactical success of England in the matter of the railway was soon to be offset by the accomplishment of a Frenchman in obtaining from the next Viceroy, Mohammed Said, the coveted canal concession.

CHAPTER III

THE CANAL CONCESSION IS GRANTED

THE Suez Canal project in modern times owed its revival, as we have now seen, mainly to the necessity felt in Europe, and particularly in France, to offset the manifest commercial advantages enjoyed by England in her traffic with India *via* the Cape by the provision of an alternative route more accessible to Mediterranean Powers. Urged repeatedly to this decisive means of settling ancient scores with England, France had attempted to seize Egypt and construct the vital waterway. She had been foiled at the time, but in making the attempt she had plainly shown her hand. Thenceforth, though alliance might replace enmity, English and French interests remained at variance on this issue, the control of Egypt, and it came to be accepted, so to say as a diplomatic axiom, that the one country was concerned to prevent and the other to secure the construction of the Suez Canal. Fifty years after Napolean's expedition the controversy had crystallised itself in the form of Railway *versus* Canal ; but it was no secret that beneath this simple and apparently innocuous formula the bitter rivalries of old lived on, and that a recrudescence of active hostility was not beyond the bounds of probability.

This was the position in 1854. The railroad, at any rate between Alexandria and Cairo, was now an accomplished fact : the canal scheme was virtually at a standstill. It is important, however, to make clear—as Abbas did—that the two schemes were regarded as falling into quite different categories. The railway could be treated as an Egyptian domestic affair, requiring only the assent of the Viceroy for its execution. The canal involved a geographical change, and therefore became an international question. Neither Mohammed Ali nor Abbas had been prepared to initiate the enterprise without an agreement between the Powers affected, and the latter, certainly, not without the formal approval of the Porte. " It is not in Egypt but in Constantinople that the question must be decided," Abbas had said. The last word was still with the Sultan, Egypt's overlord.

On the technical side also it seemed that nothing further could be done to advance the canal project. The ground had been surveyed again and again, and the difference between the levels of the Red Sea and the Mediterranean had been shown once and for all to be a fallacy by Linant Bey's final survey in 1853. That perhaps had been the greatest gain hitherto, and had permitted practical plans to be worked out. It had been confirmed that there were no insuperable obstacles to a direct canal through the Isthmus of Suez, and engineers who still favoured an indirect canal did so chiefly in the belief that a sufficient depth could not be maintained on the direct route. Only the British Government, from reasons of policy, elected to accept the biassed verdict of such men as Stephenson, and appeared determined to regard the scheme as chimerical and impracticable.

In this impasse, if the dream of a Suez Canal was ever to become a reality, it required that a man should arise gifted with untiring patience and unfailing good humour, filled with zeal and enthusiasm, qualified to handle diplomatic obstructionists, above all, a man with a world outlook and such wide human sympathies as to be capable of transcending the foolish jealousies of nations.

The Suez Canal was achieved because this man was found in Ferdinand de Lesseps. Born at Versailles on November 19, 1805, he came of a family of diplomats. His father Mathieu de Lesseps, when French Consul-General in Egypt, had been one of those who helped Mohammed Ali in his rise to power, a fact which the Viceroy always remembered with gratitude. Ferdinand was destined for the family career, and after holding various Vice-Consulships and Consulships-General he was appointed Minister at Madrid. One of his early posts was the Vice-Consulate at Alexandria. Waiting to land from his quarantined vessel, he received a parcel of books with which to occupy his enforced leisure. Among them was Lepère's report on the proposed Canal of the Two Seas. His imagination was fired by the grand concept, and he determined to make a thorough study of the subject in all its bearings.

In Egypt he was warmly welcomed by the Viceroy, and struck up a friendship with Mohammed Ali's young son Mohammed Said which afterwards was to stand him in such good stead. He also made himself thoroughly popular in the European colony and in Egyptian society by his grace, charm of manner, and superb horsemanship.

After remaining as Consul in Cairo until 1837 he was posted to Rotterdam, and it was many years before he saw Egypt again. In 1849 he was sent on a delicate mission to Rome, and it is significant that even at that time he was publicly described as " a man who has always served the cause of liberty and humanity." Governmental changes brought about his recall and a quite undeserved censure, which so affected him by its unfairness that he gave up his career and retired into private life.

Full and active though his years had been, De Lesseps had never forgotten his youthful vision of a Canal of the Two Seas, and now that nothing hindered he took up with renewed enthusiasm the investigation of the problem, and set forth his conclusions in a memorandum. A copy of this he forwarded to his friend Ruyssenaers, Dutch Consul-General in Egypt, asking whether he thought Abbas was likely to be interested. This was in 1852. " I confess that my scheme is still in the clouds," he wrote, " and I do not conceal from myself that, as long as I am the only person who believes it to be possible, that is tantamount to saying it is impossible." Like many another thinker, De Lesseps was not at the time aware how many others were similarly minded.

Ruyssenaers replied in due course that there was no prospect of making any headway with Abbas. Two years later the situation had radically changed. On September 15, 1854, De Lesseps wrote again:

" I was busy with my masons and carpenters, who are building additional storey to the old manor house of Agnes Sorel,* when the postman appeared in the courtyard with the Paris letters. They were handed up to me by the workmen, and what was my surprise to learn of the death of Abbas Pasha, and the accession to power of our early friend, the intelligent and sympathetic Mohammed Said ! I at once came down from the building, and lost not an hour in writing to the new Viceroy to congratulate him on his accession. I reminded him that the course of political events had left me idle, and that I should take advantage of my liberty to go and present him my homage, if he would let me know the time of his return from Constantinople, where he was to go for investiture. He replied at once, and fixed the beginning of November for me to meet him at Alexandria. I wish you to be one of the first to know that I shall be punctual in arrival. What a pleasure it will be to meet again on the soil of Egypt, where we first came together ! Do not say a word about the piercing of the isthmus before I arrive."

*The Manor of Chesnaye, where De Lesseps, now a widower, lived with his family.

Cutting the Sweet Water Canal at Nefriche

Cutting the Canal near Chalouf

The Isthmus of Suez Maritime Canal near Kantara

So far had the Viceroy not forgotten the friend of his boyhood, that when De Lesseps landed at Alexandria he was received in semi-state. One of His Highness's villas was placed at his disposal, and as soon as possible he was welcomed affectionately by the Viceroy in person. Said Pasha insisted that De Lesseps should join his entourage on his forthcoming military visit to Cairo, and sent him the gift of a fine Arab steed.

Nothing had yet been said about the Suez Canal; but during the progress of the Viceregal party towards Cairo De Lesseps judged the moment to be opportune. In the desert encampment of Marea dawn was breaking on November 15, 1854. The story of that notable day is best told in De Lesseps' own words.

" A few rays of the sun began to illuminate the horizon, when suddenly there appears in the west, whence the sky is cloudy, a very brilliant rainbow, running from east to west. I confess that my heart beat violently, and that I was obliged to put a rein upon my imagination, which was tempted to see in this sign of alliance spoken of in the Scriptures the presage of the true union between the western and the eastern world, and the dawning of the day for the success of my project. The Viceroy's presence served to draw me out of my reverie. . . . We rest under the shade of the carriage, while the chasseurs build up a circular parapet formed of stones which they have picked up. . . . When I leave the Viceroy to go and get my breakfast, in order to show him how well my horse can jump, I put him over the parapet and gallop off to my tent. . . . At five o'clock I again mounted my horse and came up to the Viceroy's tent by way of the parapet. He was bright and good tempered, and taking me by the hand he led me to a divan and made me sit by his side. We were alone, and through the opening of the tent I could see the setting of the sun which, at its rising that morning, had so stirred my imagination. I felt inwardly calm and assured at the moment of entering upon a question which was to be decisive of my future. I had clearly before me my studies and conclusions with regard to the canal, and the execution of the work seemed so easy of realisation that I felt little doubt as to being able to convince the Prince of this. I set out my project, without entering into details, dwelling upon the principal facts and arguments set out in my memorandum, which I had by heart. Mohammed Said listened with evident interest to what I had to say, and I begged him if there were any points which did not seem clear to him to mention them to me. He, with considerable intelligence, raised a few objections, with respect to which I was able to satisfy him, as he at last said to me: ' I am convinced ; I accept your plan ; we will concern ourselves during the rest of our expedition as to the means of carrying it out. You may regard the matter

c

as settled, and trust to me.' Thereupon he summoned his generals, bade them seat themselves upon some folding chairs which were just in front of the divan, and repeated the conversation we had had together, asking them to give their opinions as to the proposals of his 'friend,' as he was pleased to call me to these improvised advisers, better suited to give an opinion as to a cavalry manœuvre than a gigantic enterprise, the significance of which they were incapable of understanding. They stared at me and looked as if they thought that their master's friend, whom they had just seen put his horse over a wall, could not be otherwise than right, they raised their hands to their heads as their master spoke in sign of assent."

It was almost laughable that De Lesseps should obtain so readily what others had striven for in vain. A man's faith, an old friendship, and the leap of a horse, had gained the day.

The Viceroy was as good as his word. The Concession as drawn up was on broad lines. By it De Lesseps was authorised to form an international company under his own direction, the *Compagnie Universelle du Canal Maritime de Suez*. The Concession was to remain in force for 99 years from the date of the opening of the canal. With the details we are not immediately concerned, except for the provision that the firman required to be ratified by the Porte before work could be started. This original Concession was replaced by a more formal one in January, 1856,* which is the one now in operation. Later, in 1866, two Conventions between the Egyptian Government and the Company were signed.

It may be imagined that the news came as a bombshell to the assembled Consular Corps when the Viceroy made his public announcement of his undertaking. The decision had been made so suddenly that there had been no opportunity for any of the interested Governments to express an opinion. France and Austria were naturally pleased, but England had the greatest misgivings, and instructed her Consul-General in Egypt, Mr. Bruce, to make it clear to the Viceroy that Her Majesty's Government regarded the scheme with disfavour, and to represent to him that it was in every way inexpedient and impracticable.

De Lesseps was quick to realise that he would have to contend with the full force of British opposition. He therefore hastened to Constantinople to secure the Sultan's ratification before that opposition could take concrete form. He also wrote off to Richard Cobden, "friend of peace and of the Anglo-French Alliance,"

*For the text see Appendix B.

trusting that he might count on his support in case of need. It was well for De Lesseps, from one point of view, that Britain and France were jointly engaged in the Crimean War, for this at least assured that no official action would be taken that would be calculated to jeopardise still more the rather uncertain friendship existing at the time between the two countries. De Lesseps very wisely insisted at Constantinople that he was the personal representative of the Viceroy, and not of any European Power. From another point of view, however, the War was unfortunate, because it enabled the Porte under pressure to justify postponing a decision until hostilities should be ended.

The real power at Constantinople was the British Ambassador, Lord Stratford de Redcliffe, who took it upon himself, pending the reception of instructions from London, to insist that consent to the Concession should be withheld for the time being. So predominant was his influence with the Sultan and the Grand Vizier that De Lesseps could make no headway, though he did his best both directly and indirectly to overcome the "Great Eltchi's" antagonism. In a personal letter to the Ambassador De Lesseps stated:

"I venture to hope that I shall no longer have to fight against the powerful opposition of the honourable representative of Great Britain.... The question has been submitted in due course to the Sublime Porte without any sort of foreign intervention. It would not be within my province, as the agent of Mohammed Said, to place it upon another ground, as your Excellency suggested. The Viceroy of Egypt was at liberty to place it upon this ground and to keep it there. Just as he was unwilling to give it a purely French or Austrian complexion, in the same way he would not consent to give it an exclusively English aspect by transferring the discussion of it to London, and letting the solution of it depend on one Government. He is anxious that this affair of the Suez Canal should retain, above all things, its Egyptian and Ottoman initiative. Your Excellency is too enlightened a patriot and attaches too much importance to the alliance between our two countries—an alliance of which I am proud to be one of the warmest partisans—to allow a question of antagonism, in which it would be deplorable that the *amour-propre* of our two Governments should be involved, to arise in this connection."

The Ambassador would not be drawn into expressing a clear opinion. He replied:

"The various considerations which you have touched upon in a manner at once delicate and flattering to myself, are at the same time of too high a political order to be entered upon here. In a position such as mine, personal independence has its limits, and cannot but yield at times to official eventualities."

De Lesseps was not deceived by this modest language. He knew that he was being deliberately obstructed, and that things being as they were it was useless to waste further time at Constantinople. He returned to Egypt to report to the Viceroy, only to find that, due to Lord Stratford, inspired letters had been sent to Mohammed Said by the Vizier and the Viceroy's own brother-in-law containing the most offensive warnings and veiled threats. He was to be careful not to provoke England, nor to throw himself into the arms of France, and recommended in the strongest terms to drop a project which could only prove disastrous.

The letters had the very opposite effect to what was intended, and determined the Viceroy to push forward the scheme with all the power at his command. The revelation of the contents of these letters in diplomatic circles enabled the Austrian Internuncio to make such a sharp protest to the Porte that both the writers were forced to resign from office.

It was obvious that the British Government must eventually define its attitude. After an interchange of correspondence with the French Government it was finally agreed that officially both countries would refrain from active interference at Constantinople either for or against the Canal. The project was to be regarded strictly as a private enterprise on the part of De Lesseps. But this saving of face still permitted the British Government to place every possible difficulty in De Lesseps' way in the expectation that he would soon be forced to abandon his efforts, while France could give him but little encouragement.

In this situation De Lesseps decided to beard the British Lion in his den. Armed with important letters of introduction he arrived in London in June, 1855, and one of his earliest calls was on Lord Palmerston, now Prime Minister.

The policy of the elderly statesman was undoubtedly the wellspring from which flowed the British opposition to the Canal scheme. He was quite willing to take his visitor into his confidence.

" M. de Lesseps, I will not hesitate to tell you what my apprehensions are. They consist, in the first place, of the fear of seeing the commercial and maritime relations of Great Britain upset by the opening of a new route, which in being open to the navigation of all nations will deprive us of the advantages which we at present possess. I will confess to you also that I look with apprehension to the uncertainty of the future as regards France—a future which any statesman is bound to consider from the darkest side, unbounded as is our confidence in the loyalty and sincerity of the Emperor ; but after he has gone things may alter."*

The statement made it clear that England suspected French designs on Egypt to be at the back of her advocacy of the Suez Canal. At any rate, this was a more plain-spoken attitude than the suggestion that England only had the welfare of Turkey at heart and was anxious to safeguard Ottoman interests in Egypt and to prevent Egypt becoming an independent sovereign State, which it was believed would happen if the Suez Canal was constructed. This was the view expressed by the Foreign Secretary, Lord Clarendon.

Among the parliamentary rank and file Robert Stephenson was bitterly hostile, and in speech and writing roundly and authoritatively, as an engineer, declared that such a canal as was contemplated was impossible of execution. The press also was derisive at this period. *The Times* pontificated about the natural obstacles which were bound to nullify the enterprise " in a land where the face of nature is changed by a tempest of wind. . . . A single night of storm will engulf everything in the sand." The *Daily News* sarcastically stated that " the literature of fiction is not dead in the land of Alexander Dumas and Monsieur de Lesseps. The most extravagant romancers are children compared with the great discoverer of a new Pelusium, trying to convince his audience that 250 sick Europeans and 600 conscripted Arabs will accomplish this stupendous work, without money, without water, without stones . . ."

But De Lesseps was by no means discouraged and found many strong and influential supporters. In particular he sought and won the approval of the commercial and shipping world. Here were the real masters of Mid-Victorian England. Pamphleteering and lecturing he set out to convince those whom he believed would give him the backing which would impress Governmental circles.

" I have come to England," he proclaimed, " to place the matter

*Letter of Ferdinand de Lesseps to Count Th. de Lesseps, London, June 25, 1855.

clearly before the eyes of the public. I appeal to the interests and am content to rely on the judgment formed by the East India Company, the traders with Australia, Singapore, Madras, Calcutta, and Bombay, the merchants of the City, the shipowners of London and Liverpool, the manufacturers of Manchester, the ironmasters, the makers of machinery, the P. and O. Steam Navigation Company, the managers of banks and other large businesses, the commercial associations, and the owners of the coal mines who in 1854 exported nearly four and a half million tons of coal, representing a value of £2,147,156, and who, by the opening of the Suez Canal, would find these enormous exports considerably increased."

Theoretically, there could be no question of the value of a Suez Canal. But was the project practicable ? That was the fundamental question. De Lesseps's answer was the formation of an International Scientific Commission on the Isthmus of Suez Ship Canal.

CHAPTER IV

THE COMPANY IS FORMED

D E LESSEPS' International Commission, composed of eminent hydraulic engineers and naval experts of different countries—including England—met in October, 1855, at his house in Paris in the Rue Richepanse. After preliminary investigations the Commission appointed a sub-committee of five of its members to go out to Egypt and study the terrain. Their expenses, amounting to £12,000, were paid for by the Viceroy personally.

The expedition was entirely successful. Returning to Alexandria on January 1, 1856, the Commissioners submitted to the Viceroy the following report:

" Your Highness summoned us to Egypt to examine the question of the piercing of the Isthmus of Suez. While supplying us with the means of deciding, *de visu,* as to the merits of the different solutions proposed, you requested us to lay before you the one which was the easiest, the safest, and the most advantageous for Euuropean commerce. Our investigation . . . has revealed to us innumerable obstacles, not to say impossibilities, for taking the route by Alexandria, and unexpected facilities for establishing a port in the Gulf of Pelusium.

" The direct canal from Suez to the Gulf of Pelusium is therefore the sole solution of the problem for joining the Red Sea to the Mediterranean ; the execution of the work is easy, and the success assured. . . . We are unanimous in our conviction upon this point, and we will develop our reasons for it in a detailed report. . . . This is a long and minute work, which will occupy several months ; but in the meanwhile we beg to acquaint your Highness with our conclusions, which are as follows:

" 1. The route by Alexandria is inadmissible both from the technical and economical point of view.

" 2. The direct route offers every facility for the execution of the canal itself, with a branch to the Nile, and presents no more than the ordinary difficulties for the creation of two ports.

" 3. The port of Suez will open on to a safe and large roadstead, accessible in all weathers, and with a depth of about 30 feet of water within a mile of the shore.

" 4. The port of Pelusium, which, according to the draft scheme, was to be at the extremity of the Gulf, will be established about 17 miles farther to the west, at a point where there are 25 feet of water within a mile and a half of the shore, where the anchorage is good, and getting under way easy.

" 5. The cost of the canal, and of the works connected with it, will not exceed the figure of £8,000,000 given in the draft scheme of your Highness's engineers."

Following upon the basis of the Commission's report a new act of concession was granted by the Viceroy, though containing the same provisions about the duration of the Concession and the need for the Sultan's ratification. This Concession enabled the Statutes of the Suez Canal Company to be formulated in full. The central offices were to be located in Alexandria and the legal and administrative offices in Paris. The capital was fixed at two hundred million francs, divided into 400,000 shares of 500 francs each. Investors from all nations were to be invited to participate in the enterprise.

As a result of the work of the International Scientific Commission more exact details about the construction became available and were widely circulated. In England many waverers were now convinced. During a brief visit in 1856 De Lesseps was received by Queen Victoria and the Prince Consort. The latter showed the liveliest interest in the project, and asked many questions. De Lesseps was also entertained by the Royal Geographical Society, and afterwards addressed a crowded meeting, which received his remarks with loud applause.

Returning to Egypt to report progress to the Viceroy De Lesseps had an important interview with Prince Metternich, which greatly strengthened his hand. " The Viceroy of Egypt, who has so faithfully served his Suzerain during the war," he said, " will have rendered, by his conduct in regard to a work of peace, a not less signal service, and thus will be fulfilled the prediction of Napoleon I at the beginning of the century, that the execution of the canal from sea to sea would contribute to the glory and to the maintenance of the Ottoman Empire."

It began to appear that the British Government was adopting an inexcusable dog-in-the-manger attitude. De Lesseps himself hit out straight from the shoulder in a letter to Richard Cobden dated from Cairo, November 22, 1856.

" How can it be imagined," he wrote, " that people on the Continent will believe in the sincerity of England, in her zeal for universal progress, civilisation, and public wealth, if it is seen that England, where public opinion reigns supreme, allows her Government to continue its incredible opposition to the Suez Canal, a private enterprise, in the origin, constitution, and object of which there is nothing to awaken any suspicion of political rivalry ? How can the apostles of free trade and open competition propagate their doctrines when the two leading members of the Cabinet, who recently figured in their ranks, will not agree, through fear or horror of competition, to the suppression of a narrow neck of land which divides the two most opulent of seas, and stands as a feeble barrier against all the navies of the globe ? "

The peculiar ways of British statesmanship, so hard for the European mind to follow, seemed once again to be giving grounds for the charge of hypocrisy.

During April, May, and June of 1857, the intrepid Frenchman undertook an extensive tour of the great industrial and shipping centres of Britain, addressing Chambers of Commerce, Merchant and Shipping interests, obtaining signatures and declarations in favour of the canal. The complete record was at once published in book form, and dedicated to the members of the British Parliament. This mobilisation of commercial opinion about the value of the Suez Canal must, it was felt, prove effective to shake the Government at Westminster.

On July 7, 1857, Mr. Henry Berkeley, member for Bristol, rose in the House to ask the First Lord of the Treasury " whether Her Majesty's Government would use its influence with His Highness the Sultan in support of an application which had been made by the Viceroy of Egypt for the sanction of the Sublime Porte to the construction of a ship canal across the Isthmus of Suez, for which a concession had been granted by the Viceroy to M. Ferdinand de Lesseps, and which had received the approbation of the principal cities, ports, and commercial towns of the United Kingdom ; and if any objection were entertained by Her Majesty's Government, to state the grounds of such objection."

Lord Palmerston was beleagured, but he still held out with a kind of reckless bravado. His answer was both irritating and insulting, and hardly raised a laugh or a " hear, hear " even from the Government benches.

" Her Majesty's Government," he said, " certainly cannot undertake to use their influence with the Sultan to induce him to give permission for the construction of this canal, because for the last fifteen years Her Majesty's Government have used all the influence they possess at Constantinople and in Egypt to prevent that scheme from being carried into execution. It is an undertaking which, I believe, as regards its commercial character, may be deemed to rank among the many bubble schemes that from time to time have been palmed off upon gullible capitalists. I believe that it is physically impracticable, except at an expense which would be far too great to warrant the expectation of any returns. I believe, therefore, that those who embarked their money in such an undertaking (if my hon. friend has any constituents who are likely to do so) would find themselves very grievously deceived by the result.

" However, this is not the ground upon which the Government have opposed the scheme. Private individuals are left to take care of their own interests, and if they embark in impracticable under-takings, they must pay the penalty of so doing. But the scheme is one hostile to the interests of this country—opposed to the standing policy of England in regard to the connection of Egypt with Turkey —a policy which has been supported by the war and the Treaty of Paris. The obvious political tendency of the undertaking is to render more easy the separation of Egypt from Turkey. . . . I can only express my surprise that M. Ferdinand de Lesseps should have reckoned so much on the credulity of English capitalists, as to think that by his progress through the different countries he should succeed in obtaining English money for the promotion of a scheme which is in every way so adverse to British interests. . . . But probably the object which M. de Lesseps and some of the promoters have in view will be accomplished, even if the whole of the undertaking should not be carried into execution. . . ."

The last sentence veiled the Government's belief, or pretence to believe, that the French in collusion with the Viceroy would be satisfied with digging a trench deep enough and wide enough to be a military obstacle to a Turkish force advancing on Egypt through Syria. Strangely enough, the time was to come during the First World War when England herself defending Egypt against Turkey would be thankful for the barrier to invasion afforded by the Suez Canal.

Personally insulting to De Lesseps as were Palmerston's com-ments, which he reiterated in the House on the 17th, they did not have the expected effect of alienating public sympathies from the scheme in England, while they greatly increased French support. In the French Chamber, M. de Lamartine declaimed dramatically: "Nature is stronger than these wretched national antipathies. Europe and India will communicate, despite all you may do, by way of Suez. You will have but delayed this great and beneficent act of Providence ; the two worlds *will* join hands by way of Egypt, and gather new life as they do so."

Meanwhile, an unexpected factor had stressed the value of the Egyptian route. In May, 1857, the Indian Mutiny had started, and the British Government was at last forced to send troops to India through Egypt.

"Thus the Government admits," said the *Daily News* of October 2, 1857, " that the Suez route is the best for communication with India, and after stubborn resistance, broken down by necessity, resolves to send by this route some of the troops which are being despatched to the relief of our gallant soldiers in India. Nothing could be a more complete avowal of the utility of M. de Lesseps' scheme; and this action of the Government is the implicit condemnation of Lord Palmerston and Lord Stratford de Redcliffe, who have hitherto opposed the scheme. It would seem as if Providence had set itself to inflict upon them the chastisement which they deserve, by making them, so to speak, responsible before public opinion for the difficulties which their country is experiencing in putting an end to the calamities which are so preying upon its interests, its affections, and its power. . . ."

But these circumstances had in no way terminated British official opposition to the Canal project. On several occasions during the next year both under Lord Palmerston's and Lord Derby's administrations the subject was brought before Parliament. There was even a full-dress debate in the House on June 1, 1858, when sixty-two members voted in support of Mr. Roebuck's motion in favour of the Canal. Gladstone was championing the scheme, while Disraeli was urging caution. But behind the scenes British diplomatic pressure persisted at Constantinople to bring the Sultan to pronounce definitely against the Canal.

De Lesseps had been fighting unceasingly to keep the issue free from political considerations, and had been called a rogue and a charlatan for his pains. For him the value of the Suez Canal lay in the fact that it would offer far speedier communication between East and West, contributing to the commercial prosperity of all nations ; and he could not see what there was to quarrel about in that. Once evidence had been supplied that the enterprise was practicable, surely no intelligent person could raise objection to it. It did not make sense that England should oppose a scheme that was so much in the interest of her great manufacturing and shipping community, bringing India several thousand miles nearer to her shores. De Lesseps had been in the diplomatic service of his own country, and knew well the devious ways of international statesmanship. But in this matter he believed that his only hope lay in adhering strictly to the business aspect of his proposition, in the confidence that the political complications arising from the contemplated alteration in geography would in due course sort themselves out.

Writing from Constantinople in April, 1858, he said:

" We have to prove that the so-called chimera is a reality.... To avoid all misunderstandings in an affair which should retain its general and commercial character, the Company will not ask for the assistance of any of the governments of whose support it was assured. But it is about to organise itself in a definite form ; it will march resolutely forward and complete its work, backed up by the investments of its shareholders of all nations, and by the public opinion of the whole world. The Scientific Commission will meet about the end of June, and its report will settle the conditions under which the works are to be executed, in order to open the first section of the canal. A temporary board of administration will then decide how much capital is to be issued ; the shareholders will receive intimation of when they are to pay their calls, and every arrangement will be made, so that by the end of the year the work may be put thoroughly in hand, and carried on without interruption."

Nevertheless, on July 28 de Lesseps found it advisable to place his interests and that of the company under the protection of Napoleon III, while still endeavouring to preserve the principle of freedom from Governmental interference. In taking this step he had already been assured of the approval of the European Powers concerned ; but trusted that action would not be needed, and that England would not remain the only country out of tune in the European concert.

In a letter from Paris in September to his colleague De Negrelli at Vienna, De Lesseps wrote:

" Since my return here, I have been devoting my whole time to the establishment of agencies for the Company abroad and in France, as well as of scheduling the private subscriptions which have been sent to me, and which have already reached £3,200,000. The adversaries of the enterprise, our faithful allies over the water, have already lost their two first campaigns as to the impossibility of making the canal and the hostility of the Porte. All their efforts are now directed to deterring their compatriots from subscribing to it,

34

because, in their innate pride and insular ignorance, they believe that their example will prevent other nations from investing money in it. We are now in course of destroying their last illusions.

"The Emperor is in favour of subordinating the political question to the organisation of the Company, which will be strong enough to withstand opposition, and which the Continental Governments will be in a position to support if needful. This seems to me very prudent, and is quite in keeping with my view as to Government intervention, which should follow, if the necessity for it arises, and not precede the execution of a commercial and industrial enterprise."

De Lesseps had been strongly advised, and regarded it as his best course to pursue, to push ahead as quickly as possible with the formation of the Suez Canal Company. The capital was fixed at 400,000 shares of 500 francs each bearing statutory interest at 5 per cent. These were placed on the market in November, 1858.

In accordance with the desire of De Lesseps that all the Western Powers should participate financially in the enterprise blocks of shares were specially reserved for these countries. The result was very disappointing, however, and the issue would have failed completely had it not been for the fine response of France and Egypt, as shown by the following table:

	Shares reserved for various countries	Shares applied for and allotted
Egyptian Government	64,000	177,642
Turkey	—	750
Egypt	42,000	998
Tunis	—	1,714
France	80,000	207,160
Algeria	—	728
Great Britain	80,000	Nil
Malta	—	85
Austria	40,000	163
Russia-Wallachia	24,000	174
Germany	—	5
Prussia	—	15
Sweden and Norway	—	1
Denmark	30,000	7
Switzerland	—	460
Netherlands	—	2,615
Belgium	—	573
Spain	—	4,161
Portugal	20,000	5
Italy	—	2,719
Greece	—	25
United States	20,000	Nil
	400,000	400,000

More than half the total number of shares had been taken up in France, and it was symptomatic of popular feeling on the Continent that many people became subscribers in order to register a protest against the official British attitude. Mr. Gladstone had foreseen this situation. When attacking Palmerston in Parliament in June, 1858, he had declared : " There is not a State in Europe which does not declare the opposition of England to this project . . . as unwarrantable, and as a selfish policy . . . Is it not perfectly plain," he challenged, " that all Europe will conclude the real ground of your opposition is because you suppose the canal to be injurious to the British Empire, and that the alleged interest of Turkey is hypocritically thrust in for the mere purpose of justifying your policy ?"

But Palmerston's denunciation of the scheme as a " bubble " enterprise had effectively warned off British capital from participating, whatever might be thought of the political aspects.

CHAPTER V

THE CANAL IS CUT

HAVING obtained the initial capital, De Lesseps proposed to push on with his plans. At the first the Turkish Ministry had recognised the utility of the scheme, and to De Lesseps' way of thinking the Canal should be considered as much a domestic Egyptian undertaking as the railway. He therefore saw no need to continue to wait for the Sultan's ratification, and in the spring of 1859 he took steps to initiate the work. On April 25, in the presence of the labourers, staff, and engineers, he gave the first blow with the pickaxe, and shovelled the first spadeful of sandy soil on the Pelusian shore of the Mediterranean which was to be the northern terminus of the canal. On this site would hereafter arise the new town of Port Said, commemorating the name of the ruler who, against every effort at intimidation, had stood by the great scheme which he had sponsored. It had been by no means easy to do so, and there were times, especially in the early stages of the work, when the Viceroy became alarmed and despondent. Even De Lesseps, incurable optimist, was forced to realise that he could not hope to overcome on his own the forces arrayed against him. Funds also were being exhausted without sufficient compensating progress. The predicted financial crash of the whole concern seemed imminent.

The day had come when France must abandon her official passivity. England had persistently broken the agreement of neutrality*; so that France was fully entitled now to give more than moral support. The matter became pressing, because the British Government, concerned that construction had actually begun, had so worked upon the Porte that a formal order from the Sultan had been sent requiring all operations to cease forthwith.

The Viceroy was in a quandary, especially as M. Sabatier, the French Consul-General, anxious to avoid political complications, agreed that the order must be obeyed. Laroche, De Lesseps' chief engineer at Port Said, protested vigorously, and flatly refused to

*See p. 26.

37

abandon the excavations. The French Consul insisted ; but still Laroche held out, and wrote off urgently to his chief. Everything clearly depended on the attitude of the Emperor, whose vacillating character was well known.

A deputation from the Company arrived at St. Cloud. The Emperor addressed himself immediately to De Lesseps. " How is it, M. de Lesseps, that so many people are against your enterprise ? "

" Sire, it is because they think that Your Majesty will not stand by us."

Napoleon considered, then, " Do not be uneasy," he said. " You may count on my assistance and protection."

That was the end of that crisis. The ultimatum was called off, and the native labour provided for under the terms of the Concession was supplied. Operations were resumed, and by October 18, 1862, the waters of the Mediterranean had flowed as far as Lake Timsah.

The statement sounds bald enough, and gives no conception of the magnitude of the achievement, which impressed even the British observers. The Canal had been cut through an almost waterless region of sandy waste, and it had been necessary in the first instance to cut a sweet-water canal from the Nile to Lake Timsah, and from Lake Timsah to the new Mediterranean harbour of Port Said, in order to provide drinking water for the thousands of operatives engaged on the major work and to convey supplies. Port Said itself was rising on the former marshes of Lake Menzaleh, filled in with the soil excavated by the dredgers.

De Lesseps, with his love for picturesque ceremonial, saw to it that the celebrations were worthy of the occasion of the completion of this stretch of the Canal. A stand hung with bunting accommodated distinguished guests, among whom were to be seen the engineers, the Grand Mufti, and the Catholic Bishop. Along the embankments were lined up thousands of workmen. Every eye was directed towards the narrow ridge of sand, which was the only obstacle separating water from water. At a given signal the last blows were struck, and as the waters burst their way through, De Lesseps cried in ringing tones, " In the name of His Highness Mohammed Said, I command that the waters of the Mediterranean enter Lake Timsah by the grace of God ! "

Congratulations showered on the happy inspirer of the scheme.

Prince of Wales letting the waters of the Mediterranean into the
Bitter Lakes, 1869.

Opening of the Suez Canal: The procession of ships in the

who had fought so indomitably for its realisation. The Empress Eugénie sent him her greetings, while the Emperor elevated him to the rank of Commander of the Legion of Honour.

The obvious progress of the undertaking, however, served only to increase the determination of the British Government to retard it, and, if possible, to secure its abandonment. Pressure was continually being applied at Constantinople to take further action to embarrass the Company. The grounds for interference by the Porte, it was now represented, should be the alienation of Egyptian territory in the Canal Zone, conceded to the Company, and the supply of forced labour for the workings, which, it was held, deprived Egypt of the services of 60,000 persons, who otherwise might be more productively employed for the benefit of the country. Despite the spirited protest of the French Ambassador, two notes were dispatched by the Porte on April 6, 1863, the one to the Ottoman Ambassadors at London and Paris and the other to the Viceroy in Egypt, in which the restoration of the lands by the Company and the abolition of the forced labour were made conditions of ratification of the Concession.

In the meantime, on January 18, 1863, De Lesseps' friend and patron, Mohammed Said, had died. " I am grieved to the heart," he wrote in his journal, " not on account of my enterprise, in which I have the most serene confidence, despite all the difficulties which may arise, but because of the cruel separation from a faithful friend who for more than a quarter of a century has given me so many proofs of affection and confidence."

Fortunately Said's successor, Ismail, ranged himself boldly on the side of the enterprise. " I should not be worthy to be Viceroy of Egypt," he told De Lesseps, " if I was not even more a ' canalist ' than you are."

His championship did not make the new ultimatum from the Porte any less formidable, and in July, 1863, it was reinforced by another note, which insisted on the Company's compliance within six months with the conditions stipulated, or the work would be stopped by force. It was for the Viceroy and the Company to come to terms and find a *modus operandi*, which both were anxious to do.

Negotiations were transferred to Paris. The Company petitioned the Emperor on January 6, 1864, to act as arbitrator, in order that the considerable French capital sunk in the enterprise might be

D

protected. Napoleon agreed, and in March appointed a Commission to examine the questions at issue. By April 15 the Commission had settled the points which were to be the subject of arbitration, and these were accepted and signed by De Lesseps on behalf of the Company and by Nubar Pasha on behalf of the Viceroy. The evidence on these points was ready for presentation to the Emperor in June, and on July 6 he delivered his verdict.

There had been a clear agreement about the employment of the forced labour: the Company was therefore awarded an indemnity of 38,000,000 francs for giving up its rights in this respect. On the land question, in return for a further indemnity, the Company was to restore to Egypt 150,000 acres of land in the Isthmus, retaining, however, a narrow strip on either side of the Canal, amounting to 30,000 acres. The sweet-water canal had already, over a large part of its extent, been made over to the Egyptian Government: the Company was now to make over the final stretch from Lake Timsah to Suez, it being stipulated that the free use of these vital waterways should remain with the Company until the maritime canal was completed. The full amount of the indemnity, totalling a little over £3,000,000, was to be paid to the Company over a period of 15 years.

The settlement having been accepted by both parties, there could no longer be any justification for the Porte to withhold ratification of the Act of Concession, which, with the new agreements, satisfied every demand which had been made. Nevertheless, it was not until March 19, 1866, that the Sultan finally gave his sanction, so bringing to an end the long story of delays caused by Britain's obstructive tactics.

Through the patience, perseverance, and unwavering faith of De Lesseps every difficulty and every crisis had been surmounted. Not the Suez Canal itself but the imaginations of statesmen had proved to be a chimera. So often the evil intentions of nations have no other existence than in the minds of prejudiced politicians, and the public is scared into an attitude of hostility by a bogyman conjured up by suspicion and mistrust. In this case the biblical saying that " perfect love casteth out fear " received a notable exemplification.

This was true not only of De Lesseps' relations with governments but of his relations with his workmen, some of whom had

had a criminal record. Welcoming him many years later to membership of the French Academy, Ernest Renan paid to him this glowing tribute:

" In a report of one of your lectures, I remember reading : ' M. de Lesseps stated that men are trustworthy and not at all evilly disposed when they have enough to live on. Man only becomes evil through hunger or fear.' We should perhaps add : ' or when he is jealous.' You went on to say : ' I have never had to complain of my workmen, and yet I have employed pirates and convicts. Work has made honest men again of them all ; I have never been robbed even of a pocket handkerchief. The truth is that our men can be got to do anything by showing them esteem and by persuading them that they are engaged upon a work of world-wide interest.'

" . . . It is all this, sir, that in electing you we were anxious to recompense. We are incompetent to appreciate the work of the engineer ; the merits of the administrator, the financier, and the diplomatist are not for us to discuss ; but we have been struck by the moral grandeur of the work, by this resurrection of the faith, not the faith in any particular dogma, but the faith in humanity and its brilliant destinies.... Your glory consists in having set stirring this latest movement of enthusiasm, this latest manifestation of self-devotion. You have renewed in our time the miracles of ancient days. You possess in the highest degree the secret of all greatness, the art of making yourself beloved.... "

Released from the crushing weight of governmental opposition, the construction of the Canal made rapid headway. Machinery was brought in to replace the heavy labour loss. The excavations continued southward from Lake Timsah and northward from Suez until the waters of the Mediterranean and the Red Sea were united in the Bitter Lakes in the summer of 1869.

As completed, the Suez Canal was approximately 100 miles long and varied in width between 150 and 300 feet at the surface. It had a depth of 26 feet and a width at the bottom of 72 feet. The course of the Canal, a sea-level canal without locks, was singularly direct, having only 14 curves over its whole length. In its passage between the two seas the Canal traversed four lakes refilled by its waters from their former dry or swampy state, from north to south Lake Menzaleh, Lake Ballah, Lake Timsah, and the Great Bitter Lakes. Above and below the latter, reminder of the ancient past, sections of the bed of the old Canal of the Pharaohs continued visible close to the modern waterway. To enable vessels to pass in the Canal eight stations, or sidings, were provided, and here the width of the channel at the bottom was 89 feet.*

Describing a voyage through the Canal at its opening, a visitor reported of the northern stretch: " Emerging from Lake Menzaleh, after going about 20 miles, we came on the true features of the desert: unbroken sand, as far as the eye could reach, hot, dry, and arid-looking, everywhere except where the stations were. There (supplied by tapping the pipes which take the water from the fresh-water canal at Ismailia to Port Said) irrigation and Nile water had made a veritable oasis ; huts covered with verdant creepers in full bloom, cane and the date palms growing freely ; in truth, the prophesy is fulfilled. ' The desert *hath* blossomed like the rose.' "†

The date fixed for the opening of the Suez Canal was November 17, 1869. It was to be made an occasion worthy of the stature of the undertaking, and of its international character. Invitations had been issued on a most generous scale by the Viceroy, and in addition thousands of visitors flocked from all parts of the world to witness the momentous celebration. It is estimated that more than six thousand persons attended, apart from native Egyptians, workmen, the special staff, and the sailors manning the vessels. Among the Viceroy's guests were the Empress Eugénie of France, the Emperor of Austria, the Crown Prince of Prussia, the Crown Prince of the Netherlands, Prince William of Hesse, and many other notables and national representatives.

On November 16 Port Said roads were crowded with the craft of all nations, yachts, warships, steamers, boats, and sailing vessels of all descriptions. Every mast was beflagged, every deck crowded with sightseers. The sun shone brightly out of a clear sky, and the deep waters of the Mediterranean reflected the resplendent colours of flag and ensign.

At 11 o'clock, greeted by the thunderous salutes of the anchored warships and the Egyptian shore batteries, and by the din of steamship sirens and whistles, the French Imperial yacht, the *Aigle,* with the Empress Eugénie on board, moved slowly forward, while the National Anthem of France could be heard amidst the roar of gunfire and cheers. " Never have I seen a sight so lovely!" exclaimed the enraptured empress. Awaiting her on the largest of three platforms was Ismail Pasha, his uniform glittering with stars and orders. Presently the distinguished company was grouped

*For the latest alterations and improvements see Chapter XV.
†Sir Frederick Arrow, *A Fortnight in Egypt at the Opening of the Suez Canal.*

round the Viceroy, and the proceedings commenced with a religious ceremony. The venerable Sheikh of Islam intoned a prayer, and then the Grand Ulema read a discourse in Arabic. They were followed by the Christian clergy, headed by the Archbishop of Alexandria and Monseigneur Bauer, almoner to the Empress. The latter in his speech paid a glowing tribute to De Lesseps, likening him to a new Christopher Columbus. At the termination of the address the trumpets sounded, the guns boomed, and further cheering echoed round the harbour.

The evening was given up to festivities and illuminations. Fireworks cascaded a golden rain on the flashing waters. Balls were given on shore and afloat.

At eight o'clock on the morning of Wednesday the 17th the *Aigle* led a long column of 67 vessels into the Canal. At the same time a flotilla of Egyptian warships moved in from the Red Sea end to meet them at Ismailia. The passage of over 40 miles to Lake Timsah occupied 12 hours and was accomplished without any untoward incident. De Lesseps wrote that the Empress Eugénie afterwards confessed to him that " during the whole journey she had felt as though a circle of fire was round her head, because every moment she thought she saw the *Aigle* stop short, the honour of the French flag compromised, and the fruit of our labours lost. Suffocated by emotion, she was obliged to leave the table, and we overheard her sobs—sobs which do her honour, for it was French patriotism overflowing from her heart." When at sunset the two fleets made contact amidst cheers and acclamations, establishing the union of the two seas, the hero of the whole undertaking was fast asleep, worn out with the vigil of the previous night when the grounding of an Egyptian frigate in the canal had come so near to ruining the great occasion.

The next day a further stretch of the canal was successfully negotiated. After a night at anchor in the Bitter Lakes the procession steamed onwards to Port Suez, now Port Tewfik, which was reached at eleven o'clock in the morning of November 20. " The Canal has been traversed from end to end without hindrance," recorded the Paris *Official Journal*, " and the Imperial yacht *Aigle*, after a splendid passage, now lies at her moorings in the Red Sea. Thus are realised the great hopes which were entertained of this mighty undertaking, the joining of the two seas."

CHAPTER VI

COMPLICATIONS AND A CONVENTION

IT may be said for England that having consistently opposed the construction of the Suez Canal from mistaken reasons of policy she did her utmost to make honourable amends when shown to have been in the wrong. The Earl of Clarendon, Secretary of State for Foreign Affairs, wrote to De Lesseps :

"The successful opening of the Suez Canal has been received with great and universal satisfaction. In having the honour to congratulate you, as well as the French nation and Government, which have taken such a profound and constant interest in your work, I know that I faithfully represent the sentiments of my fellow-citizens. Notwithstanding the obstacles of all kinds against which you have had to struggle, a brilliant success has finally recompensed your indomitable perseverance. It affords me sincere pleasure to be the organ for transmitting to you the felicitations of Her Majesty's Government on the establishment of a new means of communication between the East and West, and on the political and commercial advantages which we may confidently expect will result from your efforts."

Queen Victoria bestowed on De Lesseps the Grand Cross of the Order of the Star of India, and he was made a Freeman of the City of London. A magnificent fête was held at the Crystal Palace.

But when the richly merited plaudits and acclamations had died away the hero of the hour and the Company which he represented had to give urgent attention to more discordant cries: they came from the shareholders. It had been anticipated that the dividends would begin to flow as constantly as the waters of the Canal. That expectation was doomed to disappointment. The difficulties which had been placed in the way of the enterprise had more than doubled the original estimated cost of construction. Part of the deficit had been met by the indemnity awards and a further sum paid to the Company for the renunciation of other rights. Yet even so, more than 100,000,000 francs were required to be found to cover the costs. The money had been raised in France, it is true, by a loan flotation in 1867-68, but this left little for working capital. It was expected that there would be an immediate satisfactory revenue from the Canal to offset expenditure and the payment of arrears of interest. It seemed, however, that the shipping companies were in no hurry to make use of the facilities of the new waterway, and in the first year of operation less than five hundred vessels passed through the Canal, yielding a revenue of only 4,345,758 francs.

In 1870, the year following the opening, the value of the 500 franc shares fell to 272 francs. The next year they fell still lower to 208. The financial problem rapidly reached an acute stage. Pamphleteers screamed about "The Agony of the Suez Canal. Barrenness of the Results. It's approaching Ruin." A further issue of bonds became imperative. These were put on the market in 1871-72 on the security of a surtax on tolls of one franc per ton authorised by the Khedive, but only sufficient were taken up to tide over the crisis. Thereafter, fortunately, the returns steadily improved and the Company prospered accordingly. In 1875 the shares for the first time rose above par value. By 1880 the number of transits through the Canal was 2,026 compared with 486 in 1870, and the number of passengers carried had risen to 101,551 compared with 26,758.

The material betterment in the Company's position was not reached, however, without a further complication, which arose out of complaints made by shipowners about the system for measuring tonnage on which the dues were levied. The Porte considered it advisable to convene a Conference at Contantinople to deal with this vital question. It met in October, 1873, and issued its report in December. It recommended that the Moorsom system for determining net tonnage should be adopted by the Company, which however was permitted for the time being to add a surtax of from three to four francs in excess of the basis of ten francs provided for. After some demur as to the length of time that the surtax should operate the Company accepted the ruling of the Conference, which took effect in the spring of 1874.

The early straits of the Canal Company were seen at the time to have a significance far wider than the interests of either stockholders or customers. What would happen to the Canal if the Company crashed? Whose property was the Canal? Could it be sold? People were asking such questions as these.

The Suez Canal, once it was completed, had become a part of the world's physical and political geography: it joined two seas and divided two Continents. Its fate was a matter of international concern. In certain English diplomatic circles it was suggested seriously that the British Government should step in and buy out the Company, and in this way obtain the control of the Canal. It was said that the Khedive favoured an English Company acquiring the Concession. If it had been possible for such a transfer to take place it would have meant the very negation of the principle which had inspired the undertaking. The Canal would have come under the domination of a single Great Power, the very thing of which the British Government itself had formerly been afraid.

Yet even De Lesseps, wrestling with financial difficulties, proposed to the Khedive against his inclination that the Canal should be sold to the European Maritime Powers jointly, hoping in this way to save the situation and to ensure the Canal's permanent internationalisation and neutrality.

The Porte, however, made it very clear that it " could not admit, even in principle, the sale of the Canal or the creation of an International Administration on its own territory. On the other hand, M. de Lesseps, having only the concession of the undertaking, could never have the right of raising questions of such a nature. The Suez Canal Company is an Egyptian Company, and therefore subject to the laws and customs of the (Ottoman) Empire."

The Canal was Egyptian property operated under an Act of Concession by an Egyptian Company, which could relinquish the Concession or seek its renewal, but could not otherwise dispose of it.

The Porte's statement fairly settled the matter at the time, though in 1874 Lord Derby, in the House of Lords, mentioned that he would not be opposed to the management of the Canal by an international syndicate—an assertion which he repeated the following year in Edinburgh after the British Government's purchase of the Khedive's holding in the Company. Lord Farrer, President of the Board of Trade, also declared " that complications and difficulties will be endless so long as this great highway of nations remains in the hands of a private company." That prophecy has not been fulfilled so far as the Company itself is concerned, since it is factors quite outside its jurisdiction and responsibility that have caused complications and difficulties. But in view of later developments, which we shall consider in due course, it is well that these early proposals for internationalisation should be remembered.

Disraeli's purchase for Great Britain of the 176,602 shares in the Suez Canal Company held by the Khedive Ismail has been unduly dramatised, not only by that remarkable statesman, with his novelist's talk of " secret emissaries in every corner," but by many subsequent writers. Such drama as there was lay rather in the swiftness with which the transaction was carried through, for, as Lord Derby declared, " there was no deep-laid scheme in the matter."

Discounting Disraeli's extravagant and inaccurate report to his lady friends, that if a French banking offer had succeeded " the whole of the Suez Canal would have belonged to France, and they might have shut it up,"* the circumstances of the purchase were briefly as follows.

For ten years the Khedive had been running recklessly into debt. to the tune of an average of nearly seven million pounds a year, borrowing at exorbitant rates of interest. In the autumn of 1875 he found himself unable to meet pressing obligations soon falling due, and was forced to seek some way of finding a further substantial sum. His only really valuable remaining assets were his Suez Canal shares. At first he did not consider selling the shares, but proposed to lodge them as security for a loan with one of the banks with which he was already deeply involved. A group of French financiers, however, made him a somewhat better offer for outright purchase, which, though it came to nothing owing to the group failing to raise the money, led him to withdraw his mortgage intentions and decide to sell. General Stanton, British Consul-General in Egypt, had reported these negotiations, and had been instructed to inform the Khedive that " Her Majesty's Government are disposed to purchase if satisfactory terms can be arranged." This was on November 17. On November 23 Stanton wired that Great Britain was offered the shares for 100,000,000 francs (£4,000,000), and that an answer was required by the 25th.

The next day Lord Derby wired Stanton to close with the offer, and on the day following Stanton was able to wire back that the agreement for the sale of the shares was signed. Speaking at Edinburgh on the 27th, Lord Derby gave the Government's reasons for

*The Letters of Disraeli to Lady Bradford and Lady Chesterfield, edited by the Marquis of Zetland.

their quick decision. " I can assure you," he said, " that we have acted solely with the intention of preventing a larger foreign influence from preponderating in a matter so important to us. We have the greatest consideration for M. de Lesseps. We acknowledge that, instead of opposing him in his great work, we should have done better to associate ourselves with him. I deny on behalf of my colleagues and myself, any intention of predominating in the deliberations of the Company, or of abusing our recent acquisition to force its decisions. What we have done is purely defensive. I do not think, moreover, that the Government and English subjects are proprietors of the majority of shares."

Disraeli was undoubtedly the driving force behind the deal. He at least was determined that the Khedive's share in the Canal should belong to Britain and to no other Power or interest. Commercially and strategically the Canal was vital to the British Empire: it was the " Key of India."

The Prime Minister was justifiably proud of his achievement. Not only had he convinced his colleagues in the Cabinet against their inclination, but in Messrs. N. M. Rothschild and Sons he had found a banking house able and willing to finance the transaction. Their co-operation, indeed, had been essential, for Parliament was not in session to authorise allocation of the requisite funds. When the House did meet, in February, 1876, the Government were treated to an energetic criticism before the motion to approve the purchase was carried.

It was immediately evident, however, that the purchase was popular in Great Britain. From the Queen to the humblest of her subjects there was a joyful recognition that the Empire had gained greatly both in prestige and practical advantages. Continental opinion, on the whole, was also favourable. " It seems to us," said the Italian journal *Opinione,* " an act of great political ability which does great honour to the perspicacity of Mr. Disraeli's Government." De Lesseps was very satisfied :

" The English nation now accepts that share in the Canal which had been loyally reserved to her from the outset ; and if this action is to have any effect, that effect, in my opinion, can only be the abandonment by the British Government of the longstanding attitude of hostility towards the interests of the original shareholders of the Maritime Canal, whose perseverence has been at once so active and so well directed. I therefore look upon the close community of interest about to be established between French and English capital, for the purely industrial and necessarily peaceful working of the Universal Maritime Canal, as a most fortunate occurrence."

The British acquisition of nearly half the Canal shares undoubtedly contributed towards the healing of old wounds between France and Britain arising out of the Egyptian question. "Great Britain and France have two essential interests in common," declared Clemenceau in a speech to the Chamber in July, 1882, "the freedom of the Suez Canal and the proper administration of Egyptian affairs." This community of interest had developed increasingly as a result of the Khedive's extravagances. Already in the spring of 1876 the numerous loans to Ismail had had to be consolidated into a general debt amounting to £91,000,000 as a measure calculated to introduce some order into the chaotic finances. Thereafter Egyptian revenues and expenditure were placed under dual Anglo-French control. This Dual Control was renewed in 1879, after Ismail had been deposed and his son Tewfik had been made Khedive, when the representatives of the two Powers were Major Baring (afterwards Lord Cromer) and M. de Blignières.

These arrangements designed to right the Egyptian Ship of State and to protect the European bondholders could not hold any quality of permanency; but in the event they terminated more abruptly than was intended. This was due to the growth of a nationalist spirit in Egypt itself.

Alarmed at the extent to which foreigners were controlling and running the country, native sentiment was aroused as well as Islamic religious zeal. Disaffection manifested itself in the Egyptian Army, and the anti-alien movement, military and civil, rapidly came to a head when it found a leader in Colonel Ahmed Arabi. Speedily the national cause assumed the character of a revolt against the authority of the Khedive, and Anglo-French "protective inter-vention" became imperative.

Rioting broke out in Alexandria on June 11, 1882, in which more than fifty Europeans lost their lives. The Sultan would not send troops, and it was left to England and France to take whatever action might become advisable. Faced with the threat of invasion, Arabi proceeded to strengthen the fortifications of Alexandria. The Admirals of the English and French fleets ordered him to desist;

but without avail. France would go no further than her formal protest, and the vacillating policy of Freycinet's administration brought about a rupture in the concert of the two Powers, and in a helpless kind of way France faded politically from the Egyptian scene.

On July 11 Admiral Seymour shelled the Alexandrian forts,* and on the 24th British forces landed and occupied the port.

England had undoubtedly done her best to secure corporate intervention. After France, she had invited the participation of Italy, and again met with refusal. Lord Granville could honestly say: "We have done the right thing; we have shewn our readiness to admit others." Mr. Gladstone now decided that a military expedition must be sent to Egypt. The command was given to Sir Garnet Wolseley.

The first business of the expedition was to occupy the threatened Canal Zone. The free passage of the Suez Canal was endangered by the revolt, and it was the Khedive himself who authorised the British forces to seize such points of the Isthmus as might serve to safeguard the Canal.

De Lesseps was deeply mortified at the failure of his own country to lend her aid. He thought he saw his own work and that of his father before him being undone in a day by the wretched political changes at home. In unreasoning excitement he telegraphed to Arabi:

"The English shall never enter the Canal, never. Make no attempt to intercept *my* Canal. *I* am there. Not a single English soldier shall disembark without being accompanied by a French soldier. I answer for everything!"

Back came the reply: "Sincere thanks. Assurances consolatory, but not sufficient under the existing circumstances. The defence of Egypt requires the temporary destruction of the Canal."

The British expedition arrived only just in time to safeguard the waterway. "If Arabi had blocked the Canal," said General Wolseley, "as he intended to, we should be still at the present moment on the high seas blockading Egypt. Twenty-four hours' delay saved us."

By August 21 the British were in possession of Ismailia, their proposed base of operations. But in retiring Arabi's forces had

*In 1951, sixty-nine years later, all public transport in Cairo stopped for fifteen minutes as an act of protest on the anniversary of the bombardment.

dammed the Sweetwater Canal, and it was with some difficulty that they were driven from its proximity. The decisive battle which crushed the revolt took place at Tel-el-Kebir on September 13, and shortly after Arabi surrendered at Cairo. Wolseley returned to England leaving behind an army of occupation.

Henceforth there was no more Dual Control. France by her own action had lost for ever her status in Egyptian affairs, and Egypt became in all but name a British Protectorate.

So far as concerned the Canal three results followed. The least important, perhaps, was that England acquired an increased share in its direction. Where, after the purchase of the Khedive's shares, the Government had been permitted to have three seats on the Board of the Canal Company out of twenty-four, now a further seven directorships were given to representatives of British mercantile interests, though at the same time the total number of Directors was increased to thirty-two, which had been the original number.

The second result was that Great Britain was tacitly recognised as the custodian of the Canal exercising on behalf of Egypt the guardianship of the Isthmus. De Lesseps had declared the landing of the English forces during the Arabi revolt to be " an act of war which constitutes a flagrant violation of the neutrality of the Canal." Here, however, he was in error, for in his own proposals submitted to the Congress of Paris in 1856 he had made a point that " no foreign troops can be stationed on the banks of the Canal without the consent of the territorial Government," and in this case the British troops were in occupation at the express request of the Khedive. After hostilities had ended, however, it became a burning question as to whether, even with Egyptian consent, Britain could be allowed to take charge of the Canal without some international safeguard which assured that she would not use her position to the detriment of other Powers.

The situation led directly to the third result. The British Government was quite ready, and indeed anxious, to enter into guarantees with the other Powers to preserve the freedom of the Canal for the passage of all ships in any circumstances. But she desired to preserve the right to defend the Canal from an act of aggression against Egypt so long as the necessity for her present occupation of the country continued.

This was by no means acceptable to the Powers primarily interested. How long was Great Britain to remain in occupation ?

Negotiations dragged on until 1888, when at last a compromise was effected accepting the French proposal that a Commission of the Consular Agents of the signatories in Egypt should be empowered to watch over the due execution of the treaty which all desired.* The Canal was not to be neutralised, but rather extra-territorialised while remaining part of Egypt.

The Suez Canal Convention as finally agreed was signed at Constantinople on October 29, 1888, by representatives of Great Britain, France, Germany, Austria-Hungary, Italy, Russia, Spain, Turkey, and the Netherlands, and subsequently ratified by their respective Governments. The first article read :

" The Suez Maritime Canal shall always be free and open, in time of war as in time of peace, to every vessel of commerce or of war, without distinction of flag. Consequently, the High Contracting Parties agree not in any way to interfere with the free use of the Canal, in time of war as in time of peace. The Canal never shall be subjected to the exercise of the right of blockade."

It could by no means be foreseen at the time what extraordinary political changes would take place in the course of the next sixty years, which if they did not make the Convention a dead letter clearly demonstrated the need for drastic revision of its terms.

*This proposal was embodied in Article VIII of the Convention of 1888, but in fact it did not become operative. Great Britain did not formally adhere to the Convention until the signature of the Anglo-French Agreement of April 8, 1904, and then on the condition that paragraphs i and ii of Article VIII should remain in abeyance. For the complete text see Appendix C.

CHAPTER VII

THE MEDITERRANEAN QUESTION

THE signing of the Convention of 1888 might have been thought to have terminated the Suez Canal controversy. In reality this was far from being the case. The Canal was an integral part of the Egyptian Question, and Egypt was a part of the rapidly developing Mediterranean Question. Linked with both these questions was European envy of the power and might of Britain.

Both France and Russia, France in particular, were dissatisfied with the prolonged British occupation of Egypt. It was felt, and not without reason, that England was steadily taking over the rights of the Ottoman Empire as Egyptian suzerain. In spite of all British protestations that her sojourn in Egypt was only temporary, it was obvious that she was becoming more and more a fixture. France had hoped some day to regain at least a part of the ground she had lost in the Arabi affair, and deeply resented the fact that this hope would have to be dismissed as an illusion. Through diplomatic channels everything possible was done to get the Sultan of Turkey to assert his sovereign rights. The Sultan made the attempt by ordering Egypt to withdraw her troops from part of the Sinai Peninsula. It was reported that Turkey was even contemplating the construction of a strategic railway across the Peninsula to the edge of the Canal at Suez. These actions and intentions of the Ottoman Empire were regarded by Britain as directly menacing both the safety of Egypt and the security of the Canal, and her reply was both prompt and characteristic. Turkey was warned off, while a British fleet appeared in Egyptian waters to indicate what might be expected if the warning went unheeded. The Sultan gave way.

This was in 1906. But for the previous quarter of a century European power politics had been increasingly complicating the situation. This was specially true of the relations between Italy, France, and Germany.

So far as Italian policy was concerned, Great Britain did not appear to Italian statesmen at the time to constitute a potential enemy, even with England's hold on Egypt. The Mediterranean Problem was not seen as one in which British and Italian interests were in conflict. Even when Disraeli had acquired for Britain nearly half the Suez Canal shares, the decision was praised and welcomed. Sir Arthur Paget reported to Lord Derby a conversation which he had had with the Visconti Venosta, in which the latter had said: " that he should consider the possession by England, who was never likely to establish exclusive regulations to the prejudice of other Powers, of a preponderating voice in the affairs of the Canal, as highly advantageous to the commercial interests of all nations, and politically speaking . . . he could not but rejoice at an act which tended to increase the influence of Great Britain in the Mediterranean, not only on account of the past service which Italy had received from England, but also in view of general considerations connected with the future."

Italy's fears were reserved for her territorial neighbour France, whom she believed threatened her national integrity. The Mediterranean Question was at first felt to be more critical on its European side. The African side only began to assume importance when the French occupied Tunis in 1881, and there was the prospect of her seizing Tripoli and so holding the coast immediately opposite Italy. France was the encircling, imprisoning, and menacing Power. It was this conviction which led Italy to seek alliance with Germany and Austria.

Germany, though by no means enamoured of Italy as an ally, was willing to accept her as a junior partner as an additional check on France ; and Austria was brought in too on the understanding that Italy would help to preserve the Balkan *status quo*. The treaty which cemented the Triple Alliance was signed on May 20, 1882. The treaty was secret, and it was operative for five years.

It was not long, however, before Italy started to use the friendly overtures made by France as a bargaining lever to extract from her allies additional promises to be incorporated in the treaty when it should come up for renewal. In this way she obtained in a special German-Italian section of the amended treaty of 1887 an undertaking that Germany would safeguard the North African coast opposite Italy against French intrusion. The third and fourth articles of this section of the treaty are eloquent. They read:

Bird's eye view of Suez Canal, 1869

The Suez Canal Company's offices at Port Said

" 3.   If it were to happen that France should make a move to extend her occupation, or even her protectorate or her sovereignty, under any form whatsoever, in the North African territories, whether of the Vilayet of Tripoli or of the Moroccan Empire, and that, in consequence therof, Italy, in order to safeguard her position in the Mediterranean, should feel that she must undertake action in the said North African territories, or even have recourse to extreme measures in French territory in Europe, the state of war which would thereby ensue between Italy and France would constitute, *ipso facto*, on the demand of Italy and at the common charge of the two allies, the *casus fœderis* with all the effects, etc.

" 4.   If the fortunes of any war undertaken in common against France should lead Italy to seek for territorial guarantees with respect to France for the security of the frontiers of the kingdom and of her maritime position, as well as with a view to the stability of peace, Germany will present no obstacle thereto ; and if need be, and in a measure compatible with circumstances, will apply herself to facilitating the means of attaining such a purpose."

This fourth article reads somewhat mysteriously ; but its import was subsequently interpreted by Bismarck the German Chancellor as being " to mollify Italy and bind her to the Central Powers by means of gifts, such as could be made in the shape of Nice, Corsica, Albania, and territories on the North African coast."

Having found the bargaining game pay, Italy tried it on again when the treaty next came up for renewal in 1892.   Relations with France had improved, which made it possible to put up the price to Germany and Austria for remaining in the Triple Alliance. Germany was forced to promise to back up Italy not only in Tripoli and Cyrenaica, but also in Tunis. France, naturally anxious to detach Italy from the Triple Alliance, had already indicated that she would not interfere in Tripoli to the detriment of Italy.

The renewed treaty remained valid by prolongation to 1903 ; but the third time for renewal found Italy herself concerned to maintain the Alliance, as in the intervening period she had embroiled herself in war with Abyssinia and had suffered the disgrace of the defeat of Adowa.   What Bismarck had described as Italy's " jackal policy " became evident to the Austrian Ambassador in Rome, who wrote of Italy's " desire to have a part in everything, eagerness for new conquests, for a great success, fear of an unexpected coup which might procure this success for someone else and not for them."

E

The French by this time had become aware of the existence of the treaty and were naturally keen to know its terms. The Italians, however, evaded showing it to them and negotiated with France, despite the Triple Alliance, a distinct treaty by which both Powers expressed the intention to remain neutral if either should become the object of direct or indirect aggression by one or more other Powers. Italy was determined to have it both ways. " This is not artifice," Tittoni told the Italian Chamber ; " it is not Machiavellianism ; it is not a double policy, as had been wrongly said : it is simply the plain road to follow which presents itself inevitably to whoever really invites the preservation of peace."

According to Isvolski, the French view of the situation was that " neither the Triple Entente (of Britain, France, and Russia) nor the Triple Alliance can count on the loyalty of Italy ; that the Italian Government will employ all its efforts to keep the peace ; and that in case of a war it will begin by adopting a waiting attitude, and then join on the side towards which victory is inclining." Both World War I and II were to confirm the truth of this forecast.

Italy's recognition of herself as a first-class Power was bound to produce colonial aspirations ; but until her position had been secured by treaties and alliances imperialistic enterprises had to take second place. Italian statesmen like Francesco Crispi were keen on expansion, but the people were never really enthusiastic. The Italian emigrant had found so little difficulty in settling down in the midst of alien nations in other lands that he had seen little reason for burdening himself with the responsibilities of colonial possession and government.

In the first instance Italy's interest in North Africa was primarily defensive, as we have already noted. She wished to prevent the opposite coast of the Mediterranean from falling completely into the hands of the French. Commercial needs and undertakings, however, inevitably began to pave the way for empire. The caravan routes into Central Africa were valuable for trade, and so was a base on the Red Sea coast. Signor Rubattino, an Italian shipper, had bought the bay of Assab in 1870, and in 1882 Assab formally became an Italian crown colony. With the consent of Britain, concerned with the pacification of the Sudan, Italy extended her hold to Massawa and Beilul, and in 1890 the narrow but strategically important strip of territory partly conceded by the Emperor Menelek of Ethiopia was given the name of Eritrea. This was followed in 1891 by the assumption of a protectorate over Italian Somaliland.

The effect of these acquisitions was to establish Italy securely on the East African coast on the direct highway to India and the Far East via the Suez Canal. In this region France and Britain also, for various reasons, had staked claims ; so that there was now beside the Italian territories a French Somaliland with its port of Jibuti, and a British Somali Coast Protectorate ard East Africa Protectorate. In addition, since 1839, Britain had been in possession of Aden on the Arabian coast, and came into control of the Sudan, with its Red Sea port of Suakin, as a result of the campaigns following upon the Mahdist rising.

The rulers of Abyssinia did not take kindly to the Italian encroachments and flew to arms. On January 26, 1887, an Abyssinian force of 20,000 surprised near the village of Dogali some 600 Italians under the command of Colonel De Cristoforis, and almost completely annihilated them. The " Disaster of Dogali " created widespread anger in Italy and desire for revenge. The Depretis-Robilant cabinet fell, and its successor authorised Italy's first major colonial campaign. This proved successful less by military than by diplomatic strategem. The Italians played off the King of Shoa, Menelek, against the heir of the Negus Johannes, rivals for the Ethopian throne ; and when Menelek triumphed they secured from him by the Treaty of Ucciali not only commercial privileges and the acceptance of the Italian colony, but also the right to represent him in foreign relations. They could thus claim to exercise a virtual protectorate over Abyssinia.

Clause 17 of the Treaty of Ucciali stated : " His Majesty the King of Kings of Ethiopia consents to make use of the Government of His Majesty the King of Italy for the treatment of all questions concerning other Powers and Governments." The treaty was ratified in 1889, but, jealous of Italy's growing influence, Menelek denounced it in 1893.

Again there was war. Italy proceeded to the conquest of Tigré. General Baratieri pushed forward his expeditionary force and reached Axum, the holy city of Abyssinia ; but the vaccilation in his tactics the following spring (1896) led to his terrible defeat at the Battle of Adowa, when the Italians lost nearly 10,000 men killed and prisoners.

The effect of Adowa at home was even more painful to the Italians than the Dogali disaster. Crispi and his colonial policy had to go, and after an uneasy peace had been patched up with Abyssinia Italy decided that she had had enough of overseas adventures for the time being. This partly accounts for Italy's failure to make any decisive move in the matter of Tripoli until 1911, although it had been acknowledged as a sphere of Italian influence both by the Triple Alliance and the Triple Entente.

The Italo-Turkish war was declared on September 29, 1911. In Italy the public mind had been prepared in the usual way—" protection of interests," " insults to the flag," " outrages on civilians," and the like, and to crown these " the genuine and beneficent work of economic progress and civilisation." Signor Giolitti announced that the primary reason for his Government's action was that, while " Western Africa, from Tunis to Morocco, was under the protection of European administration, Libya was very much behind the times. Slave markets were still held in Benghazi, and men and women taken by violence in Central Africa were sold in these markets : infamies which it was impossible to tolerate at the very gates of Europe."

In the interval between the Abyssinian and the Tripolitan campaign there had been time for a strong Italian nationalism to develop, its sabre-rattling leaders being the direct forerunners of the later Fascists. According to McCullagh, they were " jingoes of an extreme and candid type. They believe in war for war's sake. They believe that the shedding of blood makes a nation virile, unifies it, intensifies the patriotism of the individual."* These words were written in 1912.

On the other hand the Italian Labour Party was antagonistic to the war. The rather obscure socialist editor of *Lotta di Classe* (Class Struggle) proclaimed that " millions of workers are instinctively opposed to the African colonial undertakings. The adventure of Tripoli is a red herring to distract the country from facing up to its grave and complex internal problems." He was imprisoned ; but when he came out of jail next year he resumed his vituperative denunciations.

*Italy's War for a Desert, p. 4.

" International militarism," he cried, " continues to celebrate its orgies of destruction and death. Every day that passes the huge pyramid of lives that have been sacrificed rears it bloody summit upon which Mars stands waiting with his unsated and contorted mouth in an infernal grin. . . . So long as there are fatherlands there will be militarism. The fatherland is a spook, like God ; and, like God, it is vindictive, cruel, and tyrannical." The author was the future Fascist Duce, Benito Mussolini.

The war was waged by Italy with great ruthlessness. To avoid complications in Europe it was vital to secure victory as rapidly as possible. But it was the imminence of the Balkan War which really forced Turkey to give up the struggle at the end of the year. Peace was signed at Ouchy, October 18, 1912. By the terms of the treaty Libya (including Tripoli and Cyrenaica) was ceded to Italy.

In the course of the war Italy had seized the Dodecanese Islands in the Ægean, ard she continued her occupation of these islands as a guarantee that the terms of the treaty would be carried out. The islands, however, were never evacuated, and after the First World War they too were ceded to Italy by the treaties of Sèvres and Lausanne. Particularly Leros and Rhodes were to become important air and naval bases constituting a direct menace to Egypt and the Suez Canal. Thus the Tripoli campaign marked the real beginning of the attempt to assert Italian supremacy in the Mediterranean, while Italy's territorial gains in Africa brought a new Power into immediate relationship with issues which before had seemed primarily to lie between France and Britain.

How acute those issues could be had only recently been illustrated by the Fashoda incident, when in September, 1898, the French flag had been hoisted 300 miles south of Khartoum on the very line of march of Kitchener's Anglo-Egyptian army reconquering the Sudan from the Mahdi and his successor the Khalifa.

By the Anglo-Egyptian agreement of January, 1899, the eastern Sudan was constituted an Anglo-Egyptian condominium under effective British control, whereas most of it prior to 1882 had been under Egyptian government alone. Its western frontiers were settled by the Anglo-French agreement of March, 1899, which, while it recognised the French spheres of influence in that area, left that country by no means content. The taste of Fashoda was still bitter, and there was some resentment at the way in which Britain had finally ousted France from all association with Egyptian affairs. Britain, indeed, only obtained the reluctant acceptance of her position in Egypt by consenting to the satisfaction of French claims in Morocco and Italian claims in Tripoli and Cyrenaica.

West of the Suez Canal these adjustments finally brought about a situation which seemed to hold promise of accord for the Powers most directly concerned with the Egyptian and Mediterranean questions, with the exception, of course, of Turkey. With the loss of Libya and most of its Balkan territory in the wars of 1911-1913 the influence of the Ottoman Empire had been considerably reduced. Only the Arab lands still remained, and Turkey's hold on some of these was now precarious.

But what was left of the Ottoman Empire was of great strategic and economic importance, and a fourth great European Power was ready to exploit this to the uttermost. With the burgeoning of German imperialism the area of tension shifted from the west to the east of the Suez Canal.

CHAPTER VIII

DRANG NACH OSTEN

T HE year 1888 in which the ambitious German Prince
Wilhelm became the Kaiser Wilhelm II also saw the opening
of the railroad from Central Europe as far as Constantinople,
and the granting of a concession to German interests for its extension as far as Angora (Ankara). This line, completed in 1892, was to
be the first stage in the project subsequently known as the Berlin-
Baghdad Railway.

In its origin the scheme was designed to assist the Sultan to
control more effectively the outlying parts of the Ottoman Empire ;
but German commerce, seeking means of expansion, was quick to
seize on the possibilities presented by the undeveloped Near East.
Catching fire from the Emperor's imperialism, German agents
swarmed out to capture markets and plant the flag of German
culture in every region where a foothold could be gained.
" Germans," said the Emperor, " must never weary in the work of
civilisation ; Germany, like the spirit of Imperial Rome, must
expand and impose itself."

With amazing industry Germany built up her economic empire,
and beside it grew ever greater her military and naval might. Her
destiny demanded a " place in the sun," and she meant to have it.
The railway advancing into Anatolia pointed an iron finger at the
East as one area where German influence might well become paramount. Turkish fear of Russia made German assistance welcome,
and in 1898 the Emperor was being entertained by the Sultan at
Constantinople, the first Christian sovereign to be so received. The
Kaiser persuaded his host to reorganise the Turkish Army on
German lines under German officers. He also visited Palestine, and
part of the wall of Jerusalem was knocked down to permit his entry
on a milk-white steed. In grandiloquent terms at Damascus he
proclaimed his friendship for the three hundred millions of the
Islamic world. About the same time the Deutsche Bank secured

the preliminary concession for the construction of the Baghdad Railway.

It seemed as if the Kaiser had taken the Turkish domains under his particular patronage, and the mailed fist began to peep out at Morocco and elsewhere. There was as yet no serious clash with British imperialism, except in the matter of the Boer War, but it was at least clear to the Emperor and his advisers that Britain stood in the way of full German aggrandisement. Mistress of the seas, guardian of the gateways to the wealthy Orient, England was recognised as Germany's most formidable enemy and rival. To bring that enemy to her knees became the barely concealed object of German policy. It was this policy that prompted the feverish construction of a powerful German navy and the works on the Kiel Canal, and that dictated the encouragement of the Young Turk Party when the sinister Abd al-Hamid had been deposed.

The British domination of Egypt, and her use of the Suez Canal route to the Far East, could to a considerable extent be offset by the restoration of the northern overland route pioneered centuries earlier by such travellers as Marco Polo. Germany might outflank her rival through the railway system connecting Berlin with Baghdad through its extension to the Persian Gulf. Such a railway system, indeed, associated with a regenerated and German-controlled Turkey, would facilitate an eventual Turkish reoccupation of Egypt and the ousting of England.

The strategy of the whole conception was clearly set forth by such German writers as Dr. Paul Rohrbach in his book *Die Bagdadbahn*, published in 1911.

" England can be attacked and mortally wounded by land from Europe only in one place—Egypt. The loss of Egypt would mean not only the end of her dominion over the Suez Canal and of her communications with India and the Far East, but would probably entail also the loss of her possessions in Central and East Africa. The conquest of Egypt by a Mohammedan Power, like Turkey, would also imperil England's hold over her sixty million Mohammedan subjects in India. . . . Turkey, however, can never dream of recovering Egypt until she is mistress of a developed railway system in Asia Minor and Syria, and until, through the progress of the Anatolian railway to Baghdad, she is in a position to withstand an attack by England upon Mesopotamia. . . . The stronger Turkey becomes, the greater will be the danger for

England, if, in a German-English war, Turkey should be on the side of Germany. . . ."

It will be seen that the situation was in many respects similar to that which had existed a century earlier when French imperial aims had clashed with those of Britain, and France had hoped under Napoleon to destroy the power of England through Egypt. Egypt, indeed, has been recognised again and again from her geographical position to be the pivot of any ambitious imperialistic world plan conceived by a European Power.

History was inclined to repeat itself now. England was again slow to appreciate that the Baghdad Railway offered any threat to her interests and vital communications with India *via* the Suez Canal. She was even ready in the initial stages to give her co-operation in carrying out the scheme. Only at the end of 1909 did Britain demand from Germany control of the section of the line from Baghdad to the Gulf. Here Britain was to a certain extent protected by an agreement made with the Sheikh of Koweit in 1899, whereby that ruler had undertaken not to cede any of his territory without British consent.

Discussions dragged on, with Russia continuing invincibly opposed to German designs. At last an Anglo-German agreement was reached which fixed the terminus of the railway at Basra until Britain should permit of its further extension to Koweit, and gave Britain two seats on the directorate. But this was not until June, 1914, and by then war was imminent and the Convention was not ratified.

In the meantime at the end of the Second Balkan War the German General Liman von Sanders had been appointed by the Turkish Government to reorganise its army. Von Sanders was to have commanded the First Army Corps, at Constantinople, with very considerable authority. Russia, supported by France, vigorously protested against the conferment of these wide powers, and finally Germany accepted a limitation of Von Sanders's position to Inspector-General of the Turkish forces.

Elsewhere in the Middle East the German programme was being pursued in various ways. Taking advantage of the Anglo-Russian Convention of 1907 which virtually divided Persia into English and Russian spheres of influence, but promised respect for Persian independence, German missions appeared in the Persian

Gulf. Led by the German "Lawrence of Arabia" Wassmuss, appointed Consul at Bushire, brusque demands were made for equal rights for German shipping in the Gulf. These demands were resisted, and for a time Wassmuss was sent elsewhere. But he was reappointed to Bushire in 1913, and set to work very successfully to win the affection of the tribes of Dashtistan and Tangistan, adopting their dress and manners.

The effect of Wassmuss' activities was seen at the outbreak of World War I, when he was ordered to Constantinople. There he was "instructed by Enver Pasha in the Turco-German scheme to enlist the Middle East on the side of the Central Powers. The plan was this : a mission of Turks and Germans, under the leadership of Wassmuss, was to cross Persia and Afghanistan in order to inter-view the Emir at Kabul and persuade him to identify Afghanistan with the cause of a Holy War, which, in the meantime, would have been proclaimed."

All the ramifications of the Turco-German design are still not clear ; but certainly some time before the war the terms of alliance between the two Powers were being discussed, though signature did not take place until August 2, 1914.

The British Foreign Office, apparently, was largely ignorant of what was brewing. Nevertheless, it was British action which was largely responsible for cementing the Alliance by fostering anti-British feeling in Turkey. By seizing the Turkish battleship *Osman I*, nearing completion in a Tyne shipyard, the British Government created widespread resentment at Constantinople. This was at the close of July, and Germany hastened to profit by the circumstance by ordering the commanders of the cruisers *Goeben* and *Breslau*, then in the Mediterranean, to pass through the Dardanelles and anchor off Constantinople. There a fictitious sale of the two vessels to the Turkish Navy took place.

Before considering the further developments which contradicted Turkey's continued professions of neutrality, a digression is required here to bring the affairs of the Suez Canal up to date. In spite of the clouds which were steadily gathering on the political horizon, and which might well be fated to endanger the Canal, the Company responsible for its operation had devoted themselves assiduously to improving its serviceableness by enlarging and deepening the channel and reducing the dues. A very important works programme was initiated in 1908 and completed in 1914. Under this programme the channel of the Canal was widened to 148 feet over its whole length at a depth of 33 feet, and deepened to 36 feet.

The size of the ships using the Canal had so much increased by this time that a new programme was adopted in 1912 even before the previous one was finished. This programme was the most ambitious hitherto, and its principal object was the permission of the passage of vessels of a length of 720 feet, a width of 92 feet, and a draught of 33 feet. For this purpose improvements had to be made in the roadsteads of Suez and Port Said as well as in the Canal proper. Owing to the war this programme could not be fully completed until 1924.

When these programmes were initiated, since they involved very heavy financial commitments, the Suez Canal Company thought it well to approach the Egyptian Government for an extension of its Concession, which would make it easier to carry the burden.

In 1908 the Concession still had sixty years to run. It was now proposed to extend the period for a further forty years, from November 17, 1968, to December 31, 2008. The terms offered were very favourable to Egypt, and ministerial circles were by no means opposed to the idea. A strong body of opinion in Egypt, however, thought otherwise, considering that the prolongation of the Concession meant the prolongation of foreign—and particularly British—interference in Egypt's internal affairs. The Canal Company's move was regarded by the Arabic Press as British inspired, which was loud in its denunciation of the Egyptian Ministers who—they said—were prepared to sell the birthright of their country.

The nationalist outcry was such that Sir Eldon Gorst the British Agent decided that the final decision should be left to the Egyptian General Assembly. The Assembly appointed a commission to consider the agreement, which rejected it unanimously, and it was finally turned down by the Assembly itself in April, 1910, with only one vote cast in its favour out of about one hundred.

The outbreak of World War I effectively put an end to any questions affecting the future status of the Canal. Its security became a far more urgent matter.

Egypt was willy-nilly a belligerent on the side of Britain against the Central Powers, in view of the British military occupation. The pro-German Khedive Abbas Hilmi was at Constantinople at the time, and his Prime Minister, Hussein Rushdi Pasha, was acting as Regent. Rushdi realised that nothing would be gained by defying Great Britain, even though the quarrel was not the direct concern of Egypt, and the Council of Ministers decided to accept the inevitable. As was stated in their Declaration of August 5, 1914 : " Since the presence in Egypt of His Britannic Majesty's Army of Occupation renders the country liable to attack by His Majesty's enemies . . ." the Government was obliged to take the measures necessary to defend the country against the risk of such attack.

By the proclamation of August 5 the Egyptian Government ordered the Suez Canal to be cleared of enemy shipping. The order was imperative, as it was easily possible for any of such vessels to sink themselves in the Canal and block it at least temporarily. Apart from this, enemy ships, relying on the Suez Canal Convention, were clinging to the ports of access to the Canal in order to evade capture, where they helped to congest the harbour. Such vessels were given a free pass to leave ; but when they would not do so they were taken outside the three mile limit to escape if they could.

It was held by the Prize Court set up at Alexandria on September 30 that :

" Whatever questions can be raised as to the parties to and between whom the Suez Canal Convention, 1888, is applicable, and as to the interpretation of its articles, one thing is plain—that the Convention is not applicable to ships which are using Port Said, not for the purpose of passage through the Suez Canal or as one of its ports of access, but as a neutral port in which to seclude themselves for an indefinite time in order to defeat belligerents' right of capture after abandoning any intention which there may ever have been to use the port as a port of access in connection with transit through the Canal."

This was the first time where Egypt was concerned that the terms of the Convention had been tested under war conditions, and it was shown that all contingencies had not been foreseen. Nevertheless there was exhibited by the Allies a desire to operate the Convention so far as it was workable, the safety of the Canal and its unimpeded passage for shipping being understood to be the essential elements in its application. No attempt was made to seize any enemy vessel within the three-mile limit unless there was good reason to apprehend the commission of some hostile act in the Canal.

The British and French fleets so effectively controlled the eastern Mediterranean and the Red Sea that almost from the outset there was no likelihood of the Canal being injured by a naval bombardment.

A land attack was a greater possibility, especially when it was discovered in October, 1914, that the Turks were laying down roads in the Sinai Peninsula, and that German officers were supervising the arrangements. But at the time, with Turkey still ostensibly neutral, the possibility was not seriously entertained.

" It is legitimate to say of the early autumn of 1914," wrote Lieut.-Col. P. G. Elgood,* " that throughout Egypt there was no consciousness of the significance of the reported concentration in Syria of formidable Turkish Forces, or no doubt that the Sinai desert was an impossible barrier to a hostile army advancing upon the Suez Canal. Local opinion was sadly uninstructed. Not only did people complacently ignore factors directly affecting the security of Egypt, but they knew nothing of the potential resources of the Ottoman Empire, or of the arrogant ambitions of its rulers. A little more education upon the first point would have saved the foolish optimism thought and talked, when General Sir Ian Hamilton set out to force a landing on the beach of Gallipoli, and wider knowledge on the second that the Suez Canal was protected by nature from attack. One did not need to possess much military knowledge to recognise that General Maxwell had insufficient forces to hold Egypt if Turkey joined the enemy.... If the opinion in Cairo was insensible of impending danger from Turkey, the Canal Zone was equally unconscious. If it was suggested that Egypt might become in the future an actual theatre of war, the remark would be received with an incredulous smile. ' But looking at the subject from a shipping point of view,' a pessimist would ask an acquaintance, ' Have you no anxiety as to the safety of the Suez Canal if Turkey enters the war ? ' ' Not from the land. No regular army could traverse Sinai,' was the invariable reply. Strange that men should know so little of the events of history."

The real question was, did Germany see the situation in this light, or would there be an attempt to put the pre-war plan for a Turkish assault on Egypt into operation ?

The plan indeed seemed ludicrous with Turkey's still most inadequate communications in Palestine and the supply problem for a sufficiently large expeditionary force across the desert. General Liman von Sanders, Inspector-General of the Turkish Army,

*Egypt and the Army, pp. 65-7.

frankly said so, but apparently the German High Command thought otherwise, and Djemal Pasha, one of the Young Turk triumvirate, was especially keen on the venture. Von Sanders afterwards wrote :

" It seems to me that very hazy ideas must have been entertained at home about the possibility of conquering Egypt. This so-called fatal spot of England evidently was the subject of fantastic mischief in Germany and the navy was not without a share in it, though it should be stated in extenuation that the navy was wholly ignorant of the conditions surrounding a land expedition on Turkish soil in Asia."

Von Sanders was overruled, and in Constantinople there was great eagerness to regain Egypt.

With the Kaiser the destruction of the British Empire had become a mania. He fully believed in the Rohrbach thesis that this could be accomplished by ousting Britain from Egypt and the Suez Canal, and spoke exuberantly of " cutting England's jugular vein."

Towards the end of October, 1914, the Turkish Government sent an insolent note to the British Embassy declaring that Egypt was, and would always be considered, an integral part of the Ottoman Empire. The Allies responded by breaking off diplomatic relations.

CHAPTER IX

DEFENCE OF THE CANAL, 1914-1918

IN November 1914 Turkey openly joined the Central Powers and Britain declared that a state of war existed between herself and the Ottoman Empire. This immediately created a problem in Egypt, since the country was still nominally a part of the Ottoman Empire, and its *de jure* ruler Abbas Hilmi, a friend of Turkey, was at Constantinople. Feelings among all sections in Egypt were more or less strongly opposed to the British Occupation. A nationalist spirit was increasing, and many of the effendi class had both family ties and sympathies with Turkey. In these circumstances Britain could hardly hope to count on active co-operation in the conflict, and had to aim rather at achieving passivity.

Acting upon instructions from London the General Officer Commanding, General Maxwell, had declared martial law to be in operation as from November 2, and followed this up with an explanation that this measure was not intended to supersede the Civil Administration. In announcing the rupture of peace General Maxwell made clear that the sole burden of the war would be borne by Great Britain. Yet something more was wanted to assure reasonably settled conditions for the duration of hostilities. The British Foreign Secretary therefore gave notice on December 18 that Turkish suzerainty over Egypt was terminated, and that Britain was assuming a temporary Protectorate. On the following day it was further announced that H. H. Abbas Hilmi Pasha had been deposed from the Khediviate, and that the dignity with the title of Sultan had been offered to Prince Hussein Kamil Pasha.

In the meantime Turkey was proceeding with the movement of troops and supplies into Syria and Palestine in preparation for the proposed advance on Egypt. The problem of communications was a serious one, since adequate rail and road services were not available in the south, and the distance from Constantinople to the Suez Canal was approximately twelve hundred miles. Yet by successful use of such lines as there were, together with further extensions and alternative methods of transport, the difficulties were surmounted, and sufficiently formidable forces were speedily brought within striking distance of the Canal. In this movement the German officers and engineers were of great assistance.

The final concentration fell considerably below what had been intended, and was far too small for the military invasion of Egypt. But Djemal Pasha, Commander-in-Chief of the Expeditionary Force, counted with no real justification on support within Egypt which would hamper and weaken the British defence.

So cocksure was Djemal that he allowed himself to be called " The Saviour of Egypt," and as he stepped into his train at Haidar Pasha he told his friends, " I shall not return until I have entered Cairo." His German Chief of Staff, Oberst Freiherr Kress von Kressenstein, was extremely able, but took a less rosy view of the prospects. The conquest of Egypt might appeal to Berlin and Constantinople ; but it would be satisfactory to the German commanders on this front if the expedition achieved the more limited success of blocking the Suez Canal. This indeed was not beyond its power in the early days ; for if the resources of the striking force were limited, so also were those of the defence.

A considerable part of the British Occupation troops had had to be sent to Europe in August. Lord Kitchener sent out a Lancashire Division as replacement, and is said to have remarked, " Lancashire spins cotton. Not a bad thing, then, if Lancashire men see how the raw material is grown." These forces were supplemented by untrained men from Australia and New Zealand, and two Divisions of Indian Infantry. With these the double duty had to be performed of maintaining the security of Egypt and guarding the Canal.

The Canal itself was made the front line, and except for a few advance posts on the eastern bank covering the ferries the defence force was entrenched behind the Canal, a circumstance which led Lord Kitchener on a visit of inspection to enquire, " Are you defending the Canal, or is the Canal defending you ? "

In addition to the available troops units of the British and French fleets were stationed in the Canal, and to shorten the front to be held a considerable area east of Port Said lying below sea level was flooded.

Three routes were available to the invaders, northern, central,

and southern, and the central was rightly chosen as the most practicable. Here the terrain lent itself to the possibility of effecting a
successful crossing of the Canal either north of Lake Timsah over
the sill of El Guisr, or south of the Lake over the lower sill between
Serapeum and Toussoum. Curves in the Canal at both points would
be of advantage to the attackers, and by converging upon and
capturing the Sweetwater Canal behind Ismailia the defence
deprived of water supplies would be forced to capitulate. Yet it was
in the northern and southern sectors that the first exchange of shots
took place. On January 26, 1915, a Turkish patrol opened fire on a
British post five miles east of Kantara, while south of the Little
Bitter Lake at El Kubri there was another small clash. These
incidents were no doubt meant to keep the defence guessing ; but
intelligence reports and aerial reconnaissance indicated that the
main attack would come in the central sector.

On the 27th maritime traffic through the Canal was suspended
and the danger zone cleared. The attack did not develop, however,
before February 3. In the early hours of that day feints were made
towards Kantara, the Ismailia Ferry Post, and El Ferdan, while
at a well-chosen point between Toussoum and Serapeum the real
attempt to cross the Canal was made. Here the few pontoons
brought from Constantinople were launched, but only three actually
got across. The remainder were either dropped on the eastern bank
or sunk by gunfire. The attack was kept up throughout the day,
though greatly impeded by a violent sandstorm. In the end failure
was complete, and though their numerical losses were not great
the Turks decided to retire. Virtually nothing was done to harass
the retreating forces, and no provision for pursuit had been made.

Although the grand design to invade Egypt had ended so swiftly
and ignominiously to the deep chagrin of Djemal, the Suez Canal
was by no means out of danger for some months. From time to
time detachments of Turks approached the Canal, and at the end
of June one of them succeeded in planting a mine at the southern
end of the Little Bitter Lake which was struck by the steamer
Teresias. But resumed shipping through the Canal was only interrupted for half a day.

The Canal was never in jeopardy for the rest of the war, and
to-day the only reminder of its ordeal is the memorial of twin
obelisks on the Jebel Mariam and a Turkish pontoon riddled with

F

shrapnel holes which reposes peacefully in the garden of the Residency at Ismailia.

From 1914 to 1918 the passage of shipping through the Canal continued on the principle of " business as usual " with only the very minor interruptions mentioned, though considerably depleted in volume owing to German submarine activities in the Mediterranean. Two valuable facts emerged from the experiences of World War I. It had been demonstrated that the Convention of 1888 could be kept in spirit, if not exactly in the letter, and that given suitable measures for defence the Canal was by no means as vulnerable as had frequently been suggested.

In 1916 a threat to the Suez Canal still remained. The Turks had been considerably reinforced and were now serviced by a railroad through Palestine as far as Beersheba constructed under the oversight of Meissner Pasha, the German contractor who had been responsible for the Berlin-Baghdad Railway. But the British and Colonial forces, by this time operating east of the Canal, were also stronger. A substantial attack by the Turks was mounted in July against the British defensive line resting on Katiya and Romani. It was defeated, and by the end of the year the British had pushed forward across the Sinai Peninsular to the frontiers of Palestine. Behind them also came the railway from Kantara, eventually to provide a through line from Egypt to the north.

The Palestine Campaign of 1917-1918 ultimately brought about the collapse of Turkish arms and the final destruction of the Ottoman Empire. The apportioning of its remaining possessions in the Near East were to create a crop of new problems, not least among them " the establishment in Palestine of a National Home for the Jewish people " as promised in the British Declaration made by Lord Balfour to Lord Rothschild in his letter of November 2, 1917.

During the war Egypt had been attacked not only from the east but also from the west. Turkey had had to give up Libya to the Italians in 1912, but there had been no time for the new masters to consolidate their gains. The native Senussi tribesmen were a sturdy independent people, with little love certainly for the Turks with whom they had ties of faith. Their hostility to Europeans, however, was quite fanatical, and suitable bribery made their chief, Sayid Ahmed, very willing to engage in hostilities against both

British and Italians. There was, indeed, a risk that the Senussi might accomplish what the Turks could not, secure the co-operation of the Egyptian fellahin, and so provoke internal resistance to the Occupying Power which it would have been extremely difficult for the limited British forces to deal with. The Italians, who had joined the Allies eventually after sitting on the fence, could give little help, as they were forced to repatriate most of their forces to meet the invading Austrians. Almost the whole of Libya had to be abandoned to the Senussi chieftains, leaving the Italians in possession of only a narrow strip of the Tripolitanian coast covering Tripoli and Homs.

Advancing eastward the Senussi reached within striking distance of Mersa Matruh, 150 miles from Alexandria. But they were driven back, and by March, 1916, the British reoccupied Sollum. In the end, after combating grim conditions in the Western Desert, the Senussi leader was ousted from Siwa and the other oases to which he had retreated.

Yet here in Libya as in the Arabian lands on the east of Egypt bargains and promises too easily made were to sow the seeds of future strife. By the Treaty of London, April 26, 1915, various inducements had been offered to Italy to side with the Allies, and as uncertainly worded as the British promises to Arabs and Jews. Article 13 of the Treaty stated : " In the event that France and Great Britain should increase their African colonial possessions at the expense of Germany . . . Italy shall be able to claim certain equitable compensations, notably in the adjustment in her favour of questions concerning the frontiers of the Italian colonies of Eritrea, Somaliland, and Libya, and the colonies adjacent to those of France and Britain."

As directly affecting the Suez Canal, Britain herself took a step at the termination of the war designed to give her the legal right to protect this vital imperial artery which had been imperilled. In the Peace Treaties with the " enemy " Powers who had been signatories of the Suez Canal Convention they were required to consent to the substitution in the Convention of the name of Great Britain for that of the Ottoman Empire. By Article 152 of the Treaty of Versailles, " Germany consents, in so far as she is concerned, to the transfer to His Britannic Majesty's Government of the powers conferred on His Imperial Majesty the Sultan by the Convention . . ." Declarations to the same effect were signed by

Austria (Article 107 of the Treaty of St. Germain), by Hungary (Article 91 of the Treaty of Trianon), and by Turkey (Article 109 of the Treaty of Sèvres, and Article 99 of the Treaty of Lausanne).

This action made nonsense of at least one Article of the Convention, *i.e.*, Article X, since Britain did not stand in relation to Egypt in the same place as the Ottoman Empire had formerly occupied. No doubt it would have been difficult at the time to draft an acceptable new Suez Canal Convention, and the easiest course was chosen to enable Britain to secure the rights she wanted. But the resultant saddling of the Egyptian Sinbad with an apparently permanent British Old Man of the Sea could not fail to be further detrimental to the already strained state of Anglo-Egyptian relations.

CHAPTER X

MATTERS ARISING

AT no time during the previous history of the Suez Canal had Egypt been independent. Until 1914 she owed allegiance to Turkey, though from 1882, when Great Britain commenced her occupation of the country, that allegiance had been very nominal. From 1914 to 1922 Egypt was a British Protectorate, and even until 1936 certain aspects of the Protectorate continued. Only very gradually and through the determined will of the nation did Egypt secure full and unrestricted self-government.

Self-determination for peoples was the slogan of the day in 1919, and the Egyptian nationalists meant to make their voice heard. They had been vocal before the war, but now they organised themselves into the Wafd, and under their leader, Saad Pasha Zaghlul they rapidly acquired power and influence and dominated every other party in the country. Carrying on an unremitting agitation, not unattended by serious disorders, the Wafd forced Britain to concede at least part of their demands, and principally to abolish the Protectorate, though with certain significant reservations.

The important declaration that " the British Protectorate over Egypt is terminated, and Egypt is declared to be an independent sovereign State " was publicly proclaimed at Cairo on March 15, 1922, and on the same day Ahmed Fuad, who had succeeded his brother, Hussein Kamil, in the autumn of 1917, took the title of King as Fuad the First.

The Wafdists, who became the governing party with Zaghlul as Prime Minister, were by no means satisfied with the declaration, and did not accept it officially, for it included a provision which stated :

" The following matters are absolutely reserved to the discretion of His Majesty's Government until such time as it may be possible by free discussion and friendly accommodation on both sides to conclude agreements in regard thereto between His Majesty's Government and the Government of Egypt."

These affected among other things (a) the security of the communications of the British Empire in Egypt, and (b) the defence of Egypt against all foreign aggression or interference, direct or indirect. The British forces remained in Egypt, and the British High Commissioner continued to act in an advisory capacity. No change was made in the Anglo-Egyptian Condominium over the Sudan.

Successive British Governments, both Labour and Conservative, remained adamant on these reserved questions in spite of the reference to " friendly accommodation." The expression cropped up more than once, but it always seemed accommodation by Egypt to the British view.

When the Labour Party came into power in Britain in 1924 the Wafdists hoped for a modification in the British attitude ; but in this they were to be disappointed. Zaghlul Pasha saw the Prime Minister, Mr. Ramsay MacDonald, in the autumn of that year, and made five specific demands as the basis for an agreement: (1) the withdrawal of British troops from Egypt ; (2) withdrawal of financial and judicial advisers ; (3) no interference by the British Government in Egyptian affairs, particularly in the conduct of foreign relations ; (4) renunciation by Great Britain of her claim to protect foreigners and minorities in Egypt ; and (5) renunciation by Great Britain of her claim to protect the Suez Canal.

As regards the Canal it was suggested that its protection should be entrusted to the League of Nations after the British troops had been withdrawn. Mr. MacDonald made it clear that this proposal would be quite unacceptable.

" I raised the question of the Canal straight away because its security is of vital interest to us, both in peace and war. It is no less true to-day than in 1922 that the security of the communications of the British Empire in Egypt remains a vital British interest and that absolute certainty that the Suez Canal will remain open in peace as well as in war for the free passage of British ships is the foundation on which the entire strategy of the British Empire rests. . . . No British Government . . . can divest itself wholly, even in favour of an ally, of its interest in guarding such a vital link in British communications. Such a security must be a feature of any agreement come to between our two Governments, and I see no reason why accommodation is impossible given goodwill."

Out of office the Labour Party, and the I.L.P., might talk of internationalising the Canal, or placing it under the control of the

League, but there was never any probability that such talk would be translated into action. International relations were far too unstable to permit of any quixotic experiment in a matter so closely affecting British vital interests. It was felt, and Arthur Henderson endorsed this opinion, that " free navigation of the Suez Canal is already provided for by the Convention of 1888. His Majesty's Government see no reason to propose the modification of this arrangement."

Anglo-Egyptian negotiations which should make Egypt's independence a reality dragged on for years, never succeeding in reaching an agreement on all the points at issue. Draft treaties were prepared and rejected, a very meaty bone of contention being the continued presence of the British forces, which the Wafdists regarded as an army of occupation and not as the defenders of Egyptian territory against the possibility of aggression.

The problem was how to make the military occupation palatable. If the troops were genuinely intended for the defence of the Canal there seemed to be no good reason why they should be based on Cairo. Why could they not be transferred entirely to the Canal Zone, and preferably to the eastern bank of the Canal ?

The London Conference of 1930 brought a solution appreciably nearer. The British troops would be stationed on the west bank of the Canal in the proximity of Ismailia and would co-operate with Egyptian forces in protecting the waterway. Unfortunately the negotiations again broke down over the Sudan question, and it was not until 1936 that differences were hurriedly adjusted, partly under compulsion of Italian activities, and the Anglo-Egyptian Treaty was signed.*

Britain was now more evidently the ally of Egypt rather than her protector. The British troops were to continue on Egyptian soil only until such time as the Egyptian army was strong enough to take over full defensive responsibility. In the meantime they would move out of Cairo† if and when adequate barracks were provided for them in the Canal Zone, and new roads were laid down to facilitate rapid transport in case of need.

The new understanding created at the time by the Anglo-Egyptian Treaty was further improved by the action of the Suez

*See Appendix D.
†The move did not take place until after World War II, having been cancelled by the Egyptian Government in August, 1939, in view of the grave international situation.

Canal Company. In the earlier period the Egyptian people never felt the Canal was in any sense their own, though they had contributed to its construction in money and labour. The shares that Egypt held in the Company, nearly half the total, were not the property of the nation but rather the property of the Khedive. No Government, as such, had any voice in the administration of the Company. The shareholders were all private persons, who themselves elected the Directors. When the Khedive sold his shares and interest to the British Government Egypt lost even her indirect connection with the undertaking except for the ultimate reversion at the termination of the Concession. This had been a sore point with the Egyptian nationalists, who held that Egypt was deriving no benefit from a great enterprise carried on on her own soil. Actually this was an exaggeration, but there was enough truth in it to make the Egyptians very touchy. The fact that the British Government, by virtue of its purchase of the Khedive's shares, became the only Government represented on the Board did not help matters, for the Egyptians felt that Britain thus occupied a privileged position in relation to the Company which should rightfully have been theirs.

The conclusion of the Anglo-Egyptian Treaty of 1936 enabled a calmer and saner view of the position to be taken. The negotiations which had resulted in the Treaty were carried a stage further by the Company. Appreciating the store set by the Egyptian Government on having a stake in the operation of the Canal, the Company entered into conversations designed to contribute to this end.

The outcome of these conversations appeared in the 1936-1937 Convention between the Canal Company and the Egyptian Government. It was agreed that in future two Directors of the Company should be Egyptian. Further, the Company undertook to pay an annual rental of £E300,000, and to contribute as a single payment another £E300,000 towards the cost of the new strategic roads alongside the Canal provided for by the Anglo-Egyptian Treaty. The Company also promised to take each year a number of Egyptians into its employment, so that by 1958 one-third of the Company's total staff would be Egyptian. Lastly, there was an agreement affecting a new basis of valuation for the maximum chargeable for dues. The Canal Company was at all times an Egyptian Company ; but Egypt could now feel that this was true as regards operation as well as registration.

The real wealth which Egypt has derived from the Suez Canal has been the transformation of the area from desert and swamp into one of habitation, cultivation, and industry, with flourishing towns and modern amenities. It was natural, perhaps, for the Egyptian nationalists to stress Egypt's losses through the sale of her interest in the undertaking, but fundamentally these have been far outweighed by her gains.

Had the Suez Canal Company been assured of permanent occupation and administration of the Canal Zone it could not have done more for the good of the area than it has done with the certainty only of a brief tenure. At every stage a liberal portion of the profits of the Company has gone back into Egypt in carrying out its work of town-planning and reclamation on the most approved principles, and besides all this there has been the continual improvement of the waterway, its harbours, and installations.

Beneficial to Egypt as they were, and going far towards meeting her claims and desires, the fruitful negotiations which have just been considered were yet overshadowed by a mounting tension resulting directly from the imperialistic aims of the Fascist régime in Italy.

Italy's reconquest of Libya began in 1922.* General (afterwards Marshal) Rodolfo Graziani was given a free hand in the subjugation of the country. In an utterly brutal and inhuman fashion he set to work to occupy Libya " acre by acre." The task took him the best part of ten years. By 1928 the whole of Tripolitania had been subdued, including the Fezzan and the eastern oases. Finally, Senussi resistance in Cyrenaica was overcome.

In the course of the conflict Graziani well earned the name of " the scourge." Nearly half the native population of Cyrenaica perished. " An enemy forgiven," said Graziani, " is more dangerous than a thousand foes." Mercifully for the inhabitants his rule terminated soon after the conquest, and in 1934 Air-Marshal Italo Balbo was sent out to take over as Governor.

To Balbo fell the unenviable task of placating the people so terribly injured, of establishing law and order, and carrying out the Fascist programme of development and colonisation. It says much for his character and natural gift of leadership and organisation that

*What follows on this page is substantially from " Libya," by Hugh J. Schonfield, forming Chapter 8 of the Symposium, *Islam To-day*, published in 1943 by Faber and Faber.

he achieved a striking success in all these activities, and won by his personal charm and wise measures a considerable goodwill.

Libya from 1929 was divided into its two rational provinces of Tripolitania and Cyrenaica, the former with its administrative seat at Tripoli and the latter at Benghazi. Frontier rectification proceeded through a series of agreements from 1919 to 1935, when the Rome Agreement was signed by M. Laval for France and Mussolini. The various negotiations regarding Italian possessions in North Africa affected Britain and Egypt also. They represented the fulfilment by the Allies of the bargain struck in the Treaty of London. In 1925 Egypt ceded to Italy the oasis of Owenat on the Sudan frontier, and the wells of Sarra, while Britain ceded Jubaland on the Kenya border, which became part of Italian Somaliland. Awkward salients in Libya were straightened out, and the area now included the oases of Ghadames and Ghat on the west and Jarabub on the east. Italy agreed to waive her claim to a corridor linking Libya with Lake Chad and Nigeria, but more than half the length of the main caravan route, Lake Chad to the Mediterranean, came under Italian control.

The hard-won territory was by no means easy to administer or to colonise owing to lack of communications, and strategic reasons also dictated the construction under Balbo of " La Litoranea," the great coastal highway from the border of Tunisia to the border of Egypt, 1,132 miles long. The most difficult stretch of this road to complete was its 340-mile curve round the barren Gulf of Sidra. At the spot which was once the boundary between the Carthaginians and the Cyreneans, in the heart of the desert, La Litoranea was spanned by a commemorative arch towering 100 feet into the blue. The road was formally opened by Mussolini at its Egyptian end on his visit on March 12, 1937.

Originally, Italy's aim in Libya was defensive, to prevent the French from gaining control of the Mediterranean coast opposite Italy itself. But under a Fascist régime, and once full possession had been secured, policy changed from the defensive to the offensive. Libya plus the other Italian possessions on the Red Sea coast gave rise to a dream of North African empire reviving the glories of ancient Rome.

At first the defensive and apologetic aspects continued to be stressed. In an essay on *Italy, the Central Problem of the Mediterranean*, Count Antonio Cippico wrote in 1926:

" Only half the coasts of France and Spain border on the Mediterranean. If that sea were to be blocked some day, if England were to close Gibraltar and Suez to trade, France and Spain would not perish, for they could still reach the sea, could still seek freedom of action and movement on their Atlantic shores. But unlike any other great Mediterranean Power, Italy is stretched like a bridge in the very centre of that sea : its waters bathe all her coasts. Not only her liberty but her very life depends on the goodwill of those who hold the keys of Gibraltar and Suez, of those who have installed themselves, for imperial, not national needs, in Malta and Cyprus. More than forty-one millions of Italians could be starved in a few weeks if those who hold the gateways of the Mediterranean were suddenly to decide on hostilities and close those gates- to the imports of grain, coal, fuel oils, and iron, of all the raw materials, in short, essential to the life of a modern civilised nation. In view of her geographical position, which makes her a prisoner in her own sea.... Italy is to-day the gravest problem of the Mediterranean."

In Mussolini's words, what is England's highway (*via*) is Italy's life (*vita*). Once again Britain's position in the Near East and her imperial communications were seen to constitute an obstacle to the expansive needs of a European Power.

Fascism thus called for a complete change in the Italian attitude towards Egypt. No longer was it a question of maintaining a balance of influence: Egypt was definitely marked down as a prey, to fall —without war if possible—under Italian domination, if not actual occupation. Italy was to oust Britain from Egypt, and to take her place.

Until the signature of the Anglo-Egyptian Treaty it was the business of Italian agents to encourage by all means anti-British feeling, and demands for complete Egyptian independence and the total withdrawal from Egypt of the British forces. They fomented trouble among the students of the Al-Azhar University, tried to work up sympathy with the Palestine Arabs, and in the ten years from 1924 to 1934 they were the brains as well as the purse behind many of the Egyptian political agitators.

The Treaty itself, concluded in face of a barely concealed threat of Italian invasion from Libya, only temporarily checked the flow of propaganda. But later it was resumed and even doubled in intensity. Prominent in these revived activities was the *Agence Egyptienne Orientale*, the Near Eastern branch of the Stefani news service.

" The A.E.O. had been opened for the express purpose of anti-British propaganda in the Arabic-speaking countries. From its centre in Cairo it radiated throughout the Near and Middle East including Arabia, Iraq, Palestine, Syria, and the Lebanon. It had its correspondents in Hodeida (Yemen), Baghdad, Jerusalem, Beyrout, Damascus, and other centres. They sent their reports to Cairo, and it was the function of the A.E.O. office to distribute these to the Arab Press. The office also distributed the Stefani despatches from Rome. All this material—invariably anti-British in tendency—was presented gratis to the newspapers."*

Alongside the anti-British propaganda there was another kind of propaganda of the order of the snake hypnotising the bird. This was directed with many fulsome adjectives to soothing Egyptian fears about Italy's intentions. Italy, so it was said, believed in the great future of Egypt. Far from having any designs on the country, Italy was anxious to see her in flourishing independence. Italy's policy was that of the good neighbour. Her Libyan frontier coincided with that of Egypt: it was for the two countries to foster amicable relations and to advance hand in hand towards their golden destiny.

Some Egyptian politicians fell for these blandishments ; but they were a very small minority and were actuated on the whole by fear that the country could not offer adequate resistance to attack. Italy had taken little trouble to conceal the masses of troops which she was keeping in Libya, and none at all to hide the perfection of the coastal road. It was even said that Marshal Balbo had gone out of his way to inform the Egyptian Premier that a method had been found of ensuring a water supply through the desert. As none of these activities sounded in the least friendly it is not a matter for wonder that most Egyptian statesmen found it hard to credit Italian neighbourliness.

George Martelli, in his important book just quoted, reports that somebody had once said to him that " there would be peace in the Mediterranean if Mussolini decided he could not take Egypt in his own lifetime." At the time no one could know what the Duce had decided as regards Egypt, but from the decision to attack Abyssinia the worst was to be anticipated.

*Martelli, *Whose Sea?* p. 169. The author deals with the Italian propaganda at considerable length.

CHAPTER XI

SANCTIONS AND SUEZ

MARSHAL DE BONO has confessed in his book *Anno XIII* that already in 1933 he had advised Mussolini to annex Abyssinia. " I put the following considerations to the Duce," he says : " ' the political conditions in Abyssinia are deplorable ; it should not be a difficult task to effect the disintegration of the Empire if we work it well on political lines, and it could be regarded as certain after a military victory on our part.' "

The die was cast. In the spring of 1934 there was much speechmaking on Italy's civilising mission in Africa, just as there had been before the Tripoli war in 1911. But this time Mussolini was the instigator instead of the opponent of aggression. Military preparation was hastened on. There followed the deliberately exploited Wal-wal incident, a territorial claim on an undemarcated frontier. War supplies began to pour increasingly through the Suez Canal.

Menaced by aggressive acts and threatening force the Ethiopian Government, as a member of the League of Nations, appealed to the League in January, 1935, for the application of Article XI of the Covenant in order to preserve peace. A settlement of the problem became urgent. Britain and France were alarmed, and there were vain attempts at a compromise solution. On September 11 the anxious Assembly at Geneva was rallied by the statement of' Sir Samuel Hoare that Britain would adhere to the Covenant. " The League stands and my country stands with it," he stated, " for the colllective maintenance of the Covenant in its entirety and particularly for steady and collective resistance to all acts of unprovoked aggression."

Mussolini snapped his fingers at the League : it had failed over Manchuria ; it would fail again. As an extraordinary measure Britain despatched the Home Fleet to the eastern Mediterranean. Italy concentrated troops in Libya. It was a near thing ; but Mussolini was confident that Britain would not act on her own.

Either it was the League as a whole, or no intervention. There was no *casus belli* between Italy and England: Mussolini was not planning to attack the British Empire but that of Abyssinia. Counsels at Geneva and elsewhere were divided.

The British naval gesture actually gave to Mussolini just the needed touch of dramatic circumstance to line up the Italian people solidly behind him. On October 2 he came out on the balcony of the Palazzo Venezia amidst the roars of massed thousands crying hysterically, " Duce ! Duce ! Duce ! " It was his great moment.

" Blackshirts of the Revolution ! " he cried, " Men and women of Italy ! Italians scattered throughout the world, across the mountains and across the ocean !

" A solemn hour in the history of the fatherland is about to strike. Twenty million Italians are gathered at this moment in public squares throughout Italy. It is the most gigantic demonstration which the history of mankind recalls. Twenty millions are there, with a single heart, a single will, a single decision.

" We refuse to believe that the real people of France can associate themselves with sanctions against Italy. The ' Bayards of Bligny,' who perished in a heroic attack which drew admiration from the enemy, would rise from beneath the grass that covers them.

" Until it is proved to the contrary, I refuse to believe that the real people of Great Britain want to spill blood and send Europe to the verge of catastrophe in order to defend an African country universally stamped as barbarous and unworthy of a place among civilised nations.

" But we must not ignore possible eventualities.

" To economic sanctions, we will reply with our discipline, with our sobriety, with our spirit of sacrifice. To sanctions of a military nature, we will reply with military action.

" No one should so delude himself as to think he can bend us. He will surely be beaten.

" It is against this people of heroes, poets, artists, navigators, and administrators that one dares to speak of sanctions.

" Italy, proletarian and Fascist Italy, Italy of Vitorrio Veneto, and of the Revolution, to your feet !

" May the core of your very firm and unbreakable decisions fill the skies and reach to our soldiers, ready to fight in East Africa ! May their power be a spur to friends, a warning to enemies, and may it carry the word of Italy across the mountains, across seas, and throughout the world !

" The cry of Italy is the cry of justice, a cry of victory ! "

The following day Italy invaded Abyssinia, and fifty nations **at** Geneva denounced her as the aggressor.

Abyssinia, to her undoing, placed implicit confidence in the carrying out of the Covenant. Its great test had come ; for once Italy had been declared to be the aggressor it was the business **of** the League to proceed to the application of Article XVI—Sanctions.

It was laid down in this Article, as amended by the Fifth Assembly in September, 1924, that :

" Should any Member of the League resort to war in disregard of its covenants under Articles XII, XIII or XV it shall *ipso facto* be deemed to have committed an act of war against all other Members of the League, which hereby undertake immediately to subject it to the severance of all trade or financial relations. . . . The Council will notify to all Members of the League the date which it recommends for the application of the economic pressure under this Article. . . . It shall be the duty of the Council in such case to recom- mend to the several Governments concerned what effective military, naval, or air force the Members of the League shall severally con- tribute to the armed forces to be used to protect the covenants of the League. The Members of the League agree, further, that they will mutually support one another in the financial and economic measures which are taken under this Article."

The Council contemplated its obligations under Article XVI with the utmost timidity. To fulfil them would mean, they felt, not an Abyssinian War but World War ; and whatever the Article might say the Member States did not regard themselves as at war with Italy, neither did they feel able or desirous of going to war. Half- heartedly Limited Sanctions were applied, financial and economic, but so limited that the essential embargo on oil supplies to Italy was not included.

A chain is only as strong as its weakest link : the weak link in this case was M. Laval.

" M. Pierre Laval wished to run with the hare and hunt with the hounds : to keep Italy's friendship by placating Mussolini without breaking with Great Britain. When directly asked to state his policy, notably with regard to the embargo on petrol, and to declare himself either for or against Italy, he thought of nothing but how to gain time. . . . He did not perceive that the Duce was only looking for a backer or worse, an accomplice, to help him towards the realisation of his dreams of Empire."*

*Mme. Tabouis, *Perfidious Albion—Entente Cordiale*, pp. 266-267.

How much was the British Government of the time in earnest ? Had the sending of the Home Fleet into the eastern Mediterranean been nothing but a warning gesture, or did it mean business ?

Major-General A. C. Temperley has written:

" I could not see eye to eye with Sir Samuel Hoare in the view that we could take the lead in economic sanctions against Italy and remain on friendly terms at the same time. Nor could I escape the conclusion that, after Sir Samuel Hoare's burning words at Geneva . . . we ought to have blocked the Suez Canal against Italian shipping. This drastic step would probably have meant war with Italy, but it would have saved the League."*

Many were saying at the time that the Canal should be closed to the Italians. It seemed such an obvious thing to do. The war was being fought in Abyssinia at the southern end of the Red Sea. To reach the theatre of operations Italy had to send all her troops and war material through the Suez Canal. Blockade the Canal and you automatically stopped the war. It was as simple as that—apparently. Why then was it not done ?

The possibility had been canvassed in League circles even before the outbreak of hostilities. It had been one of the Sanction measures in contemplation, the refusal to support which by Great Britain had given Pierre Laval an excuse for temporising. Alexander Werth has referred to an unpublished note by the French Minister dated October 18, 1935. In this note M. Laval recalled a conversation with the British Foreign Secretary on September 9 :

" Sir Samuel Hoare had spontaneously informed him that in no circumstances would the British Government apply to Italy any sanctions other than financial and economic sanctions ; and that such measures as a naval blockade of Italy or the closing of the Suez Canal were out of the question."†

If this information is correct, the British spokesman no doubt had in mind the Suez Canal Convention guaranteeing the freedom of the Canal from blockade in time of peace or war. What cannot be denied is that Britain did not rule out the possibility of war with Italy as an extreme outcome of the measures proposed in Article XVI of the Covenant. But she would not take unilateral action, even if she made preparation for eventualities and adopted certain precautionary measures.

*The Whispering Gallery of Europe, p. 330.
†The Destiny of France, p. 179.

An aerial view of the Canal prior to the British evacuation of the
Canal base

The statue of Ferdinand de Lesseps at Port Said before
its destruction in 1956

The statue of de Lesseps at Port Said after being dynamited
by Egyptians in 1956

Had it come at the time to war between Britain and Italy no doubt the Canal would have been closed to Italian shipping on grounds of the defence of Egypt as well as the Canal under Article X of the Convention. The Italians were well aware of this, and it was one of the considerations that led them afterwards to make claims for representation on the Board of the Suez Canal Company.

One of their writers later pointed out :

" It would be illusory to suppose that in case of a conflict the Convention would be respected, all the more since the expression 'defence of Egypt' in Article X might give rise, in case of need, to the most tendentious interpretations against the right of anyone. The defence of the Canal deserves therefore to be examined and solved in a way favourable to us, if only to enable us to be on the spot and to have guarantees as to the non-existence of works which under the pretext of defence would in fact be aimed against us."*

The strict and quite proper adherence to the Suez Canal Convention by Great Britain made the Limited Sanctions which were imposed so utterly futile and ridiculous that before many months they had to be called off. It was only too patent that there was no heart or drive behind them, and the Dictators rightly felt that henceforth they could snap their fingers at the League and at the Collective Security system.

Writing in 1938, Madame Tabouis was quite convinced that the European catastrophe really dated from that ineffective year 1935. On page 265 of the book already quoted she has this pregnant statement :

" What the situation needed was that Great Britain and France, forgetting past quarrels and mindful of their obligations as guardians of the peace, should have left in the mind of the aggressor no possible doubt as to their common resolve, integrally and without faltering, to apply those sanctions to which they were pledged, whether military or by the stoppage of petrol supplies, in the latter of which they were assured of the co-operation of the United States.

" There was also the possibility of closing the Suez Canal to Italian shipping, a measure, however, whose validity, in view of the 1888 Convention, appeared doubtful to international jurists. On the other hand, it could be argued on the theory of reprisals that Italy's violation of international justice condoned a violation of the 1888 Convention as a consequence.

*Article in the Italian Review *Gerarchia*, February, 1939.

G

" As a justification of the weakness actually displayed, it is often urged to-day (*i.e.* in 1938) that positive action involved the risk of a world war. That danger did not, in fact, then exist.

" In order to avoid that risk in the future and to stop any further blackmail on the part of the Dictators, a precedent should have been created, proving to the world at large the value of the system of collective security to which all the democracies, all the Central European and Balkan States, and even the neutral powers remained attached.

" Europe would have found herself to-day in a very different situation from that which has led her into an armament race and made the fear of war her incessant companion."

The Emperor of Abyssinia to his undoing had relied completely on the Collective Security system. He was applauded, but he was not heeded. The League of Nations faced its obligations under the Covenant with extreme discomfort and reluctance. The members foresaw the direst consequences and were unprepared for them.

In a challenging statement made to *The Times* special correspondent on April 30, 1936, Haile Selassie, King of Kings, Lion of Judah, pronounced these fateful words :

" Do the peoples of the world not yet realise that by fighting on until the bitter end I am not only performing my sacred duty to my people but standing guard in the last citadel of collective security ? I must hold on until my tardy allies appear. And if they never come then I say prophetically and without bitterness, the West must perish."

He at least was clear on the issue. And already mustard gas (yperite) shipped through the Suez Canal had rained upon his defenceless people blinding and maiming hundreds of helpless women and children.

The problem of whether wrong must be met by wrong, force by force, hangs over us yet. The Collective Security system is being tried again to-day under the auspices of the United Nations with a will and determination absent in 1935. But it has not yet been proved to be successful in producing a condition of permanent peace. There is the melancholy merit in the present policies that the Powers having subscribed to them are endeavouring conscientiously to carry them out. But that does not make the policies right or good. It does not touch the root causes of aggression, and seek to eliminate them.

On the other hand, whether resisted or not, it has surely been established that aggression does not pay. Its immediate rewards are delusory. The gains often fall far short of expectations, or turn out to be no gains at all, but rather liabilities. Conquest gives incentive to or necessity for further conquest, which brings the aggressor in the end to utter loss and ruin. Abyssinia was a striking case in point.

"Since the conquest of Ethiopia," wrote Ambrosini in *I Problemi del Mediterraneo*, "the Suez Canal has acquired for Italy such importance that for her also as and even more than for Great Britain, it must be considered an essential line of communication. That is why Italy, more than any other Power, is interested in assuring for all time free navigation through the Canal."

George Martelli, who quotes this statement, aptly comments upon it as follows :

"It is only necessary to look at a map to appreciate the truth of this utterance. If anything it is an understatement. For the Abyssinian War every soldier, every gun, every load of material had to pass through the Suez Canal. Since the war was over, most of the food required to feed the garrison and the colonists, and the whole of the equipment necessary to build the new empire, from bedsteads to steel girders, bootlaces to cement, has had to take the same route. So far from becoming gradually self-supporting Abyssinia to-day is more dependent on supplies from Italy than ever and there is only one way these supplies can come. If we imagine what we would feel about a foreign Power ensconsed in Egypt we may equally realise what Italy thinks of our position astraddle the Suez Canal. From the point of view of the Italian Empire it is as if a vice were fitted about one's neck with somebody else controlling the screw.

"Having given hostages to fortune, she (Italy) would naturally like to redeem them, and she can only do so by herself assuming the stranglehold which is at present the monopoly of Great Britain. If Spain is important because a high proportion of Italian imports pass through the Straits of Gibraltar, if the possession of Tunis is desirable both for strategical and colonial purposes, both these interests take second place when set beside the question of the Suez Canal. Mussolini can afford to be blockaded in the Straits ; he can renounce his claim to Tunis without much loss of face ; but to have to give up Abyssinia would mean the defeat of all he stands for."*

To acquire for Italy an empire undoubtedly proved a financially ruinous proceeding. One of Mussolini's grievances was the French possession of the key port of Jibuti and her control of the

*Whose Sea ? p. 167-168.

main transport line to it from the interior, the Addis Ababa Railway. To get goods to and from the coast was an expensive business. Before the Second World War France was very concerned about the possibility of a seizure by Italy of French Somaliland; for to consolidate and reap the fruits of one aggression meant inevitably embarking on further aggression.

The Fascist Government had gained little more than a certain prestige at home by the conquest of Abyssinia, and that prestige had to be maintained however great the cost. With an overburdened exchequer Mussolini made his difficulties the subject of further complaint against the Democracies. The reason the cost of Empire was so heavy, he declared, was because of the high charges which had to be met for transit through the Suez Canal, run by a company consisting principally of English and French shareholders and directors. If the dues were lower Italy could make a profit.

With two unfruitful provinces in Libya and Abyssinia, Italy was in the position of a man who, at enormous expense, has built the wings of a huge edifice which are comparatively valueless to him until he can complete the centre block ; and this he is prevented from doing by the wretched landowner in the middle who refuses to sell out at any price.

Italy was really interested in the Suez Canal because she regarded it as a key to a privileged position in Egypt. If she could not acquire the property she coveted she would like to make sure of having a duplicate of the key so that she could have access to the premises. The question of the Suez Canal dues was a secondary consideration, as Italian writers admitted. In fact what Italy had paid did not represent more than about 1 % of what the Abyssinian adventure had cost her. What was of more importance was to gain a share in the control of the Canal.

Talk of Italy's " colonising and civilising enterprise in East Africa " was so much hot air. Even after the war in Abyssinia was over the larger part of the dues paid by the Fascist State in 1937 and 1938 represented the passage of warships and troopships through the Canal. In the latter year the Italians dispatched on the outward journey through the Canal 30,570 troops, and on the inward journey 61,372. The British figures for the same year were 19,588 outward and 27,988 inward in the service of her whole vast eastern Empire.

Prior to 1934 Italy for many years had occupied the fifth place among users of the Suez Canal. In 1934 she rose to fourth place, due to the fact that she had already begun to mass troops in Eritrea towards the end of that year. In 1935 the Abyssinian war brought her up to second place. The peak year of Italy's traffic through the Canal was 1936, and even then did not exceed 20.2 per cent of the tonnage passing through the Canal. By 1938 the percentage had dropped to 13.4.

Incidentally, the complaints against the Canal Company had no justification whatever, since it had been a consistent policy of the Company continually to review and reduce transit charges as much as possible. Between 1935 and the end of 1938 the tariffs on Suez Canal tonnage were lowered from 7s. 6d. per ton to 5s. 9d. for laden vessels, and from 3s. 9d. per ton to 2s. 10½d. for ships in ballast.

On March 26, 1939, in the Olympic Stadium at Rome, the Duce delivered a twenty-six minutes' speech for which all Europe had been breathlessly waiting. In certain respects it struck a note which is curiously up-to-date from the viewpoint of 1952 in its references to Bolshevism and need for a foreign loan.

Mussolini went on to say:

" We do not ask the world for justice, but we want the world to be informed. In the Italian Note of December 17, 1938, Italian problems in respect of France were clearly established—problems of a colonial character. These problems have a name : Tunisia, Jibuti, the Suez Canal."

Apart from Tunisia, Jibuti, and the Suez Canal, there was the reference in the speech to the Adriatic which no one understood until twelve days later on Good Friday Italian troops occupied Albania.

CHAPTER XII

RUMOUR RUNS RIFE

THE attack on Albania, a Muslim country, was a great shock to Islamic sentiment, especially as the Duce, imitating the Kaiser before the First World War, had posed as the champion of Islam, and for much the same reason to embarrass and weaken the British and French.

At the very beginning of the Fascist régime Mussolini had declared in the Chamber of Deputies in November, 1922:

" The situation in the Balkans and in Islam merits attentive watchfulness. Let us not forget that there are 44,000 Muslims in Rumania, 600,000 in Bulgaria, 400,000 in Albania, and 1,500,000 in Yugoslavia—an entire world that the Crescent's victory has exalted."

It was pointed out by George Slocombe that:

" More than one foreign observer in Rome has noted the increasing interest shown by the Italian dictator in Moslem affairs. The American writer Carleton Beals, in his work *Rome or Death*, states that ' particularly is Fascist policy interested in a *rapprochement* with the peoples of the Orient, Far and Near. The Fascisti desire that Italy dominates the Mediterranean with the co-operation of the Mussulman world, for the sake of dispossessing France and England ; besides, Italy's geographical position actually suggests her as a mediator between the Occident and the portals of the Orient.' "*

To achieve the desired Islamic co-operation Italy used the full force of her propaganda machine. We have already briefly referred to the working of this machine in the Arab countries† which busied itself with fomenting disaffection with French and British rule. Here we would add that Mussolini had the benefit of a propaganda weapon which pre-1914 Germany did not possess, and which other Powers have subsequently found of the utmost value—the Radio. The Oriental mind is strongly responsive to rumour, and once a

*The Dangerous Sea, pp. 108-109.
†See pp. 81-82.

story really gets going it is the hardest thing to stop or contradict it. It is repeated, exaggerated, and embroidered upon with the utmost relish, and the last thing which appears to be done is to question its veracity. Coming over the air it is in any case regarded by the uneducated as having a special authority.

Italy was the first country to exploit the radio for propagandist purposes among Arab peoples. The broadcasts of the Bari station undoubtedly exercised a very considerable influence, ladling out anti-British information especially connected with the spread of false statements about British " atrocities " in Palestine. The difficulties of Great Britain as the Mandatory Power in dealing with the Jewish-Arab problem lent themselves admirably to the purposes of Fascist mischief-making. The " news " being sandwiched between excellent native music and singing, so much appreciated by the Arabs, made the programmes doubly welcome. Until the founding of Sharq al Adna Radio Station the British radio response both in news and music was dull and insipid by comparison and exhibited little comprehension of native psychology.

In a Muslim country, such as Libya, entirely under Italian rule, the policy of posing as the protector of Islam could be fostered in other ways. Old mosques were repaired and new ones built.

The climax of all this careful cultivation of Islamic sentiment came in March, 1937, with the personal visit of the Duce himself. A group of native dignitaries was shepherded into his presence, and duly presented him with a symbolic sword, on receipt of which Mussolini declared the sympathy of Fascist Italy for Islam and the Muslims of the entire world.

The main object of his visit, however, was to bless Italy's colonising efforts and to open the strategical coastal road. " This journey is imperialist," he announced, " in the sense that has always been given to this word, and will always be given to it by virile peoples. But it has no hidden designs or aggressive aims against anybody."

This was said with the aggression against Abyssinia already committed and that against Albania in contemplation.

Pietro Silva had given an interesting picture of the Libyan situation as its real purpose was understood by the Fascists.

" With the completion of the coastal road the great Mediterranean colony was equipped, in the first year of the Empire, with the power adequate to the needs and development of an imperial policy. During the Mediterranean crisis which accompanied the Abyssinian enterprise, the conditions in the colony, its equipment, its air bases, its ports, the possibility of defence and offence offered by its geographical situation, dominating as it does a large zone of the Central Mediterranean, had played an essential rôle in determining a solution favourable to Italy. The immense importance of Libya in the Mediterranean system had then appeared in full. With the end of the crisis and the creation of the Empire its importance was still further emphasised : the visit of the Duce with the consequent decisions regarding the increase of the military, naval, and air forces permanently stationed in the colony constituted the clearest recognition of this."*

The Islamic world of Africa and Palestine could swallow the Italian propaganda so long as it voiced Arab grievances and served the cause of Arab independence outside the Libyan zone. But faith in Italian expressions of goodwill became rather less definite for a time with the seizure of Albania.

In April, 1939, President Roosevelt asked for an assurance by the Dictators that they had no aggressive intentions against certain specified countries. Egypt was on that danger list.

Egypt's immediate response to the situation was to pass an emergency measure increasing the police force. " Should an emergency arise," wrote the *Daily Telegraph's* correspondent, " it would be of paramount importance to guard against widespread panic among the civilian population of Cairo and Alexandria." It was rumoured that German troops were pouring through the Brenner Pass *en route* for Libya.

"London knows the value of the Duce's word," wrote *Paris-Soir*, " Like that of the Fuehrer it is worth its weight in air. Machiavelli is not to be trusted. What is the meaning of the tons of material and of the troop transports which are crossing the Adriatic ? While the Dodecanese, including Rhodes, is the scene of troop concentrations the other end of the Axis is also moving, and the soldiers of the Reich are crossing Berlin on their way—whither ? "

Still the tension increased. Leave was stopped for the French troops in Morocco. The French Mediterranean Fleet put to sea for an unknown destination. British forces were transferred from Palestine to the Egyptian frontier with Libya. German headlines screamed : " The climax of democratic impudence has been reached

*'Il Mediterraneo Dall ' Unita de Roma All ' Impero Italiano, p. 489.

—England means to let her warships sail before the very gates of the Roman Empire!"

On Thursday, April 13, important declarations condemning Italian aggression were made by both the British and French Governments. Almost as if he had heard them Mussolini was proclaiming at Rome: " The historical events which have just come to an end are are the result of our will, our faith, and our strength. We go towards nations who are our friends ; against hostile nations we shall have a clear resolute attitude of hostility. The world is asked to leave us alone to our great daily labours. In any case the world must know now that we, to-morrow as yesterday, to-day as always, will go straight ahead."

"Everybody knows," wrote the *Egyptian Mail* on April 19, " that in the event of another aggression by the totalitarian Powers war may easily ensue, a war into which most if not all of the Mediterranean countries will automatically be swept, and that Egypt presents a desirable target for the enemy forces. The struggle for the control of the Mediterranean in general, and the Suez Canal in particular, makes this country the inevitable centre of conflict, especially with the Italians on the Libyan frontier and a potential menace beyond the Sudan."

Wide currency was given to an article in *Le Temps* by General Catroux on Italy's threat to Egypt. After dealing with the prospects of invasion favourable to Italy, he had pointed out that Italy's gains would be considerable. " From the strategic viewpoint Britain's prestige in Levant, Arabia, the Persian Gulf, and even India. And Egypt, with all her resources, would be invaluable to the Axis."

But the General had added significantly:

" One hundred and forty years ago, a conqueror who thought on the same lines as Italy failed to keep Egypt because he lost the battle of Aboukir. Can Italy hope for a better fate ? Some of her citizens have been heard to say proudly that there will be no naval battle because Italian 'planes and submarines can clear the sea. The Admiralties think otherwise, however. They are not worried by such talk. They know that, thanks to the considerable superiority of the means at their disposal, they can sooner or later be masters of the seas. When that day comes, it will spell ruin for Italian enterprise in Africa, however much success it may have met with in the early stages."

These words were destined to prove prophetic. At the time they made little or no impression on the Axis leaders.

In one matter, however, not all the Fascist propaganda and political manœuvring had produced the desired results. No concessions to the Italian demands were made regarding the Suez Canal. They wanted not only substantial reductions of the dues, but seats on the Board of Directors of the Suez Canal Company, and finally the substitution for the Company's administration of some form of international administration in which Italy would share.

The campaign was carried on indirectly rather than directly by a sustained bombardment with paper ammunition in which argument, vilification, and misrepresentation all played a part. The campaign had reached a climax in the winter of 1938-1939. At the very beginning of the year the British Prime Minister (Mr. Neville Chamberlain) and the Foreign Secretary (Lord Halifax) had talks at Rome with Mussolini and Count Ciano ; but the Suez Canal questions were not discussed. Before Mr. Chamberlain left he was asked in the House of Commons by Mr. Arthur Henderson if he would give an assurance that the Government would not agree to any alteration of the status of the Suez Canal without consulting all the signatories to the Suez Canal Convention, and securing the approval of the Egyptian Government.

The Prime Minister replied : " The status of the Suez Canal cannot be altered without the consent of the parties to the Convention of 1888 and of Egypt." He added that in the Anglo-Italian Agreement of April 16 (1938) H. M. Government and the Italian Government had reaffirmed their intention always to respect and abide by the provisions of the Convention of 1888 as at that time in force, and that they had communicated this declaration to the Egyptian Government.

This was confirmed by the Egyptian Minister for Foreign Affairs in January, when replying to a deputy, he said:

" The Egyptian Government had not been the object of any demand concerning the Canal, and that so far it had engaged in no international discussions of the subject. Nevertheless, the Government had taken the necessary measures to safeguard the rights of Egypt and clearly to reveal that nothing could be done without her consent, and that for three reasons : first, the Canal traversed Egyptian territory ; second, it was Egypt which had given the Concession ; and third, the Canal would go back to Egypt."

According to Italian propagandists the claim to two or more seats on the Board of Directors of the Suez Canal Company was founded on Article XXIV of the Statutes of the Company, which states: "The Society is administered by a Council composed of thirty-two members representing the principal nationalities interested in the enterprise."

The Italian *Revue Gerarchia* of February, 1939, argued as follows:

"There cannot be the slightest doubt as to the interpretation of this Article : by ' nationalities interested in the enterprise ' is to be understood nationalities interested in the traffic, and not, as some have wished to maintain, nationalities financially interested ; for that would not square with the sale of shares to individuals at the time of the foundation or with the universal character of the Company.... Italy, therefore, is first of all interested in obtaining the immediate recognition of her right to be represented on the Board of the Company by a number of members proportionate to her traffic through the Canal."

The facts did not support the Italian contention. The Company's Statutes containing the Article concerned were made public nearly two years before the subscription list was opened, when the financial backing of all the civilised States was being solicited. "Nationalities interested in the enterprise " certainly meant at that time nationalities providing the financial backing which would enable the Canal to be constructed.

The Article could have no bearing on traffic because some of the countries were not even Maritime Powers. The intention of De Lesseps in making his Company " universal " was to secure the widest possible participation in the cost of the venture, so that all nations could feel that they had a stake in it. Indeed, as we have already seen,* he actually reserved a percentage of the share for each of the States whom he hoped would contribute. As it transpired, the bulk of the shares were taken up by France and Egypt. England took up none of the shares set aside for her, and only came in with her purchase in 1875 of the Khedive's holding. Italy's financial interest amounted to little more than that of Belgium, hardly 1 per cent of the total. It was inevitable in the circumstances that the Administration should be initially Franco-Egyptian in complexion, and subsequently Franco-British. Nevertheless persons of other nationalities have been given seats on the Board. These

*See p. 35.

Directors have been appointed by the shareholders, as with all Companies, for their personal qualifications, and not as representatives of their respective Governments or specially on account of the magnitude of the traffic of their countries through the Canal.

There was nothing to prevent the appointment of an Italian Director, if the shareholders approved any individual as a fit person to hold office and a vacancy on the Board arose. But there could be no justification for any arbitrary imposition of an Italian nominee, which would be a gross interference with Company rights, either of the Suez Canal or any other Company. Neither an International Conference nor a bilateral pact of sovereign States could have any power whatever to effect such action as was demanded. In face of this the further Italian proposal for a proportionate redistribution of the shares was quite fantastic.

Hardly less so were the demands for international control of the Canal as they were voiced by Italy. They represented no more than a high-sounding excuse for getting rid of the two obstacles to Fascist ambitions, the Concession granted to the Suez Canal Company by Egypt which does not terminate until the end of 1968 and Britain's position as defender of the Canal under the amended Suez Canal Convention. The relationship of Egypt to the Canal as the territorial Power were studiously ignored in these demands. It was assumed that she would be forced to yield to whatever external pressure was brought upon her.

The concern of Fascist Italy, like that of no other country using the Suez Canal, was to obtain a voice in the enterprise with the sole object of ultimately wrecking the administration and substituting for it by threats and intrigue a puppet administration subordinate to her will. Italy would not have been content that her representatives should sit quietly in council with the other Directors, considering harmoniously in what way the Canal could be run for the benefit of the mercantile needs of the world.

As Martelli has said:

" Desire to escape from an irksome inferiority is one thing; hankering after superiority with a view to expansion is another. Most Italians would like to see Italy take Britain's place in the Mediterranean. They have been taught to regard history as a dynamic process in which Empires rise and fall and one nation succeeds another. The history of the Mediterranean is the history of such changes and they regard the latest as being already in motion. Apart from prestige and material advantage, Italians feel that their East African Empire will never be safe as long as another Power commands the Suez Canal."*

Having agreed to uphold the Suez Canal Convention, the Italian demands were in themselves a violation of it, for it is clearly laid down in Article XII that: " The High Contracting Parties (which included Italy) . . . agree that none of them shall endeavour to obtain with respect to the Canal territorial or commercial advantages or privileges in any international arrangements which may be concluded."

It remained to be seen whether, after the complete failure of the propaganda attacks, Italy would risk war with her former allies to gain her ends. It was almost certain in that fateful spring and summer of 1939, filled with rumours and alarms, that she would not do so on her own. Everything waited on the outcome of the actions taken by Nazi Germany, with which Power a political and military alliance was concluded in May.

*Whose Sea? p. 294.

CHAPTER XIII

THE CANAL IN THE SECOND WORLD WAR

THE Second World War began on September 1, 1939, when Germany invaded Poland. On the 2nd, Italy proclaimed her neutrality, or more exactly her non-belligerency. On the 3rd Great Britain and France declared war on Germany. In view of the military alliance with Germany the Italian decision was significant, as significant indeed as the non-aggression pact concluded between Germany and Russia on August 23. It meant that Germany could attack France without fighting on a second front with Russia, and if and when France was subjugated Italy could enter the war without having to fight on a second front with France. In fact, on the collapse of France, Italy declared war on France and Great Britain on June 10, 1940, a week before Marshal Pétain sued for peace.

The Axis leaders were in a state of elation. Hitler, as one historian of Axis relations writes,

" thought in terms of continents now, and Africa had become his key to everything, whether in stategy or economics . . . He had decided to seize Gibraltar and Suez without further delay by sending German detachments, in the ' corset role ' they had played in the Austro-Hungarian armies in the previous war, to brace up the Spaniards and Italians . . . "

This is what he had in mind when he went to Florence on October 28, 1940, to give Mussolini his directives for the prosecution of the Mediterranean War.*

At the same time Hitler discussed with Admiral Raeder, the Chief of his Naval Staff, the further implications of this strategy. It was laid down that

" the Suez Canal must be taken. It is doubtful whether the Italians can accomplish this alone; support by German troops will be needed. An advance from Suez through Palestine and Syria as

*See Elizabeth Wiskemann in *The Rome-Berlin Axis*, Oxford University Press, 1949.

far as Turkey is necessary. If we reach that point Turkey will be in our power."*

It was an ambitious conception, as grandiose as that which Germany had entertained before the First World War, when she had Turkey as her partner instead of Italy. Circumstances now appeared to be much more favourable to the design since with the capitulation of Tunisia all threat from the west to the Italian forces in Libya had been removed. The French Mediterranean fleet was immobilised, and with the capitulation of Syria also the wings of the defensive system covering Egypt and the Suez Canal had folded up. Britain was left alone facing an imminent possibility of invasion of her own shores, and with the additional problem of running the gauntlet in the now hostile Mediterranean, and defending with slender forces and material Malta, Cyprus, and Egypt.

Undoubtedly, as has been succinctly remarked, " the decision to hold on in the Eastern Mediterranean, not only with an army assisted by air and light naval forces, but with a fleet which was prepared to face anything Italy could send against it, was one of greater boldness and danger than is easily realised in the light of after events. At that time no one knew how much might be achieved by enemy aircraft operating from Rhodes blocking the Suez Canal, and in damaging the fleet's inadequately defended base at Alexandria . . . It might well be that ships damaged in those waters would be bottled up there, unable to regain fighting trim and unable to withdraw."†

Completely to dominate the Mediterranean and as far as possible deny the Suez Canal to British shipping was clearly as essential to the triumph of the Axis Powers as the success of a land attack on Egypt from Libya. Without full command of the sea and air a North Africa campaign, whatever its initial gains, could ultimately be as disastrous as Napolean's invasion of Egypt had proved and the Turco-German efforts of 1915-16.‡

The position of the British forces in the Canal Zone itself were, during the period immediately preceding Italy's entry into the war, both diplomatically awkward and strategically dangerous.

*Fuerhrer Conferences on Naval Affairs, 1940, p. 106, quoted in The Rome-Berlin Axis.
†Sea Warfare: A Short History, John Cresswell, 1950, p. 79.
‡For the information regarding the Suez Canal which follows, the author is much indebted to the interesting book, Limelight for Suez (Cairo, 1946), by Claude Dewhurst, who writes from personal knowledge and experience.

A state of siege had been declared over the whole of the Canal area, which nevertheless left the Canal Company administratively in control.

The fall of France and the " Oran incident " greatly aggravated the situation. The *President Doumer,* a French liner of 17,000 tons, moored in Lake Timsah to protect Ismailia against hostile aircraft, was a source of extreme embarrassment: but both this ship and the *Felix Roussel,* another French liner, were handed over and eventually re-manned as troopships, in the Allied cause. Meanwhile the Italian danger grew more imminent, for not only was the Dodecanese air base only 350 miles from Port Said but a large potential fifth column was organising itself both at Port Said and Suez. Still more threatening was the fact that ships laden with Italian troops and stores passed up and down the Canal as before. On one occasion three ships carrying either military personnel or armaments were within the Canal Zone simultaneously. Important installations, such as naval workshops and oil-depots at Port Said, and the Suez Oil Refinery added further to the acute security problems.

Gradually more troops began to arrive and air defence was stiffened. Guards were put on board each Italian ship, to keep an eye on the activities of the crews, in case it might drop mines, or be scuttled just before hostilities broke out. A sizeable ship sunk in the Shaluffa reach, where the canal is cut through a rocky gorge, would have immobilised traffic perhaps for months. Constant watch was kept against submarines of the potential enemy; a boom ship was put into place at Port Said, and swung across the canal at dusk. The Italians, however, failed to strike any shrewd initial blow, nor is it known that they had any plans to do so. Only one notable incident occurred at the moment war was declared. Four hundred Italian potential fifth columnists, most of whom cried off at the last moment and threw away their arms, were arrested.

Though the Mediterranean itself was closed to Allied merchant shipping for a considerable time, the northern terminal of the Canal at Port Said did not, as might have been expected, decrease in importance. The facilities at Suez were quite unable to cope with the huge convoys that began to reach the Gulf and so the bulk of the shipping was moved up the Canal to Port Said for

British troops outside wrecked police headquarters in Port Said,
November, 1956

A British soldier watches a minesweeper at work in the Canal
after the cease-fire. November 1956

unloading, while convoys under heavy escort made the further run on to Alexandria. This presented a major problem for the Navy, but the vulnerability to air attack of the concentration of ships that might be waiting at Suez made this process the safest one.

It was generally expected that Italy would at once attack by air. The Canal was virtually immune to damage by high explosives, so the only danger was mining, and the bombing and sinking of ships actually passing through the Canal and providing a sitting target. All shipping therefore moved in convoys with added A.A. protection. It was not till the very end of August that four Italian 'planes tried to bomb Port Said, but their bombs fell either in the desert or in Lake Menzaleh. An attack on Suez at the end of September was hardly more successful.*

Italian ineffectiveness in the Mediterranean war was fully demonstrated in September. Marshal Graziani had accumulated a force of about 250,000 men when the Italians began their advance into Egypt from Libya on September 13, 1940. The British forces under General Wavell were heavily outnumbered and contented themselves at the outset with fighting a delaying action. Graziani had only managed to round the Gulf of Sollum and reach Sidi Barrani by September 16. Here quite unaccountably the advance stopped just east of the village. The halt was fatal to the Italians, as it transpired, though it may have been part of the general plan. They may have over-estimated the opposition and intended to proceed only so far initially, for Graziani wired to Mussolini: " The great success of our advance into Egypt has surpassed all expectations."

What was considered the safe strategic course seems to have been followed, and while Graziani dug in and tied down the relatively small British forces, the Italians now proceeded to the invasion of Greece. Here they met with resistance that completely surprised them, and in the six months from October 1940 to April 1941 they suffered heavy losses and defeats, eventually having to appeal for German help. Had the Greeks not been able to more than hold their own, British forces needed in Egypt to throw back the Italians would have had to be diverted to support them, as they were later, thus weakening the defence of Egypt. As it was, valuable

---

Vide: Limelight for Suez.

H

time was gained, and when Graziani was about to go ahead with the drive on the Nile Delta, as ordered, he was anticipated by Wavell, who on December 9, 1940, launched his counter-offensive. Within a week the Italians were back where they had started, and within two months had been driven as far as the Gulf of Sirte. The Italian threat to Egypt and the Suez Canal, built up over a long period, was thus entirely destroyed. No less than 113,295 prisoners were taken as well as quantities of war material.

This victory enabled troops and supplies to be diverted to the expeditionary force that was being planned and built up to cross the Eastern Mediterranean, and come to the aid of the hard-pressed Greek forces. The lack of success of the Italians in Greece made it inevitable that Hitler should come to their rescue. The German descent on the Balkans occurred on April 6, Yugoslavia receiving a most .violent assault without warning. The natural defences of Greece were more formidable, and it was hoped that a British stiffening would enable the German advance to be halted.

Preparations for this operation had been going on for many weeks. One of the factors that had to be taken into consideration in planning it was the danger that the Suez Canal might be blocked for a long-enough period to prevent the passage of the necessary shipping. Mr. Eden and General Dill were sent to Cairo to co-ordinate diplomatic and military arrangements, and on February 20, after a conference, Mr. Eden sent a cable to the Cabinet which reported among other matters, that:

" Timings cannot yet be given as these depend on discussions with the Greeks and shipping. It is estimated that to move these forces at least 53 ships will be required. These can of course only be obtained by holding ships of convoys arriving in the Middle East, with all that that implies. Additional to present anxiety is the menace of mines in the Suez Canal. Energetic measures are being taken to deal with this, but until they are fully organised and material arrives from home there is always a risk that the Canal may be closed for from five to seven days."*

It was of course the German hand in bombing the Canal that had so completely changed the defence situation there from the previous year. As early as July, 1940, Hitler was offering Mussolini to send German aircraft to bomb the Canal,† but it was in fact

*W. S. Churchill, *History of the Second World War*, Vol. III, p. 64.
†See *Ciano's Diary*: entry for July 2nd, 1940.

not until the night of January 30-31, 1941, that the Luftwaffe made the first mine-laying raid. These mines, though falling by parachute, were not plotted and when shipping began to move again two days later the *Derwent Hall* exploded a mine near Shallufa and had her rudder blown off. Two days later the Greek ship *Aghios Giorgios* was blown up ten kilometres beyond her. The following day the *Ranee* was blown up at kilo. 83, near the monument at Lake Timsah. She broke her back and completely blocked the fairway. On the following day, February 6, two Admiralty " hoppers " were sunk in Lake Timsah.

In these first raids the Germans employed magnetic mines. These could in part be countered by placing the least valuable ships in the convoy first, but the Germans then evolved a magnetic mine with a delayed-action apparatus, allowing four or five ships to pass over before exploding. It was clear that unless properly trained observers were stationed along the whole length of the Canal to report accurately where the mines fell, further disasters would occur. The Egyptian army was brought in to perform this rôle.

The next raid was by five Junkers 88 aircraft, which flew at 300-500 feet. One answer that would at least keep the enemy higher, and make accurate dropping of mines more difficult, was a balloon barrage, either concentrated over vital areas or moved about so as to deceive. Claude Dewhurst has described the network of anti-aircraft defence that was achieved at this time. Coming from the North the attackers would meet first the A.A. umbrella at Port Said, next a barrage of machine-gun and Bofors fire, thickened in depth by heavy A.A., then—at Kantara—rockets with long trailing wires, fired by a naval section ; the whole area of Ismailia would be lit up by flares or searchlights, with night fighters operating around them. There was a false channel on the Bitter Lakes and massed fire from anti-aircraft batteries at Shallufa, while Suez was protected by a balloon barrage five sections deep, and its anti-aircraft fire augmented by the guns of a hundred or more ships moored in the bay.

Attacking planes were thus kept fairly high, but it was still difficult to plot the mines that did fall in the Canal. Observers were actually placed at 50-yard intervals to do this. When a mine had been plotted it was buoyed, and a " Wellington " aircraft, specially equipped with a huge magnetic metal ring, flew over it very low to detonate it. Minesweepers were also used. More amazing, the crucial Shallufa area was covered at night by a huge net so that any mines dropping through it could next morning be at once pin-pointed.

On March 3 nevertheless, six enemy aircraft succeeded in dropping twelve mines into the Canal, and a week later a further eight. Shipping came to a standstill. It was these raids that, during the crucial period when the expeditionary force for Greece was about to be concentrated, caused the British war effort so much trouble and which Mr. Churchill has described as adding to his burden of anxiety when he was wondering whether or not to go ahead with preparations for the hazardous operation.

The most important passage of any ship during this period was, however, that of the aircraft carrier *H.M.S. Formidable*. In February, 1941, *H.M.S. Illustrious* was crippled while escorting a convoy from Alexandria to Malta. So important was it to have an aircraft carrier with the Fleet in its regular sweeps of the eastern Mediterranean that the British Admiralty decided to replace her immediately with the *Formidable* from the East Indies station.

The problem was how to bring her up the Canal, which was then obstructed by more than half a dozen wrecks and several un-detected mines. The *Aghios Giorgios*, sunk at Shallufa, and around which a new channel was being dredged with the utmost speed, was the biggest obstruction. But when the *Formidable* arrived at Suez there was practically no safety margin. The story of her passage amid the greatest anxiety and secrecy (vividly described by Mr. Dewhurst in his book) was a veritable feat of skill and ingenuity. It can truly be said that the arrival of the *Formidable* to take her place in the Mediterranean Fleet was the turning point of the sea war in the Middle East. Once again the Canal had proved a decisive strategic link in the salt water lanes guarded by British sea power.*

After the Greek campaign had begun the Canal underwent a test of a different kind. The Luftwaffe, having been forced to fly too high for the accurate dropping of parachute mines, tried substi-tuting a bomb-mine. However, the delicate mechanism of this new type of weapon could not stand the impact when dropped from

*See official Admiralty publication, " *East of Malta, West of Suez*," H.M.S.O., London.

the necessary height, so in practice they were no danger to shipping. From May 8-11 a series of consecutive attacks took place but the defences were by now becoming extremely efficient, and on the night of May 17-18, half the raiders were shot down and the mines that fell into the Canal quickly dealt with. In June there was a lull, but in July the Luftwaffe returned with changed tactics. Now the terminal point of the Canal, harbour installations and the convoys riding at anchor became the target. On the night of July 13-14, when over 135 ships and liners were anchored at Suez, there was a most spectacular attack. Sixteen aircraft concentrated on the *S.S. Georgic* alone and turned her into a burning torch.

Meantime the expeditionary force sent to help the Greeks had been hurled back and, together with the remnants of the Greek army, forced to evacuate to Crete, abandoning their heavy equipment, tanks and guns. On May 21 Crete was invaded by air and in ten days occupied by the Germans.*

British intervention in Greece had been costly, and had considerably weakened the forces in North Africa. A withdrawal had already begun at the beginning of March in the face of substantial forces dispatched to Libya by the Germans, including the specially trained Afrika Corps under the command of General Rommel. The Italians also had received replacements. Almost the whole of Cyrenaica was relinquished, except for Tobruk, where for eight months a garrison successfully repulsed attempts to dislodge it.

Elsewhere the possibility of a new land threat to the Suez Canal had been averted by the occupation of Syria by the Allies, and the suppression of a pro-Axis rising in Iraq instigated by Rashid Ali. By these measures and the building up of a Middle East army the eastern wing of the defensive system covering the Canal was restored. Had the Germans been able to land in strength in Syria an attack on Egypt from both sides could have been developed. By securing the Middle East the Germans would also have been in a position to deliver a flank attack against Russia, which they invaded from their European positions on June 22, 1941.

A few months were available, scarcely more, in which the British and Empire forces might do something by offensive action

*What may seem a disproportionate amount of space has ben devoted to this period of the war because it was at this time that the Suez Canal came in for the most serious attacks before it could be anything like adequately defended.

to hamper and delay an all-out effort by the Axis Powers to win Egypt and the Middle East. By every means, and every available route, including an air ferry service across Equatorial Africa, troops and armaments were rushed to the area. At the end of August, British and Russian forces invaded Iran and established a new Persian régime favourable to them, which would permit the opening of a supply line to Russia *via* the Persian Gulf. This was particularly important as, by the end of October, the Germans had reached the Crimea.

Air attacks on the Suez Canal Zone did not abate. The climax was reached in August when Port Said, Ismailia, Suez and Port Tewfik were almost nightly targets, but except for one night and day, that of August 11, the Canal was never blocked. Despite losses and supply problems, the strength of the Middle East forces was continually augmented. By the late autumn the whole of the Italian forces in East Africa were overcome and Abyssinia liberated. Moreover, the year 1941 ended with a successful offensive by British Commonwealth forces in the Western Desert. Tobruk was relieved and the Axis forces once more driven back on the El Agheila line. But Rommel was beaten back, not beaten. He was able to counter-attack, reoccupy Benghazi, and move forward to a line west of Ain Gazala. There for some months he was compelled to wait, building up strength for the major offensive which had been interrupted.

By this time the war had assumed world proportions. Japan had commenced hostilities against the United States and the Allies in December, 1941. The entire Far East was ablaze, and the spectacular conquests made by the Japanese in an incredibly short space of time brought them, by the beginning of March, 1942, to the Indian Ocean. Java was conquered. The Japanese were on the frontiers of India and also moving ever nearer to Australia. Here was a Power with a formidable fleet, which Germany and Italy lacked, an accession to the Axis strength which, at this critical stage of the conflict, might well prove decisive.

The summer of 1942 marked the climax of the war, and for the Middle East it was the period fraught with the gravest peril. It was conceivable that the Germans might break through to the Caucasus, that Japanese naval forces should reach the Persian Gulf, or even the Red Sea, that Rommel should break through to the Nile Delta and be master of the Suez Canal.* All these possible contingencies had to be taken into account.

But the summer passed, and the Russians held the Germans at Stalingrad. The widely extended Japanese had reached the limit of their advances. Rommel, having won brilliant successes in the renewed Axis offensive launched in May, was halted at El Alamein, the last strategically defensible position west of Alexandria.

On August 10, 1942, Mr. Churchill was in Cairo, and his examination of the situation brought several changes in the military command, notably General Alexander as Commander-in-Chief, Middle East, and General Montgomery as Commander of the Eighth Army.

Reinforcements began to arrive in great numbers, together with large quantities of equipment, made available partly as a result of America's entry into the war the previous spring. An interesting development at this time was the coming into operation of train services across the Suez Canal by means of the swing bridge which had been constructed at Kantara. This replaced the previous train ferry and enabled trains to run right through from Cairo to Beirut. It also connected up with the railway along the eastern side of the Canal from Kantara down the Suez Road.

In October the refurbished Eighth Army launched its famous counter-offensive, and exactly three months later occupied Tripoli. On February 8, 1943, General Alexander dispatched a telegram to Mr. Churchill which stated:

" Sir: The orders you gave me on August 15th, 1942, have been fulfilled. His Majesty's enemies, together with their impedimenta, have been completely eliminated from Egypt, Cyrenaica, Libya and Tripolitania. I now await your further instructions."

The new Roman Empire in North Africa had had its swift decline and fall.

Meanwhile, in a startling fresh development of the war, British and United States forces had landed in strength at various places in Algeria and Morocco held by the French Vichy administration. Plans had been concerted between President Roosevelt and Mr. Churchill to make North Africa the base of operations for an attack on Italy, the weaker Axis partner, or as Mr. Churchill described it, " the soft underbelly of Europe."

*With regard to British plans in this eventuality, see p. 111.

The closing stages of the war in Africa were fought out in Tunisia. The end came in May when, with no chance of escape across the sea, thousands of Germans and Italians surrendered to the two Allied forces which had advanced from the East and West.

During 1943 the tide of battle turned on every front. Italy's old fear of attack from North Africa, which had dictated her alliance with Germany towards the close of the nineteenth century, was now to be abundantly justified. For the occupation of the North African coast made possible not only the relief of Malta but landings in Sicily and Italy. With the elimination of Italy from the war the Mediterranean was once more open for convoys from the Atlantic. Now it was no longer necessary to divert the bulk of seaborn forces and supplies to the long route round the Cape of Good Hope. The short route through the Mediterranean was again available, and traffic from north to south could pass through the Suez Canal with aid for Russia and to contribute to the liberation of the lands still in the hands of the Japanese. During the critical year of 1942 traffic through the Canal had fallen to its lowest ebb, about seven million net tons, approximately one fifth of normal; but by the end of 1943 it had risen again to eleven and a quarter millions, and thereafter rapidly increased.*

Once again in the chequered history of Egypt and the Suez Canal a dream of domination had brought disaster to the aggressor. The most ambitious bid for the worldly power offered by possession of the Gateway of the Orient had catastrophically failed, and the desert sands were strewn with its pitiful wreckage.

But the experience of the Second World War had been very revealing as to the attitude of the Great Powers towards the Canal. When it came to the point the struggle for mastery came before everything else, and the Suez Canal Convention was for the duration of hostilities so much waste paper. If the Canal was of service to either side then so much the worse for the Canal, and the question of respecting its integrity as an international artery simply did not arise. It was expressly laid down in Article IV of the Convention:

The Maritime Canal remaining open in time of war as a free passage, even to ships of war of belligerents, according to the terms of Article I of the present Treaty the High Contracting Parties

*See Table of Figures in Appendix E.

(and these included Great Britain, Germany and Italy) agree that no right of war, no act of hostility, nor any act having for its object to obstruct the free navigation of the Canal, shall be committed in the Canal and its ports of access, as well as within a radius of three marine miles from those ports.

In complete defiance of this Article both Italy and Germany had mercilessly bombed and mined the Canal and Canal Zone as long as they had ascendency in the air to do it. Even neutral shipping using the Canal and its ports of access had not escaped.

And what of Britain which had covenanted to protect the Canal on behalf of all nations? Was it true that Churchill had said in 1940 that if Great Britain were conquered the British army would destroy the Suez Canal? There is at any rate on record the telegram which President Roosevelt and his personal representative Harry L. Hopkins drafted on June 30, 1942, and which was dispatched to General Marshall at the time when the British position in Egypt was so serious. Part of this telegram reads:

" On the assumption that the Delta will be evacuated within ten days and the Canal blocked, I ask the following questions: What assurances have we that the Canal will be really blocked? Do we know the specific plan? Could you talk to Dill (*i.e.* General Sir John Dill) about this at once? An effective blocking of the Canal is essential."

Marshall had replied that the British could block the Suez Canal so effectively that it was estimated that six months would be required to reopen it.*

Clearly, only the strategic value of the Canal was considered by both sides, and both sides were fully prepared to put the Canal out of action if it assisted their cause. This fact must surely be given its due weight in any thinking or any agreements on the defence of the Canal. It is abundantly evident that only lasting peace can offer the Suez Canal any real protection.

*The White House Papers of Harry L. Hopkins: An intimate history by Robert E. Sherwood (English edition, Vol. 2, p. 598).

CHAPTER XIV

AFTERMATH

THE defence of the Middle East against the Axis Powers had been of vital importance to the Allies, and to Great Britain in particular. Failure in this area could well have lost the war, or at least very considerably have prolonged it; while the triumph of the Axis in this quarter, even if only temporary, would have brought far more suffering and oppression to the native peoples than some of their leaders were prepared to admit. To many in Egypt and in the Arab world Great Britain was not regarded as a friend, but as an obstacle to the full realisation of national aspirations. To bring about the end of British occupation of the Canal Zone and the termination of her mandatory authority in Palestine were objects which seemed to justify passivity in the struggle, and in the case of certain politicians and extremists direct or indirect assistance to Britain's enemies. Judgment was warped by bitterness, a sense of frustration, and even in a few instances by personal animosity and ambition, so that the implications of an Axis victory were either not contemplated or ignored.

For the Jews in Palestine and the Near East there could be no illusions. Thousands of them were refugees from Nazi persecution. These and thousands more had had members of their families tortured to death or otherwise exterminated. For them desperate resistance to the Axis Powers meant not only saving the Jewish national home in Palestine from extinction, but fighting for life itself.

In general the Arabs had no hatred for the Jews, and indeed there was a good deal of sympathy with them in their sufferings. But they were fundamentally antagonistic to the aims of Zionism. They felt that the Jews were a western people in their outlook and culture, and that the solution of their problem lay in their reception into western countries under conditions of complete religious tolerance and with full civic rights. The Arab world was in revolt against

112

imposed western influences and domination. A Jewish State would make permanent and absolute in what was regarded as an Arab land a westernised power, which, even if contained and localised, could not fail to perpetuate, and in all probability would extend, western economic pressure and political interference which all Arab countries were striving to eliminate. Zionism in the eyes of Arab Nationalists was wedded to western capital, to oil wells and pipe lines, to western defensive strategy and imperialistic interests. It could not be considered apart from them. If it was intolerable to endure the British and the French, it could not be less so, if one may so express it, for the fiery and freedom-loving Arab steed to be saddled with the Zionists.

So in the war was born the British-inspired formula of the Arab League, a formula which Arab Nationalists were prepared to accept as an attempt to concert common policies and present a united front in matters affecting the interests of the Arab lands.

But the horrors experienced by European Jewry during the war had equally confirmed the Zionists in their belief that nowhere in the world except in Palestine could Jews be safe from discrimination and oppression. Only upon their own soil and under their own government could they live a life from which the age-old nightmare of persecution and antisemitism would be lifted. Zionism could no longer be regarded as a doctrine for the idealists, but as the only chance of survival. There was but one country upon which the Jews had a claim, the land which had once been the Land of Israel. Particularly by those Jews who had escaped from Germany and eastern Europe the extreme Zionist position was now espoused with desperate zeal. There were relatives in the camps of Europe, and orphaned children, thousands of victims of the war and persecution, who could not be allowed to have their fate determined by political expediency. No quota bar must keep them out. The British plan for a Jewish-Arab State in which the Jews would be in a perpetual minority and hampered by restrictions was completely rejected by the Jews, while it was unacceptable to the Arabs.

The Zionists bitterly resented Arab opposition and completely failed to sympathise with its cause. To them it appeared that the Arabs were adopting a dog-in-the-manger attitude, that being too backward and indolent to make productive use of Palestine themselves they were obstinately determined to keep out those who could

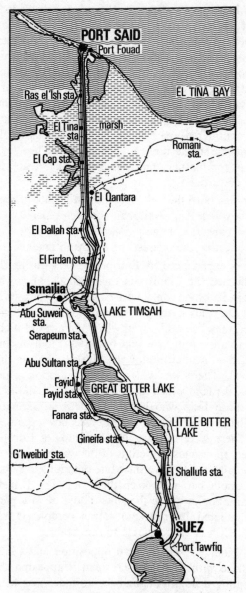

Sketch map of the Suez Canal Region

make the country prosperous. The Arabs had secured independent states for themselves, and denied that right to the Jews in their ancestral home. If that was the way of it they were prepared to maintain to the end a struggle to make the Jewish State a political reality.

The war stores accumulated in the Near East gave opportunity to both sides to acquire arms and ammunition, often illicitly. The pre-war Jewish defence organisation, the Haganah, found its authority challenged by the more militant elements of the Irgun Zvai Leumi and the Stern Gang, which became a law unto themselves. Directing Arab operations was the Higher Committee of pre-war days.

Britain's position in Palestine was now one of great difficulty. For failing to implement the Balfour Declaration she had been taken to task before the war by the League of Nations, from which body she had received the mandate, and now that the League was defunct, and had been succeeded by the United Nations, it was questionable what authority in Palestine she still possessed, since the mandate had not so far been renewed by the successor organisation. It was clear that if the Labour Government elected in 1945 did not speedily solve the Palestine problem it must be turned over to the United Nations. Mr. Ernest Bevin, the Foreign Secretary, publicly staked his political reputation on solving it.

The problem, however, even if a compromise acceptable both to Jews and Arabs could have been found, was complicated by Britain's need for defensive bases in the Near East. Would any solution in Palestine assure her the right to such bases under treaty ?

This question was specially important in view of the urgent demand of the Egyptian Government for revision of the Anglo-Egyptian Treaty of 1936. Now that there was no Power threatening Egypt's independence or the security of the Suez Canal, the Egyptian Government held that there was no last shred of excuse for the British to continue to maintain forces on Egyptian soil. If they were not so maintained they would have to be removed to an adjacent country, and only Palestine and Libya were available. And for how long ?

British forces at this time were not confined to the Canal Zone. They were also stationed at Cairo and in the Delta, as due to the war the clause in the 1936 Treaty had been suspended which required their removal to the Canal Zone on completion of the necessary roads and facilities.*

It was perfectly proper for the Egyptian Government to ask for a revision, since Article 16 of the Anglo-Egyptian Treaty stated:

" At any time after the expiration of a period of twenty years from the coming into force of the treaty, the High Contracting Parties will, at the request of either of them, enter into negotiations with a view to such revision of its terms by agreement btween them as may be appropriate in the circumstances as they then exist.... Nevertheless, with the consent of both High Contracting Parties, negotiations may be entered into at any time after the expiration of a period of ten years after the coming into force of the treaty, with a view to such revision as aforesaid."

Of course it was in the power of the British Government to refuse to enter into negotiations at this first possible moment as provided by the Treaty, and it is to its credit that it did not refuse.

A mission led by Lord Stansgate was despatched to Cairo in April, 1946. Britain was willing for the withdrawal of all her forces from Egypt, the stages of evacuation to be determined, and for a mutual defence treaty to replace that of 1936. It was made clear, however, that Britain regarded the provisions of the earlier treaty as standing if the new treaty was not negotiated and ratified by the respective governments.

The chief bone of contention was not the Canal Zone but the future of the Sudan, where an Anglo-Egyptian Condominium had existed since 1899. The British position in the Sudan had been as galling to Egypt as the presence of British forces on Egyptian soil. Indeed the Sudan was regarded as Egyptian soil, and the Government of Egypt wished to see it under the Egyptian Crown, though willing for the country to enjoy a considerable measure of autonomy. Britain, on the other hand, took the view that the Sudanese should be allowed to develop full self-government, with the right if they wished it to complete independence and national sovereignty.

The negotiations, which continued over the summer, were in the autumn transferred to London when the Egyptian Prime Minister, Ismail Sidky came on a visit to England in October. Out of the discussions the draft of a new Anglo-Egyptian Treaty emerged to replace that of 1936. This provided for the setting up of a joint

*See Appendix D.

Board of Defence " composed of the competent military authorities of the two Governments, assisted by such other representatives as the two Governments may appoint." The Board was to be an advisory body, meeting as often as necessary, and it was added:

" If need arises, the Board shall also examine, on the invitation of, and on the information supplied by, the two Governments, the military repercussions of the international situation, and, in particular, of all events which may threaten the security of the Middle East, and shall make in this respect suitable recommendations to the two Governments, who, in the case of events threatening the security of any one of the neighbouring countries of Egypt, will consult together in order to take in agreement such measures as may be recognised as necessary.*

To this document were attached two Draft Protocols, one on the Sudan (Annex 2), and one on Evacuation (Annex 3). The former read:

" This policy which the High Contracting Parties undertake to follow in the Sudan within the framework of the unity between the Sudan and Egypt under the common Crown of Egypt will have for its essential objectives to assure the well-being of the Sudanese, the development of their interests and their active preparation for self-government and consequently the exercise of the right to choose the future status of the Sudan. Until the High Contracting Parties can in full common agreement realise this latter objective after consultation with the Sudanese, the Agreement of 1899 will continue and Article 11 of the Treaty of 1936† together with its Annex and paragraphs xiv to xvi of the Agreed Minute annexed to the same Treaty, will remain in force notwithstanding the first Article of the present Treaty."

The text of the Draft Evacuation Protocol was as follows:

" The High Contracting Parties agree that the complete evacuation of Egyptian territory (Egypt) by the British Forces shall be completed by 1st September, 1949. The towns of Cairo and Alexandria and the Delta shall be evacuated by 31st March, 1947. The evacuation of the remainder of the country shall proceed continuously during the period ending at the date specified in the first paragraph above (*i.e.,* by 1st September, 1949). The provisions of the Convention of 26th August, 1936, concerning immunities and privileges will continue provisionally to be applied to the British

---

*Annex 1, Article 3, *Papers regarding the Negotiations for a Revision of the Anglo-Egyptian Treaty of 1936,* H.M. Stationery Office, 1947.
†Chiefly affecting the position of the Governor-General of the Sudan.

Forces during the period of their withdrawal from Egypt. Such amendment of the agreement as may be necessary in view of the fact that British troops will after 31st March, 1947, be withdrawn from the Delta and the two cities shall be settled by a subsequent agreement between the two Governments to be negotiated before this date."

The entire draft covering these various arrangements was initialled by the Egyptian Prime Minister and the British Foreign Secretary on October 25, 1946. It represented a personal agreement between the two ministers, and expressed their views at the time. It could not become operative, of course, unless accepted and ratified by both Governments.

In the event the agreement proved unacceptable to the Egyptian Government, which could not see its way to granting the Sudanese the right to secede from Egypt if they wished. While among the parties in the Sudan working for its independence the impression was gained that Britain had betrayed them, in Egypt the opinion was held that Britain desired to foster Sudanese independence for her own ends.

It was most unfortunate that differences over the Sudan which had disturbed Anglo-Egyptian relations after the First World War should again strain relations after the Second. The attitude of the Egyptian Government was understandable. There had for too long been too much consideration by Britain of the requirements of her imperial interests when dealing with Egypt, and too little consideration for the right of Egypt to absolute sovereignty over her own territory. The Condominium over the Sudan was a relic of vassalage, as was the continuance of British Forces on Egyptian soil under the 1936 Treaty. It was difficult for the Egyptians to imagine a concern by Britain for Sudanese independence that did not have strings to it which would be pulled for British convenience and self-interest.

At the very time the Condominium had been established, in 1899, an informed British writer had used these words:

" The reconquest of the Sudan is the rehabilitation of the Tutelary Power (*i.e.*, Britain). It is *not* a theatrical revenge for a hero's death."* Rather, it is the answer to French chauvinism and Gallic aggression which was registered at Fashoda. . . .

" No quickened sense of duty towards the Sudanese hurried

*That of Gordon at Khartoum.

118

An aerial view of the ships sunk by Nasser to block the Canal, 1956

Contrasts—a passenger liner and an Arab craft laden with cotton

British battalions up to the walls of Omdurman. It was a race for Fashoda, or what Fashoda implied in the scheme of the French annexationists.... The truth is no longer hid from us. But it is a matter of historical importance that this point should be noted, on account of its bearing on the question of domination of the Nile Valley."*

So often the present has to pay for the mistakes of the past, and the British Foreign Secretary in his utterly sincere desire to do what was equitable and just was being frustrated and embarrassed by the policies of some of his predecessors.

Mr. Bevin felt deeply the storm which had arisen over the Sudan Protocol. In his explanation to Parliament on January 27, 1947, he said :

" I regret that all my efforts have failed to reach anything in the nature of an agreed interpretation, whether in the form of an exchange of letters, or of agreed statements to be made by the spokesmen of both sides, or even of agreed statements in which the difference separating the parties would be honestly declared in the hope that it could be composed later, since the question at issue cannot become a live one for at least some years. I offered in addition, if any of these proposals were adopted, myself to make a public statement to reassure Egypt as regards the aims of British policy in the Sudan. I have offered every guarantee for the safeguard of Egyptian interests in the Sudan—for no one realises more clearly than His Majesty's Government how vital, for instance, is Egyptian interest in the waters of the Nile—I have offered to sign the treaty of mutual assistance and the evacuation protocol, and thus realise one of Egypt's most eager aspirations—and to discuss the Sudan question *de novo* at a conference with ourselves, the Egyptians, and the Sudanese. To all these proposals I have received either an uncompromising negative, or proposals which would involve my re-entering negotiations committed to the thesis that the right of the Sudanese to self-determination must be subject to permanent union between Egypt and the Sudan.... My hope is that broader and less stubborn counsels may come to prevail in Cairo, for it is evident that the interests of both countries call for a fresh treaty, and would justify a further effort to reach agreement so as to enable the two countries to co-operate for their mutual interest and defence."

On its side the Egyptian Government referred the matter to the Security Council of the United Nations, but no resolution obtained the requisite votes.

*A. Silva White, *The Expansion of Egypt under the Anglo-Egyptian Condominium*, p. 382.

I

THE SUEZ CANAL IN PEACE AND WAR

But although the Sidky-Bevin agreement was never ratified it remained on record as evidence of how far agreement could go. It was a pity that the Sudan issue had to be included in the negotiations and entered into the draft treaty ; for had it been possible to set it on one side for later discussion, and to proceed solely with the other proposals contained in the treaty, relations between the two Governments would have so much improved that there would have been an excellent chance of a distinct treaty to be negotiated subsequently dealing with the Sudan and the termination of the Condominium. By 1949 there would have been no British Forces on the soil of Egypt proper, not even in the Canal Zone.*

As it was, the failure to achieve the new treaty worsened relations and intensified anti-British feeling in Egypt, while the march of events made it much more difficult for the British Government to renew the 1946 proposals. At that date Britain still held Palestine and could use it as an alternative base if she evacuated the Canal Zone. The termination of the Mandate in May, 1948, and the Proclamation of Israel gave the Egypt base a heightened importance. The whole question of Middle East defence had also been revolutionised in the meantime by the mounting tension between the Western Powers and the Soviet Union.

From 1947 onwards American leadership of the Western Powers was so much in evidence that the Arab countries felt they could no longer regard Britain as having a completely independent policy or freedom of action. Whatever commitments they might enter into with Great Britain meant in effect alignment with the American-dominated West, a taking sides against Russia where prudence dictated neutrality. Britain still had powerful friends and sympathisers in the Near East, where help and financial assistance had been freely given, but with significant exceptions there was now a cautious consideration of fresh overtures.

There was far from being any unanimity between the members of the Arab League. But they were agreed on the weakness of Britain in the matter of Palestine, where an undeclared war between Arabs and Jews was rapidly undermining effective administration of the country. If anything, British sympathies were with the Arabs, but the Mandatory Power was required to act in the interests of both

*British Forces were, in 1947, withdrawn from Cairo, Alexandria, and the Delta, in accordance with the provisions of the 1936 Treaty.

peoples, and the United States strongly favoured the Zionists, and was chiefly instrumental in getting a two-thirds majority of the United Nations Assembly to vote for the partition of Palestine on November 29, 1947. Britain abstained from voting, believing the partition plan to be quite unworkable. Only an army could enforce it, and Britain was not prepared to lose the vestiges of her prestige in the Muslim world by embarking on such warfare. If the United Nations wanted partition let them carry it out. Britain would surrender her mandate, remove her troops, police, and administration, and leave them to it.

The United Nations Commission on Palestine had to agree in the end that the partition plan could not be enforced unless the United Nations were prepared to send adequate troops. The British would allow their own to be employed only in conjunction with others furnished by other members of the U.N., and only if the partition plan was accepted by both Arabs and Jews. Since this appeared out of the question, Britain declared that she would get out of Palestine on May 15, 1948. Belatedly the United States attempted to abandon its support of partition in favour of a United Nations Trusteeship, but by this time the Jews were fully determined to create their State in the area allotted to them under the partition plan. The U.N. resolution of November, 1947, had given them an authoritative basis on which they could act.

Britain has been criticised for abandoning her Mandatory responsibilities in Palestine precipitately knowing that the Arabs would resort to open warfare against the Jews upon her departure; but there had been no evidence that anything effective would be done by the United Nations to stop the war.

The war, of course, should never have been fought, and with more good will and understanding on both sides an honourable settlement could have been arrived at. Once full hostilities had begun, however, peacemaking became more difficult and has not yet been accomplished.

Egypt as a member of the Arab League was involved in the conflict and Egyptian forces finally held a small part of the southern coastline of Palestine known as the Gaza strip. This area had been allocated to the proposed Arab State under the United Nations partition plan.

But Egypt's association also affected the Suez Canal, since she was concerned by all means to stop supplies reaching Israel, particularly oil and commodities which might be used for military purposes. The Government proclaimed a State of Siege on May 13, and named the Suez Canal as one of three Special Zones. A service of inspection of vessels was instituted at the ports of Alexandria, Suez, and Port Said, and special powers were conferred on the Governor of the Canal Zone.*

As a result of these instructions ships bound for Palestine were seized, and all or part of their cargoes confiscated.† British vessels were among those held, and protests were made by H.M. Government against this breach of the terms of the Suez Canal Convention of 1888, which guaranteed the free use of the Canal to the shipping of all nations both in time of war as well as in time of peace. A situation such as this had never been contemplated when the Convention was drafted, and it was certainly hard on Egypt to be forced to assist an enemy under its provisions. It was of course permissible for units of the Egyptian fleet to seize Israeli vessels, not in the Canal but outside the three-mile limit at either end. But here materials for Israel were being carried by vessels of neutral Powers, and stopping and searching them as in the case of the *Empire Roach*, even elsewhere than in the Canal, could be regarded as an act of war. So far as Britain was concerned, Egypt might retort that since Britain was in treaty alliance with her she was in duty bound not to give comfort or assistance to Egypt's enemies.

These incidents did not contribute to the improvement of Anglo-Egyptian relations, and there was strong feeling in Egypt against the reluctance of Britain to supply Egypt with 'planes and war material. Once the State of Siege was ended,‡ however, and previously as a result of conversations in 1949 between the British Foreign Secretary and the Egyptian Foreign Minister, there was an improvement in the position, and normal commercial cargoes and foodstuffs destined for Israel were permitted to use Egyptian ports. This still did not apply to oil, and since direct supplies from the Middle East for the Haifa refineries were denied by the Arabs, some of this commodity intended for Israel had to be carried by the long and costly route round the Cape of Good Hope or from South America.

*Official Journal of the Egyptian Government, No. 51, May 15, 1948.
†Arabic Official Journal, Nos. 98, 100, and 105, of July 12, 15, and 21, 1948.
‡On May 1, 1950, except in the Sinai and Red Sea areas.

During the first half of 1948 only one Palestinian vessel made the transit through the Suez Canal, compared with eight during the corresponding period of the previous year. But it was not to be denied that with the State of Israel a new maritime Power had come into existence in the Mediterranean ; and though with others now using the Canal—including Liberia for the first time in 1948—she was not a signatory of the Suez Canal Convention, yet the terms of the Convention expressly excluded any discrimination.

The Convention was certainly long overdue for revision or replacement. Had the United Nations been really united it might have sponsored a new Convention with universal consent, and indeed become its guarantor. But in the prevailing circumstances this was out of the question.

So long as the existing Convention stood—and this was an international instrument not a bilateral agreement like the Anglo-Egyptian Treaty—Britain could claim the right to protect the Canal. This right she had acquired under the peace treaties after the First World War. It was not to be set aside, whatever might happen to the Anglo-Egyptian Treaty itself, unless a new international Convention came into operation. If Egypt wished to see Britain no longer occupying a privileged position in respect of the Suez Canal she had not assisted her cause by impeding the transit of vessels and cargoes on account of the conflict with Israel. It would be fantastic to suggest that any threat to the Canal had existed. Egypt here lost a great opportunity to demonstrate both in the letter and spirit her particular respect for the universal right of usage of the Canal as an international artery, more especially as it passed through her territory.

CHAPTER XV

ANGLO-EGYPTIAN DISAGREEMENT

THE year 1950 brought to a head the long-drawn-out controversy between Egypt and Britain over the Canal Zone and the Sudan question. Ever since the abortive Sidky-Bevin agreement of 1946 the determination of Egypt to put an end to the British occupation had grown steadily in intensity and concentration of purpose. Britain for her part was increasingly concerned with the general problem of Middle East defence in which Egypt held a key position. The sharp conflict of viewpoint, however courteously expressed in discussion, clearly offered no prospect of any easy accommodation or reconciliation. Talks in 1949 had failed on the main issues, and when the Wafdist Party came into power in Egypt in January, 1950, it was almost certain that any renewal of them would bring agreement no nearer. This, indeed, proved to be the case ; for the conversations which took place in Cairo in the summer of 1950 on the subject of Middle East defence made it abundantly evident that only if Egypt were actually attacked would she tolerate the presence of British Forces on her soil.

The report of these conversations is given exclusively in the Green Book published by the Egyptian Foreign Ministry in Cairo in February, 1952, following upon the White Paper presented to Parliament by the British Foreign Office in November, 1951.* The latter, entitled, *Anglo-Egyptian Conversations on the Defence of the Suez Canal and on the Sudan, December, 1950-November, 1951,* contains only incidental reference to these conversations.

The chief spokesman on the British side was Field-Marshal Sir William Slim, Chief of the Imperial General Staff, and on the Egyptian side the Prime Minister, Nahas Pasha, and the Foreign Minister, Salah ed Din Bey. Sir William, according to the Green Book, expressed his belief that the Soviet Union expected war with the West, and that in the event of war Egypt would be one of the Russian objectives, since he who holds Egypt holds the Middle

*Egypt, No. 2, H.M. Stationery Office, 1951. The texts of the British proposals quoted throughout this chapter are derived from this source unless otherwise stated.

East. He was convinced that Russia was planning for war, she wanted to get into Africa. Air attacks on Egypt would come in a matter of hours, and by way of Iran or Turkey the Russian forces could reach Egypt in about four months using ten to fifteen divisions. If Turkey held out the Russians could be delayed, and if countries from the Middle East joined the United Kingdom and United States the danger could be driven away from the Middle East. Sir William looked forward to defence arrangements with Egypt that would make it clear that no meaning of occupation was attached to the presence of British troops.

Nahas Pasha said that the Egyptian people were angry and resentful and would be unwilling to accept new conceptions which aimed at maintaining foreign troops in Egypt under any name or in any capacity. No power on earth could convince the Egyptian people that Egypt would be attacked because of herself. It would be the presence of foreign troops that would lay Egypt open to attack and be the target for Russian aggression. Why, he asked, did Britain not transfer her troops from the Canal Zone to Palestine or Gaza ? From there, if need arose, they could be in Egypt within a week. They would find Egypt fully co-operative once these troops were outside her borders.

Sir William urged that there must be some British air forces in Egypt, since those of Egypt were inadequate. Nahas Pasha replied that Egypt would welcome more 'planes, and if war came they would be used in the British interest and all necessary preparations would be made. Sir William Slim did not agree that defence could be confined to one service : it required a combination of all. It would be very difficult to advise the British Government to accept complete evacuation. If Britain withdrew from Egypt it would have a disastrous effect on the Cold War. Nahas Pasha pointed out that Britain had in fact agreed with Sidky Pasha to complete evacuation by September, 1949. " We advance in our conception of defence," Sir William rejoined.

Later, Nahas Pasha said that if the existence of a threat of war was held to justify the maintenance of British troops in the Canal Zone the occupation would last for ever, because the danger of war would never disappear. Neither Iran or Turkey were occupied by foreign troops, yet they were in danger of direct invasion.

It appeared that both Britain and Egypt could agree on an

alliance in replacement of the Anglo-Egyptian Treaty. But the only condition upon which Egypt was prepared to conclude it was evacuation, and nothing but evacuation. To this decision Britain at this time was not prepared to commit herself. There was no confidence that Egypt could maintain bases in sufficient readiness to be immediately serviceable in case of war. Nothing had really been accomplished by this exchange of views, except on the Egyptian side to appreciate the weakness of the British case. Nothing had been put forward by the British representatives to establish that there was any acutal threat to Egypt in the existing international situation, only a conceivable threat, and British concern for Egypt's safety appeared too palpably if quite naturally concern for her own safetly. The inevitable outcome was a hardening in the Egyptian attitude.

If the strength of Egyptian feeling was fully understood in London it was by no means so easy to respond to it in the way that Egypt wanted. The Egyptian base was now regarded as essential for Middle East defence not only to Britain but also to her Western allies. The letter of the bond—the Anglo-Egyptian Treaty—was therefore relied upon in justification of maintaining the existing state of affairs until such time as Egypt should show herself more amenable to the requirements of the Middle East defensive system.

The consequence was that Egypt determined on a show down. After a statement made by the Egyptian Delegation at Lake Success a direct challenge was offered in the speech from the throne at the opening of the Egyptian Parliament on November 16. This declared :

" The Egyptian Government believe that the 1936 treaty has lost its validity as a basis of Anglo-Egyptian relations, and the decision is inevitable that it should be abrogated. It therefore becomes inevitable to decide upon its cancellation and arrive at new clauses based on other principles, namely total and immediate evacuation, and the unity of Egypt and the Sudan under the Egyptian Crown. My Government proclaim they will never depart from these fundamental principles. They will resort to every possible means, the chief whereof is to announce the termination of the 1936 treaty on the grounds that it openly conflicts with provisions of the United Nations Charter, and that the conditions in which it was concluded have changed."

In response to this Mr. Bevin made a statement in the House of Commons on November 21. The Egyptian declaration was not accepted as a challenge.

" The Egyptian Government," the Foreign Secretary said, " has stated that it wishes all British Forces to be withdrawn from the Canal Zone in time of peace. The principle of common defence measures in time of peace has been accepted by all the Western Powers as fully compatible with national independence and sovereignty. Other countries in the Middle East are co-operating in this way. This is not a matter which merely concerns the United Kingdom and Egypt. What is at stake is the independence of other countries also. I assure them that the Government has no intention of taking steps or agreeing to any measures which would leave the Middle East defenceless, or would prejudice the safety of free and friendly countries in that area or elsewhere."

What emerged from this statement as from other Anglo-Egyptian conversations both before and subsequently was that the specific reason for the presence of British Forces in the Canal Zone, namely the protection of the Suez Canal, no longer applied in the British view. Rather was Egypt regarded as the pivotal point for the general defence of the Middle East in the interest of the British Commonwealth and of the North Atlantic Treaty Powers. During the talks which the Egyptian Foreign Minister Salah ed Din had with Mr. Bevin in London in December, the former tried hard to get the British Foreign Secretary to express a willingness for British evacuation within a year. In this he was unsuccessful. Mr. Bevin first wished to have clarified Egypt's willingness to come into the Middle East defensive system of the Western Powers. He did not want to leave a vacuum between the termination of the existing treaty and the conclusion of a fresh agreement of alliance. The question of the period evacuation might take was secondary, but the conditions of it must be such as would assure at every stage that full defensive capacity existed. It would take considerable time to bring the Egyptian forces, especially the air force, up to the strength essential for that purpose. A year would obviously be inadequate for this development. There was also the question of the conditions under which the British Forces would be allowed to return in the event of a threat of war, and the consideration of the integration of the Arab States in the defensive system. Mr. Bevin assured the Egyptian Foreign Minister that there would be immediate expert study of the Middle East defence problem with the object of putting forward H.M. Government's considered view as to what provisions a settlement should contain. These would be presented in January or as soon after as possible. Salah ed Din said he was glad the study would be undertaken with speed and he would await the results.

The British proposals were put forward on April 11, 1951, and in so far as they related to the question of defence are here quoted in full from the White Paper of November, 1951.

(1) DEFENCE

His Majesty's Government in the United Kingdom are prepared to resume negotiations for the revision of the 1936 Treaty of Alliance in accordance with the provisions of Article 16 of that Treaty.

His Majesty's Government in the United Kingdom are aware of the Egyptian Government's great difficulties in the matter. They cannot, however, in view of their commitments to their other allies in the North Atlantic and in the Middle East, accept the responsibility of making any arrangements which prejudice their ability to contribute to a successful defence of this region against an aggressor. Such a defence will only be possible if in the future the Egypt base continues to function in such a manner as to be immediately available in war and if the air defence of Egypt is assured.

In these circumstances His Majesty's Government in the United Kingdom propose that the 1936 Treaty of Alliance be revised so as to provide for the following:

(a) The phased withdrawal of British troops from Egypt beginning within one year of an agreement on revision of the Treaty and ending in 1956. (It should be noted that rate of withdrawal of combatant troops and of General Headquarters depends largely on the rate at which accommodation can be provided for them elsewhere.)

(b) The progressive civilianisation of the base which it is suggested should be completed by 1956, essential British civilian personnel being introduced as military personnel are withdrawn. The base thereafter to be entrusted to the Egyptian Armed Forces for security purposes but to be operated in accordance with British military policy under the overall administrative control of an Anglo-Egyptian Control Board. (His Majesty's Government in the United Kingdom would be prepared to pay rent for base installations and sites.)

(c) The creation of a long-term Anglo-Egyptian co-ordinated air defence system in which there should be both Egyptian and British components.

(d) The provision at an early date of arms and equipment on training scale for the Egyptian forces and thereafter the provision of whatever further arms and equipment may be necessary in equal priority with other nations with whom Great Britain has working defence agreements. (His Majesty's Government in the United Kingdom would also be prepared to render any assistance required by the Egyptian Government in the training of Egyptian forces.)

(e) In the event of war, imminent war or apprehended international emergency, Egypt would agree to the return of British Forces for the period of emergency and would grant to them and to the forces of Britain's allies all necessary facilities and assistance including the use of Egyptian ports, aerodromes, and means of communication.

These proposals were completely rejected by the Egyptian Government in their reply of April 24, which expressed " deep regret and bitter disappointment at the contents." Eight matters were listed which were deemed particularly objectionable. These included the date at which it was proposed evacuation should begin and be completed, the rate of withdrawal being made dependent on the rate at which accommodation could be provided elsewhere, and the suggested return of British Forces to Egypt in the event of imminent menace of war or apprehended international emergency. Further, the Egyptian Government rejected the British Government's claim to share in the defence of the Middle East on the plea of their obligations towards their other allies in the North Atlantic and the Middle East. The following counter-proposals were put forward :

1. The evacuation of British troops from Egypt to begin immediately upon concluding the agreement and the necessity of completing this evacuation by land, sea, and air within a period not exceeding one year.

2. The base to be handed over to the Egyptian armed forces immediately upon the completion of evacuation in accordance with the preceding paragraph.

3. Special priority for the provision of necessary arms and equipment to be given to the Egyptian Army at the earliest opportunity, considering that Egypt is situated in a sensitive strategic area.

4. The unity of Egypt and the Sudan under the Egyptian Crown and self-government for the Sudanese within two years in the framework of this unity.

5. British Forces and British officials to be withdrawn from the Sudan and the present régime in the Sudan to be terminated immediately upon expiry of those two years.

6. The conclusion of an agreement between the two parties

129

whereby British forces may return to those places to which, in the agreed opinion of the two Governments, it is necessary that they should return for the purpose of assisting in the defence of Egypt in the event of an armed aggression upon her or in the event of the United Kingdom's being involved in war as the result of an armed aggression on the Arab countries adjacent to Egypt.

7. In the event of their returning to Egypt in accordance with the preceding paragraph, British troops will begin to withdraw from Egyptian territory immediately upon the cessation of hostilities. This withdrawal to be completed by land, sea, and air within a period not exceeding three months.

8. The Treaty of Alliance signed in London on August 26th, 1936, together with the Agreed Minute, notes, and Convention, also the two Agreements of 1899 regarding the Sudan to be abrogated immediately upon the entry into force of the new agreement.

In concluding the reply the Egyptian Government gave a clear indication that they would be forced to denounce the 1936 and 1899 Agreements if the counter-proposals were not accepted.

No doubt Egypt would have been content with a modification in certain respects, but no indication was forthcoming of any willingness to make suggestions that would approximate to the Egyptian position. There were exchanges of views in June and July on the Sudan question without achieving agreement in principle, and it was now evident that the possibility of reconciling the opposing attitudes on both issues in a mutually satisfactory manner was remote. It was held by Egypt that Britain was directly responsible for the breakdown of conversations in so far as no reply had been made to the counter-proposals. On the other hand, Britain claimed there should have been no breakdown since she had informed the Egyptian Government that she was working on a completely new approach to the defence question. As it was patent, however, that this approach—not yet stated—would in some way involve Egypt with the North Atlantic Treaty Powers she could not see anything hopeful in this piece of information.

The climax came quickly. On October 8th, 1951, the Egyptian Government announced its intention of denouncing the Anglo-Egyptian Treaty of 1936 and the Sudan Condominium Agreements of 1899, thus anticipating by two days the date at which Mr. Herbert Morrison, then British Foreign Secretary, had intimated the new proposals whould be ready for presentation. They were in fact presented by the British Ambassador on the 13th, and promptly rejected by the Egyptian Government on the 15th. On the same day the Egyptian Parliament passed decrees abrogating the 1936 Treaty and the 1899 Agreements.

There is no difficulty in seeing why the fresh proposals did not appeal to the Egyptian Government. They exhibited not the slightest intention of complying with Egypt's requirements, and putting an end to the intolerable tradition of occupation. What was offered was that several foreign devils should take the place vacated by one foreign devil. Egypt was invited to become a full and equal founding partner with Britain, France, Turkey, and the United States of an Allied Middle East Command. It was stated that Australia, New Zealand, and the Union of South Africa, had also agreed in principle to participate in this Command. Britain would agree to the suppression of the 1936 Treaty and withdraw from Egypt such forces as were not allocated to the Command by its co-founders. The detailed organisation and its relationship to the North Atlantic Treaty Organisation would be worked out in consultation with all the Powers concerned.

In view of all that had gone before there was a special sting ir the Annex to the document which may here be quoted in full.

1. In common with the other participating Powers who are making similar contributions to the defence of the area

(a) Egypt will agree to furnish to the proposed Allied Middle East Command Organisation such strategic defence and other facilities on her soil as are indispensable for the organisation in peacetime of the Middle East, and

(b) she will undertake to grant the forces of the Allied Middle East Command all the necessary facilities and assistance in the event of war, the imminent menace of war, or apprehended international emergency—including the use of Egyptian ports, airfields, and means of communication.

2. It would also be hoped that Egypt would agree to the Allied Supreme Commander's Headquarters being located in her territory.

3. In keeping with the spirit of these arrangements it would be understood

(a) that the present British Base in Egypt would be formally handed over to Egypt on the understanding that it would simultaneously become an Allied Base within the Allied Middle East Command with full Egyptian participation in the running of this base in peace and war ;

(b) that the strength of the Allied forces of the participating nations to be stationed in Egypt in peacetime would be determined between the participating nations, including Egypt, from time to time as progress is made in building up the forces of the Allied Middle East Command.

4. It would also be understood that an Air Defence Organisation, including both Egyptian and Allied forces, would be set up under the command of an officer with joint responsibility to the Egyptian Government and to the Allied Middle East Command for the protection of Egypt and the Allied Base.

The whole approach of Britain and her Western Allies was extraordinarily onesided. They seemed to assume that they had the right to impose on the Middle East a defensive system favourable to themselves because of their fears of the area falling into the hands of a Power inimical to them. A defensive steel chain must at all costs be drawn round the Soviet Union and her associates ; and since a chain is only as strong as its weakest link—and the Middle East was that weakest link—therefore it must be made at least as strong and secure as its fellows.

All this was a radical departure from the position of the amended Suez Canal Convention that Britain, and Britain only, had the right to defend the Suez Canal in conjunction with Egypt in case of war, and if Egyptian forces should prove inadequate for the purpose. And moreover that the protection of the Canal was so that it might serve as an international waterway both in war and peace in the interests of all nations—incidentally including Russia which was a signatory of the Convention. That whole conception as a result of two world wars appeared to have gone by the board. Perhaps it was more straightforward for Egypt to denounce the Agreements of 1936 and 1899—however illegal it might be to act unilaterally—because these agreements no longer corresponded to the realities of the situation, than for Britain to profess to uphold the Suez Canal Convention when it had demonstrably lost its validity.

The Conservative Government which took office at this juncture in place of the Labour Government in Great Britain upheld the action of its predecessor. Egypt formally declared on October 27th that her alliance with Britain had ended, and that therefore the latter had now no authorisation to station forces in the vicinity of the Suez Canal. Britain's reply on November 6th was to the effect that the alliance was still in force together with the other agreements. One would have thought that if an ally becomes hostile he ceases to be an ally, and despite her words Britain certainly seems to have acted on this assumption by substantially reinforcing the Canal Zone and placing the ports of access to the Canal under heavy naval and military guard. Egypt accused Britain of aggression.

Without any declaration of war or breaking off of diplomatic relations the two countries were now to all intents and purposes in a state of war. No provision had been made in any instrument affecting the Suez Canal for such a contingency. The Suez Canal Company was inevitably placed in a dilemma, at least temporarily. It was reported that an Egyptian Customs official at Port Said had asked the Company to deny pilots to British shipping using the Canal. The Company announced that it would " abide by its Concession which made it a duty to treat all ships in transit identically so long as they observed the regulations."

From this time the Wafd administration did everything that could be done by imposing and promoting terrorist activities to endeavour to make the British position in Egypt as intolerable as possible. But pressure, isolated attacks, and acts of sabotage by individuals and small groups, could obviously do no more against the reinforced British military strength than express Egyptian national feeling. On both sides there was some loss of life, but also a great deal of self-control by responsible officials both British and Egyptian. There were only two really black spots during a prolonged period of disturbance, the battle between British troops and Egyptian auxiliary police at Ismailia with heavy casualties to the latter, and the rioting in Cairo which took place the day following, January 26th, which resulted in the death of a number of people including several British nationals and widespread destruction of property. Subversive elements had made use of the opportunity afforded by the inactivity of the police and popular reaction to the news from Ismailia, and strong measures had to be taken by the Egyptian Government to bring the situation under control. Even so the king felt compelled to dismiss the Government of Nahas Pasha and called upon Aly Maher Pasha, an Independent, to form a new Cabinet.

The change did not mean any weakening in Egypt's resolve to terminate the British occupation of the Canal Zone ; but it did inspire hope that conversations might be renewed and lead to an acceptable outcome. It was most unfortunate at this juncture that Mr. Churchill should refer in Washington to the possibility of

United States forces joining the British in Egypt, and no less unfortunate was his language in reporting to the House of Commons on January 30th. In his speech he said:

"Now that we no longer have available the former Imperial armies which existed in India, the burden of maintaining the control and security of the international waterway of the Suez Canal is one which must be more widely shared. It is upon an international basis that the most hopeful solution to our Middle East difficulties will be reached. I trust that all the Powers concerned will play their part, working together and sharing the burden and responsibilities for the peace and security of the Middle East. It may be a long time before that is to be achieved, but that should clearly be our aim and our goal."

Not only was there in this speech a reiteration of the last British proposals which had been summarily rejected by Egypt; but for one most careful in his choice of words to speak of "control" of the Suez Canal was an unwarrantable addition to the letter of the law. No existing treaty or international agreement gave Britain any authority to maintain control of the Canal. The use of this expression could but emphasise the divergence between the British and the Egyptian points of view. It still remains to be determined how and in what way they can be reconciled.

Widening the Canal after 1956. Egyptian labourers removing soil from the existing bank and piling it up behind the proposed new bank

An Israeli soldier stands guard at Kantara after the Six-Day War

CHAPTER XVI

THE EGYPTIAN REPUBLIC
AND
NATIONALISATION

AFTER the riots of Black Saturday, January 26th, tension relaxed very gradually. Spasmodic incidents, such as the derailment of a British army train at Kantara on February 15th, kept troops in the Canal Zone on the alert, but there was at last a breathing space for diplomacy. In the Commons Mr. Anthony Eden expressed Britain's desire for an agreement which would ensure the security of the Middle East and the Canal. Aly Maher, in the face of bitter Wafd criticism, reciprocated this sentiment and on March 1st talks were resumed in Cairo, designed to cover not only the Anglo-Egyptian dispute but also the future of the Sudan.

The subsequent replacement of Aly Maher by Neguib el-Hilaly Pasha as Prime Minister portended no change in Egyptian policy. The main issues under discussion remained the conditions for a total British withdrawal from the Canal Zone and the unity of the Nile Valley. On the latter point Egypt was prepared to accept the Sudanese right to self-government provided Egyptian sovereignty were first recognised. The fact that Farouk was still pointedly describing himself as "King of Egypt and the Sudan" hardly provided, in Britain's view, the basis for an impartial debate.

The Sudanese question proved indeed to be the stumbling block and after a month the talks were switched, at Egypt's request, to the calmer atmosphere of London. Sir Ralph Stevenson the Ambassador to Egypt, and Sir Robert Howe, Governor-General of the Sudan, were recalled for consultations and new proposals for a solution to the problem were handed over to the Egyptian Government on May 4th. But Britain's affirmation of Sudan's right to self government by the end of the year, as embodied in the draft of a new constitution drawn up in London early in April, was again challenged by Egypt on the sixteenth anniversary of King Farouk's accession when Hilaly Pasha stated publicly that an Eygptian-Sudanese union under the Egyptian crown was still the only answer.

Egypt, in fact, miscalculated popular feeling in the Sudan. In

Khartoum there was no great disposition to respond to the blandishments of a neighbour who had virtually ignored Sudanese interests for a quarter of a century and whose main objective appeared to be to gain complete control of the Nile waters. In the less developed, less prosperous southern region, however, suspicion of Egyptian motives was a secondary consideration to the genuine fear of political and economic domination by Khartoum. Only on the necessity for withdrawal of all foreign troops was there general agreement, and it was with this in mind that Britain's draft constitution was approved, on the understanding that the Sudan should retain the right to decide the date and method of eventual self-determination.

Meanwhile, in Cairo, a train of events was being set in motion which would shortly render all previous discussions and decisions meaningless. On June 29th, to the surprise and dismay of the British Government, Hilaly Pasha was ousted by Hussein Sirry Pasha, a former premier. His term of office lasted only three weeks. On July 21st Hilaly Pasha returned. Two days later, however, a bloodless military coup took place, led by Major-General Mohammed Neguib, president of the Cairo Officers' Club. Aly Maher was again installed as Prime Minister.

The situation was now radically transformed. The new régime, backed by the army and air force, pledged itself to eradicate all vestiges of the old landlord-dominated political structure. There were wholesale arrests and resignations as the Government proclaimed its intention to put an end to corruption and initiate a programme of reform. Within three days King Farouk abdicated and left the country with his family. His infant son, Ahmed Fuad II, was proclaimed king and a three-man Regency Council set up. The fall of the monarchy was accepted without protest or surprise. There were no popular demonstrations and after a few days the troops disappeared from the streets of Cairo and Alexandria.

The dramatic turn of events caused alarm in British Government circles. Although Neguib assured the British Ambassador that there was no reason to fear an upsurge of nationalistic, anti-foreign sentiment, he openly announced Egypt's firm intention of ridding the country of British troops at the earliest opportunity. But despite his promise of elections the following February, the hallmarks of a rigidly imposed military dictatorship were evident in his warning to political parties to reform, in the increased pace of the political and military purges, in the reimposition of outgoing press censorship and in the summary trial and execution of the ring-leaders of the riots in the textile centre of Kafr el-Dawar on August 13th.

On September 7th the iron grip of the army tightened as Neguib took over as Prime Minister from Aly Maher. Yet public support for the Government was assured by proclamations of a new deal for the *fellahin*, involving the breaking-up of the great estates, the limitation of land holdings to 200 acres and the redistribution of one-fifth of the available cultivated area of land.

Agreement with Britain over the Canal Zone was a matter of priority, not only for reasons of national prestige but also on solid economic grounds. A slump in world cotton prices was having serious repercussions in the export field. Egypt had drawn heavily on her sterling balances in 1951, to the tune of £E55 million, and her reserves were ominously low. Furthermore, the precarious political situation was having an adverse effect on a normally flourishing tourist trade. A hopeful sign of the régime's intentions was seen in Egyptian overtures to the Sudan in October, whereby Egypt agreed to recognise the Sudanese right to independence by the end of 1965.

There was much speculation at this time concerning the future of the Suez Canal Company. This is a good moment to interrupt the sequence of events and to take a brief look at the Company as it was constituted and as it operated during the post-war years.

The Company was in effect an Egyptian joint-stock company, operating the Canal under a Concession which was due to expire in November, 1968. While its official headquarters were in Egypt, its principal administrative office was in Paris. As has already been mentioned, the British Government had the right to appoint three directors to the board of the Company as well as seven other non-Government directors. France had eighteen directors and there were two Egyptian, one American and one Dutch director.

Apart from the Board there was a Management Committee, consisting of the President of the Board and four others specially delegated.

The essential activities of the Company were carried on by three departments, the Department of Administration, the Transit Department, and the Engineering Department. The last named was concerned with the Works Programmes for the development of the

Canal and the various improvements decided upon from time to time. It was also responsible for maintenance and upkeep, repairs to installations, and the considerable fleet of dredgers, salvaging craft, etc. The Transit Department naturally dealt with all matters concerned with navigation, passage, pilotage and signalling.

At the end of 1948 the Board of the Suez Canal Company decided to embark on the Seventh and thus far the largest Works Programme in its history, including the cutting of a by-pass canal, seven and a half miles long, to speed up convoys in the northern section of the Canal. The programme also involved the deepening of the Canal by twenty inches over its entire length and the enlargement of anchorage facilities in the harbour of Port Said.

The Egyptian Government had long been dissatisfied with the minor role played by Egyptian nationals both on the Board of the Company and in the operation and maintenance of the Canal itself. It was to increase Egyptian representation in these spheres that the Government concluded with the Company a new Agreement which came into operation on August 19th, 1949, following upon signature by both parties on March 7th. The principal clauses of that Agreement are quoted in Appendix E of this book. It went considerably beyond the previous Agreement of 1937, giving recognition to the fact that the Concession was due to terminate in 1968, when the Canal would revert to Egypt. In these circumstances the Canal Company appreciated and accepted the need for a greatly augmented and growing number of Egyptian nationals to gain experience in all departments of its work in Egypt.

It was made abundantly clear after the army coup of 1952 that Egypt would not consider any extension of the Suez Canal Company's Concession beyond the expiry date of 1968. On October 15th Sabry Mansour, Minister of Commerce and Industry, announced the formation of a department to prepare for taking over the Company at that time, stressing that Egypt had no intention of jumping the gun. On November 25th this department was set up, responsible to Mohey el-Din, Under-Secretary for Commerce and Industry, one of the Egyptian directors on the board of the Company.

Rumours were now circulating of internal Government dissension and imminent changes. On November 17th the Cairo correspondent of *The Times* reported the local *Rose el-Youssef* as expressing the general belief that Lieutenant-Colonel Gamal Abdel

Nasser would shortly "share the burden" with Neguib. He was said to possess patience, coolness and intelligence, and to enjoy the full confidence of Army officers. "It would therefore not be surprising," wrote *The Times*, "if Colonel Nasser were brought forward to take publicly the position he already enjoys in the Army movement and ease the strain on General Neguib." During the following months Nasser indeed emerged as the Government's principal spokesman on the Canal.

On the six-month anniversary of the coup, January 23rd, 1953, General Neguib and his temperamental aide, Major Salah Salem, produced some stirring words for popular consumption. Salem, soon to become the *bête noire* of the British press, spoke of a struggle, if necessary with bloodshed, against the "imperialist forces". But behind the scenes it appeared that more moderate counsels might prevail. On February 12th Britain and Egypt signed an agreement on the Sudan, guaranteeing immediate self-government with self-determination in three years. Eden expressed the hope in the Commons that this would clear the way for talks on the Canal Zone and Neguib spoke of "a new era in the relations of Egypt and Britain".

Throughout the Arab world expectation was voiced of a bright new age of Anglo-Arab co-operation. There was no excuse for delaying the talks on evacuation of the Canal Zone, which opened in Cairo on April 27th. In the meantime Stalin had died and the western world looked vainly for signals of the new régime's policy. The Soviet Foreign Minister called on Mahmoud Fawzi, his Cairo counterpart, to express concern about possible Egyptian participation in a Western-inspired Middle East defence pact. Equally, from the Conservative back benches in the Commons and the columns of *The Times*, came the urgent plea to the Government not to consider "scuttling" from Suez. On the Egyptian side there was no equivocation. "Unconditional evacuation" and "Evacuation or death" were the mottoes of the day.

Although the strategic importance of the Canal Zone in the context of Middle East security was a vital issue, its value could not be calculated solely in military terms. This huge industrial network, with its power stations, cold storage and sewage plants, docks, railways, roads, communications systems, airfields, oil and ammunition dumps, provided employment for some 10,000 technicians.

Britain was adamant that the problem of the future maintenance of the base and the conditions under which British troops would be permitted to return in an emergency should form a crucial part of any discussions. There was also the perennial question of freedom of navigation for all users of the Canal—a point on which, where Israel was concerned, Egypt refused to budge. Egypt, for her part, approached the talks primarily from the political angle. It was a simple question of national rights, of prestige in the eyes of her own people and the whole Arab world.

On June 18th all pretence of a monarchy was abandoned. Neguib proclaimed Egypt a Republic, with himself as President and Prime Minister, Nasser as Vice-Premier and Salem as Minister of National Guidance. A week later, Britain, in common with the other major powers, gave *de facto* recognition to the new Government. One of its first steps was to announce an austerity programme to reverse the trend of the £E38 million budget deficit of 1951-52. The four-day celebration of the Revolution's first anniversary could not conceal the gravity of the economic situation.

The talks continued informally throughout the late summer, with disagreement occurring over the right of British troops to return in an emergency and the question of the maintenance staff wearing uniforms. Egypt would not concede that a possible attack on Turkey constituted such an emergency. Meanwhile, elections took place in the Sudan, against a background of British and Egyptian accusations and counter-accusations of bad faith and political pressure. The year ended with no solution in sight.

Egypt hardly contributed to an amicable settlement of the free navigation issue by her decree of November 30th extending the blockade against Israel to include "foodstuffs and all other merchandise that might increase the military potential of Israel". It could now be argued, however implausibly, that all cargo bound for Israel came into this category. Moreover, she declared her intention to blacklist any vessel of any nation refusing to support this boycott. Although permitted to use the Canal they would be denied port facilities. On February 5th Israel brought the matter again before the Security Council, arguing that the blockade was in flagrant defiance of the Council's 1951 Resolution. The Egyptian reply that only eight seizures had taken place and that two or less vessels in every thousand had been subjected to inspection hardly affected the legality of the case. But Egypt refused to end the restrictions either in the Canal itself or in the Gulf of Akaba where her guns commanded the Tiran Straits.

On February 25th the long-expected reshuffle took place as Neguib resigned in favour of Nasser. He was accused of having quested for "more power and authority than he could be granted under the spirit of the Army Revolution." The strain of office was clearly affecting his health and he was criticised for delaying tactics on reforms. Three days later he returned but confusion reigned until on April 18th Nasser again took over as Premier. A return to parliamentary government after elections was promised for the end of June. Trouble flared up once more in the Canal Zone and Britain refused to resume discussions until order was restored.

In Paris, on June 1st, the Suez Canal Company held its Annual General Meeting. Chairman François Charles-Roux announced favourable results for the year, a rapidly increasing volume of traffic and over ten billion francs to be distributed among shareholders. He also reaffirmed the Company's policy towards the disturbing events of the day, which, in retrospect, had a flavour of tragic irony:

"From time to time, rumours and hearsay have involved your company in local disputes centred on the Canal Zone and in international controversies about the Convention of 1888 for the free navigation of the Suez Canal. The truth is your company has never interfered in the one or the other. I can tell you again . . . Your company's policy is essentially to take no part in politics."

Yet a solution was near. The decision of the British Government to move its military Headquarters in the Middle East from Egypt to Cyprus (June 23rd) heralded the initialling, on July 27th, of the Agreement on the evacuation of troops from the Canal Zone. The Agreement*, which was formally signed in Cairo on October 19th, provided for the complete withdrawal of British troops within twenty months of signature. It was to operate for seven years, during which time the base was to be maintained in working order and capable for immediate use in the event of armed attack by any outside power on any Arab League State or on Turkey. Article Eight stated:

* The text of the Agreement is quoted in full in Appendix F.

"The two contracting Governments recognise that the Suez maritime canal, which is an integral part of Egypt, is a waterway economically, commercially, and strategically of international importance, and express the determination to uphold the Convention guaranteeing the freedom of navigation of the canal signed at Constantinople on October 29th, 1888."

Egypt would assume responsibility for the security of the base and its equipment, and an agreed number of British technicians would assist in the upkeep and operation of installations such as ammunition dumps, workshops and engineers' stores. Britain would be granted staging rights for the R.A.F. Public utilities, communications, bridges, wharves and pipelines would be handed over to the Egyptian Government.

Colonel Nasser described the Agreement as "a turning point in the history of Egypt . . . the biggest single achievement in Egypt's national aspirations to date." Britain had bowed gracefully to the inevitable, though doubts in varying degrees were voiced by the Labour Opposition and the Tory back-benchers who called themselves the "Suez Group". World opinion, for the most part, hailed it as a triumph for wisdom and statesmanship. Even Farouk cabled his congratulations from Rome. *Pravda*, however, warned Egypt against going along with America in her plans for a Middle East Command. In Russian eyes it guaranteed "neither territorial integrity nor sovereignty, avoidance of interference in her internal affairs, not equality in her relations with the Western countries." And in Israel the imminent departure of British troops was regarded with concern as likely to leave the nation dangerously vulnerable to the hostile aims of her Arab neighbours.

Three weeks after the Agreement was signed Israel resolved to test the intentions of both Egypt and Britain on the question of free navigation. The 500-ton *Bat Galim*, bound from Massawa to Haifa with a cargo of meat, tried to enter the southern end of the Suez Canal and was promptly detained. The Security Council was convened on October 5th to consider Israel's complaint. The ensuing debates were inconclusive and Egypt released the captain and crew of the *Bat Galim* on January 1st, 1955, though not the vessel itself. It was evident that Egypt was not prepared to compromise on the blockade and that the United Nations was powerless to intervene.

October 19th in Cairo was predictably a day of rejoicing and firework displays. But for Nasser trouble erupted a week later when shots were fired at him in Alexandria. Angry citizens burned the offices of the Muslim Brotherhood in Cairo and Neguib was removed from the Presidency for the last time. Press reports, not denied by the Government, suggested his implication in the assassination attempt but no steps were taken to arrest him. Nasser, however, as undisputed Head of State, dealt drastically with the Brotherhood, arresting over a thousand members, of whom six were executed, and officially dissolving the movement.

During this agitated period the Suez Canal Company optimistically announced a new scheme for improving the Canal's facilities over the next five or six years. It was the eighth and largest improvement programme to date, and was to involve the expenditure of some $2\frac{1}{2}$ million pounds, the excavation of over 80 million square yards of soil, and deepening to allow passage of vessels of 36 ft. draught. It was an imaginative and urgent scheme inasmuch as the existing Canal was inadequate for coping with the increasing volume of traffic and size of vessels, and obviously the Company could not afford to wait on political developments.

The year 1955 opened ominously for the Canal as the 11,000-ton oil tanker *World Peace* collided with the railway swing bridge at El Ferdan, bringing 350 tons of metal crashing down on her decks and causing a four-day blockage of the Canal. But this was a minor incident in what was to prove a fateful year for Egypt and her relationship with East and West.

On January 31st two Jews were hanged in Cairo for spying, creating intense anger in Israel and exacerbating an already tense situation. That month a meeting of Arab League leaders had been convened in Cairo, to which Iraq was pointedly not invited. Pressure was brought on the Arab statesmen to condemn Iraq's flirtation with the West and this assertion of Egyptian natural supremacy in the Arab world caused a rift in loyalties which Nasser regarded with concern. When Iraq finally signed a military alliance with Turkey in Baghdad on February 24th, Egyptian fury was boundless. Apart from the overt alignment of Iraq with Western defence plans in the Middle East, Egypt was indignant that she should link herself to a nation which recognised Israel. Israel was equally suspicious of the Pact, though for different reasons. Whatever transpired, she was excluded from joining the alliance and the combination of Britain and Iraq was not viewed with much enthusiasm.

It was clear that Egypt was veering from a position of strict neutrality towards a closer link with the Soviet Union. Already she had concluded a number of commercial agreements with Russia and other East European nations, which had helped her to dispose of large surpluses of otherwise unsaleable cotton. Now, as America and Britain voiced doubts about Egypt's reliability in a Middle East security system, the problem of arms supplies became a burning issue. Alarmed by a renewal of fighting in the Gaza Strip— the first big clash since the Armistice—and determined to stake his claim for leadership of the Arab League, Nasser began to give serious thought to approaching Moscow for the arms which, in his opinion, were vital for Egyptian security.

The Bandung Conference of Asian and African States in May gave Nasser the opportunity to emerge as the natural spokesman for Arab self-determination and champion of every nation struggling to throw off the colonial yoke. He returned with his prestige much enhanced. At home, as the first results of land reform and city development were visible, his popularity with the masses was un-challenged. Meanwhile, on April 6th, Anthony Eden took over from the ageing Winston Churchill as Prime Minister. At the end of May he won a convincing victory at the polls, strengthening his hand against a temporarily divided Opposition.

There were regular outbreaks during the summer in the Gaza area, and General Burns, the Canadian Chief of Staff of the Truce Supervision Organisation, appealed to the United Nations for help. Egyptian *fedayeen* penetrated deep into Israel, causing numerous civilian casualties, while Israel's reprisal raids resulted in the deaths of soldiers and civilians in and around Gaza. Not until early September was a cease-fire arranged.

In August Nasser announced Egypt's first sale of cotton to Communist China and accepted an invitation to visit Moscow. The news was received phlegmatically in London where, it was asserted, it was known that the Colonel was no lover of Communism. But *The Times* of August 18th pointed accurately to signs of increasing Soviet involvement in the Middle East and speculated as to whether Nasser was not unwittingly risking becoming a tool of Soviet foreign policy in an area where she had long dreamed of getting a foothold. The signs were indeed there for all to read. On September 27th Nasser announced that he had concluded a deal or deals with

Russia and Czechoslovakia for the supply of MIG fighters, tanks, artillery and other heavy equipment, and naval craft.

Now the Western powers sat up and took notice, starting with an expression of "grave concern" by the new British Ambassador, Sir Humphrey Trevelyan. The *New York Times* described it as "playing with fire" and as a significant political victory for Russia, no matter that Nasser was convinced he was not opening the door to Communism at home. Nasser himself had no qualms about initiating a new arms race, asserting he had warned the British Ambassador in June, and adding, "I never bluff; I always say what I mean."

To the perplexing problem of arms for the Middle East and the increased danger of an Arab-Israeli war was now added a fresh one—the financing of the new High Dam at Aswan. This scheme, symbolising Egypt's determination to pursue an independent course and improve the country's industrial and agricultural potential, had been under consideration for some time and was now projected in detail. The High Dam, replacing the existing one, would be three miles in length, 364 ft. high and would be designed to store 130,000 million cubic metres of water. It would double Egypt's potential hydro-electric power and increase the area of cultivable land by some 30%. It was likely to take about sixteen years to complete and its estimated cost was $1,300 million. This massive undertaking obviously required substantial financial and technical assistance from foreign countries. In February 1956 it was confirmed that the World Bank had agreed to lend $200 million and that America and Britain would furnish initial grants of $56 million and $14 million respectively.

Egypt, however, was irritated by the conditions accompanying the offer. Not only did the Bank insist on an assurance that the loan would be used exclusively for the intended purpose but it made it contingent upon Egypt first coming to an agreement with neighbouring Sudan on the use of the Nile waters. For the Sudan stood to be vitally affected. A large portion of her territory would be flooded, the lives of thousands of peasants disrupted and her own industrial future perhaps transformed. Her leaders were also in militant mood for on December 19th, 1955, she had declared outright independence and was pressing for a speedy revision of the obsolete 1929 Agreement whereby her share of the Nile waters was only about one-twelfth of Egypt's. Nor was she prepared to wait for the dam to be built before discussing the problem of surplus water, as Egypt now suggested.

Nasser was in no mood to be hamstrung by such conditions. $270 million only went a small way towards the total cost, and already Russia had expressed a desire to participate in the scheme. At 6.45 a.m. on June 13th, 1956, the last British troops pulled out of the Canal Zone, and the Union Jack was hauled down from Navy House, Port Said, symbolising the end of seventy years of uninterrupted occupation. Egypt celebrated with a four-hour military parade in Cairo's Republic Square. General Sir Brian Robertson was invited; so too was Soviet Foreign Minister Shepilov.

Although Nasser admitted that Britain had fulfilled her obligations and announced that he wished to be on good terms with everybody, it was clear that relations with the Soviet bloc were now closer than ever. Trade with the Communist nations had increased in a year by more than 65%; anti-British and anti-French propaganda poured daily from the "Voice of the Arabs" radio; and the supplies of Soviet and Czech arms were revealed to be on a much more substantial scale than had originally been thought.

The Canal itself was very much in his thoughts and talks had taken place early in the year to discover means of binding the Company more closely to Egyptian Government interests. On June 7th the terms of an agreement with the Company were published. Under it the Company undertook to invest £E21 million of its funds in the Egyptian economy, 10 million in 1956, 3 million in 1957, 2 million in 1958 and 1 million annually until 1964. The Company also agreed to increase the roster of pilots (there were 156 in December, 1955), taking on 26 Europeans and 32 Egyptians during the next two years. The Egyptian Government had once more made it quite plain that in no circumstances would the Concession be extended after 1968.

The day following the Cairo parade it was rumoured that Russia was offering Egypt a loan of $1,200 million, repayable over 60 years, at the low interest rate of 2%. By implication there were no strings attached. The West suspected a bluff. Ahmed Hussein, the Egyptian Ambassador to Washington, appeared anxious to conclude the original deal. Astonishingly, on July 19th, Secretary of State John Foster Dulles turned the Egyptians down. In the words of the State

Department, "It is not feasible in present circumstances to participate in this project." Next day Britain followed suite, giving similar vague reasons, and the World Bank offer automatically lapsed.

Although the reasons for this abrupt policy switch were allegedly economic, it was clear that it was also politically motivated. Doubts as to Egypt's reliability in a Middle East defence organisation, her arms deals with the Soviet bloc, her recognition of Communist China on May 17th, and the State Department's resolve to call the Russian bluff, were all recognisable considerations. Nor was there much doubt as to which party was responsible for the maladroit decision. Sir Anthony Eden commented on it ruefully in his *Memoirs*:

"We were informed but not consulted and so had no opportunity for criticism or comment . . . We were sorry that the matter was carried through so abruptly, because it gave our two countries no chance to concert either timing or methods, though these were quite as important as the substance. At this moment Colonel Nasser was in Brioni at a meeting with Marshal Tito and Mr. Nehru, and the news was wounding to his pride."[*]

This was an understatement, as was soon made clear. Yet the British Government must share the responsibility for failing to see how near the brink Egypt was being pushed by the West. During the course of the Prime Ministers' Conference in London, lasting from July 7th until July 14th, the Aswan Dam and the Suez Canal were not even mentioned.

The climax came on the night of July 26th, as Eden was dining at Downing Street with his old friend King Feisal of Iraq. A Private Secretary interrupted the meal to inform Eden that Nasser had seized the Canal. In a two-and-a-half-hour speech in Alexandria he had that evening announced Egypt's intention to take over the Suez Canal immediately and to nationalise the Suez Canal Company. Revenues from the Canal would be used to finance the High Dam project. "This Canal," he shouted to a wildly applauding crowd, "is an Egyptian Canal . . . The income of the Suez Canal Company in 1955 reached £E35 million—100 million dollars . . . We, who lost 120,000 persons who died digging the Canal, receive only 3 million dollars . . . We shall build the High Dam as we want it . . .

---

[*] Sir Anthony Eden, *Memoirs—Full Circle*, p. 422.

We shall be victorious and will defend our freedom to the last drop of blood."

The Company funds in Egypt would be frozen, its property in Egypt and abroad confiscated, its assets and liabilities taken over by the Government. Company employees were ordered to continue at their posts at risk of imprisonment and forfeiture of the right to indemnity. Compensation would be paid to shareholders in due course, after delivery of assets and properties of the nationalised Company. Management would in future be in the hands of an independent authority attached to the Ministry of Commerce. Heading it would be Mahmoud Younes, an engineer, who had already taken control in Ismailia. The Company's officers in Cairo, Ismailia and Suez were in process of being seized.*

As the full text of President Nasser's speech became available, the Western Governments finally realised the gravity of the crisis which they had helped to instigate.

* The text of the Nationalisation Law is quoted in Appendix G.

CHAPTER XVII

THE SUEZ WAR

THE events of the late summer and autumn of 1956 which culminated in the Israeli attack on the Sinai peninsula and the Anglo-French invasion of the Canal Zone have been the subject of many controversial articles and books during the last twelve years. Apart from official sources, many versions have been submitted of the incidents which provoked a major international crisis and which, for a brief time, threatened to give rise to a situation where the intervention of the two super-powers might have been inevitable. With the passage of time, new facts have come to light, some of them providing factual evidence of what was at the time mere suspicion and speculation, mainly concerning Anglo-French motives and allegations of collusion with Israel. Though it is not appropriate in this book to analyse these conflicting versions nor to pass judgment on the actions of the main protagonists, the sequence of events must be related and some account taken of these later revelations in order to understand how the actions of the British and French Governments brought about the very thing they had pledged themselves to prevent—the closure of the Canal.

The Canal was, of course, the central issue, although the highly emotional reactions of the main parties concerned did little to clarify the essential basis of the controversy. From Egypt's point of view the issue was a simple one. Expropriation of the Universal Maritime Suez Canal Company was an exclusively domestic concern. Whether the Company was technically French or Egyptian was of no importance. The Canal was indisputably Egyptian. Provided adequate compensation was offered to shareholders for the un-expired period of the Concession, the act of nationalisation was both morally justified and legal. In the view of the majority of Canal users this was an over-simplification. This was not an ordinary Company nor an ordinary property. This was a Company controlling an international waterway. Any change in the ownership of such a Company was therefore of prime concern to all nations using the

Canal. They were entitled to obtain assurances from the new authority that the objectives and governing conditions of the original Concession should continue to be observed, that there should be no impediment to free navigation, no discrimination against any vessel of any nation and no arbitrary control of the conditions of passage in order to further the political or economic interests of any one nation.

The legality of the expropriation was never the prime consideration. The situation would have had to be faced anyway in 1968. What caused dismay and anger was the abrupt method and timing. As far as Britain and France were concerned it boiled down to the simple question—could Nasser be trusted? What reliance could be placed in the promises of a man who had only a few months previously announced that he had no intention of curtailing the Concession? Could Egypt, who had already defied the Security Council and world opinion by continuing her blockade of Israel, be expected to operate the Canal in accordance with the terms of the 1888 Convention? If Nasser were allowed to get away with this coup, might he not be encouraged to foment nationalistic risings in other Arab countries, notably Iraq and Jordan, and to threaten the free flow of Middle Eastern oil? These possibilities worried Britain especially. France, moreover, was disturbed at the conclusive evidence of material aid given by Egypt to the Algerian rebels. The United States, not so immediately involved as a Canal user, was particularly concerned about the long-term political consequences in the Middle East, where the shadow of Russia was already looming large, and the threat of serious trouble erupting in an election year.

On August 2nd, therefore, the Governments of the United Kingdom, France and the United States issued a statement condemning "the arbitrary and unilateral seizure by one nation of an international agency which has the responsibility to maintain and to operate the Suez Canal." They proposed convening a conference, to be attended by all parties to the Convention and other Canal users, whose object would be "to establish operating arrangements under an international system designed to assure the continuity of operation of the Canal as guaranteed by the Convention of 29th October, 1888, consistently with legitimate Egyptian interests,"*

* Cmd. 9853, pp. 3-4.

The ruins of the Nasr Oil Refinery at Suez after shelling by Israeli guns, 1967

Smoke pours from the Nasr Oil Refinery at Suez after shelling
by Israeli guns

This Conference of Twenty-two Nations was held in London from August 16th to August 23rd and resulted in the presentation of a plan, supported by a majority of eighteen countries, calling for an international operating Board for the Canal. An alternative plan, sponsored by India and supported by the Soviet Union, Indonesia and Ceylon, recommended the operation of the Canal by Egypt, assisted by an international advisory body of Canal users. The majority proposal, which had been presented by U.S. Secretary of State Dulles, was adopted, and a delegation of five nations, headed by the Australian Prime Minister Mr. Menzies, was detailed to submit the plan to Colonel Nasser.

Meanwhile, Sir Anthony Eden had announced to the Commons on August 2nd that "certain precautionary measures of a military nature" were being taken by the Government. Reservists had been called up and units of the army, navy and air force transferred to the Eastern Mediterranean. In France similar "precautions" were also being taken. Britain and France had made it quite clear that they were prepared to restore the situation by force if peaceful methods failed. The United States joined Britain and France in blocking Suez Canal Company funds in their respective countries and in freezing Egyptian assets. America, however, would not condone the use of force in any circumstances.

The Menzies mission, not unexpectedly, was rebuffed. On September 9th Nasser formally rejected the proposal and the Anglo-French military build-up gathered momentum. In the Commonwealth, only Australia and New Zealand unswervingly supported Britain, while at home opinion was sharply, often acrimoniously, divided. India and Pakistan were sympathetic to Egypt and Nehru was believed to be advising Nasser behind the scenes. Canada, though not directly concerned in the dispute, was determined to seek a peaceful solution through the United Nations. America, thoroughly alarmed by the impetuosity of Eden and Mollet, vacillated, playing for time. In a press conference on September 11th Eisenhower pledged that America would not become involved in a war, to the intense dismay of Britain and France and the obvious relief of Egypt.

Dulles then came forward with an entirely new scheme—a Suez Canal Users' Association (SCUA). This body would hire its own pilots, collect all transit dues (paying Egypt for technical co-operation), and conduct all convoys through the Canal. It was completely unrealistic and stood no chance whatsoever of being acceptable to Nasser. But Eden was persuaded to give it approval since it did seem to provide a means of witholding Canal dues from Egypt. A second International Conference was therefore called in London for September 19th to consider setting it up.

Meanwhile, the Suez Canal Company, almost certainly under pressure from the British and French Governments, had stepped into the centre of the arena and provoked a new crisis. On July 29th the Board of Directors had announced that shipping lines would be expected to continue paying dues to the Company in the normal manner, in the expectation that two-thirds of the total tolls collected would go on flowing into London and Paris bank accounts. It condemned as unrealistic Nasser's proposal to divert the relatively small Canal profits into building the Aswan Dam. On August 6th the Company instructed its non-Egyptian personnel to fulfil their contracts by ceasing work and leaving Egypt. Egypt was already weeding out foreigners on the clerical and administrative sides, whilst prudently leaving alone the essential pilots and key executives for the time being. Working conditions were therefore becoming increasingly difficult. But the Company's employees were recommended to continue working until the end of the month.

By the end of August the Company claimed that the situation of their employees was becoming unendurable. Additional strains were put on the pilots by the substitution of one convoy daily instead of two, which did not alter the average number of ships passing through the Canal each day. The Company supported the idea of an international authority and told its staff to await the outcome of the Menzies mission. But it was clear that, given the word, almost all the foreign pilots, of whom 61 were British and 53 French, representing more than half of the total roster, were packed and ready to leave. Although Mahmoud Younes condemned the Company's plans as "sabotage" and threatened reprisals, it was merely a matter of time. After the failure of the Menzies mission the Company took decisive action and in a statement dated September 11th instructed its employees to stop working immediately and seek repatriation.

On September 15th, a few days before the second London Conference, 141 foreign pilots left Egypt. Meanwhile the new

Authority had been advertising widely through the world press for new recruits and had received an encouraging initial response, particularly from Russia and other Eastern European countries. The official Western line was that without experienced pilots the Egyptians could not hope to run the Canal efficiently. Since this would inevitably interfere with free navigation an excuse could then be found to intervene. Other nations, including Norway, the second largest Canal user, were not so convinced of Egyptian ineptitude, and Nasser himself was optimistic. But already some shipping lines were making plans to divert their vessels round the longer and more expensive Cape run, insurance companies were raising war risk rates, and commodity prices, such as tin, were showing sharp increases.

Even before the London Conference began Dulles had virtually torpedoed the plan he had himself devised. At a press conference on September 13th, asked about American intentions regarding sending a SCUA convoy through the Canal, he flatly dismissed any idea of using force, whatever the provocation, concluding with the mystifying words:

"The association is not intended to guarantee anything to anybody. I think that each nation has to decide for itself what action it will have to take to defend and if possible realise its rights which it believes it has as a matter of treaty. I do not recall just exactly what Sir Anthony Eden said on this point. I did not get the impression there was any undertaking or pledge given by him to shoot their way through the Canal."

Later he commented, "I can't understand this talk of the United States pulling the teeth out of the users' association. There never were any teeth in it as far as I am aware." With some justification, Eden regarded this as a betrayal of their joint intentions, remarking, in his *Memoirs*:

"The Users' Club was an American project to which we had conformed. We were all three in agreement, even to the actual words of the announcement. Yet here was the spokesman of the United States saying that each nation must decide for itself and expressing himself as unable to recall what the spokesman of a principal ally had said. Such cynicism towards allies destroys true partnership. It leaves only the choice of parting, or a master and vassal relationship in foreign policy."*

* Sir Anthony Eden, *Memoirs—Full Circle*, p. 484.

Anglo-American relations had indeed reached their lowest point since the war. The disarray of Western policy and opinion stood exposed. Even on the vital question of dues Britain had not been able to bring America round to her way of thinking. By this time Egypt was already pocketing some 45% of tolls collected, 10% more than before.

The second London Conference duly met, but only as a prelude to referring the entire dispute to the United Nations. America refused to sponsor or even to support the Anglo-French draft resolution which was to be submitted to the Security Council. Three days later, on September 26th, Eden and Foreign Secretary Selwyn Lloyd met their French counterparts, Mollet and Pineau, in Paris. The French still favoured immediate action, showing scepticism both towards the Users' Club and the United Nations. Eden felt that a solution should be sought through the United Nations before embarking on drastic action.

The dire predictions of the pessimists about the smooth operation of traffic through the Canal was, in the meantime, not borne out by facts. During the days and week following the foreign pilots' departure, Mahmoud Younes and his nucleus of trained Egyptian and Greek pilots managed to keep traffic moving steadily, The day after they left 42 ships passed through, the next day 36. By the end of September the daily average of 42 ships was being maintained. Thanks to the good response to the advertisements, 92 pilots were said to be working, with a further 90 in training. There were only a few minor mishaps and delays and Lloyd's removal of the insurance surcharge previously imposed indicated their confidence in the new management.

On October 5th the Security Council met to discuss the Suez controversy, the ground being laid by the indefatigable Lester Pearson. The crucial discussions, however, were not in the Council chamber but took place behind closed doors between the three Foreign Ministers, Lloyd, Pineau and Fawzi. Out of these discussions emerged a two-part draft resolution. The first part, which was accepted by the Security Council, including Egypt, embodied six principles, and read as follows:

"The Security Council, noting the declarations made before it and the accounts of the development of the exploratory conversations on the Suez question given by the Secretary-General of the

United Nations and the Foreign Ministers of Egypt, France and the United Kingdom, agrees that any settlement of the Suez question should meet the following requirements:

(a) There should be free and open transit through the Canal without discrimination, overt or covert—this covers both political and technical aspects.

(b) The sovereignty of Egypt should be respected.

(c) The operation of the Canal should be insulated from the politics of any country.

(d) The manner of fixing tolls and charges should be decided by agreement between Egypt and the users.

(e) A fair proportion of the dues should be allotted to development.

(f) In case of disputes, unresolved affairs between the Universal Maritime Suez Canal Company and the Egyptian Government should be settled by arbitration, with suitable terms of reference and suitable provisions for the payment of sums found to be due."

The second part of the resolution declared that the proposals of the Eighteen Powers corresponded to these requirements and were suitably designed to bring about a settlement of the Suez Canal question by peaceful means. This part was unacceptable to Egypt and vetoed by Shepilov on behalf of the Soviet Union.

Britain and France saw this rejection as a turning point. The six principles had been unanimously agreed but there was clearly no way of putting them into practice. As Eden remarked in his *Memoirs*, "The truth was starkly clear to me. Plunder had paid off."* From that moment Britain and France accelerated their plan to impose their own solution, in conjunction with the Israeli plan for a pre-emptive attack on Egypt.

On October 16th a vital meeting took place in Paris between the two Prime Ministers and the two Foreign Ministers. It was held in strict secrecy, without any advisers present. Here, according to Eden, the role of Israel was first mentioned and here the final plans were worked out for the assault two weeks later. There was no longer any question of consultation with the United States. Troop movements were speeded up, a smoke-screen of silence descended between the two capitals and Washington, and the Israeli ambassadors in key European capitals were recalled home.

* Sir Anthony Eden, *Memoirs—Full Circle*, p. 506.

The accusation of "collusion" was hurled at Eden and his ministers soon after the fateful decision to bomb Egyptian airfields and land forces in the Canal Zone. In the dozen years that have elapsed it has become abundantly clear that official versions of the events of October, 1956, concealed much of the truth. What was then conjectured by many has to a large extent been substantiated by official and unofficial spokesmen both in France and Israel. Neither France nor Israel was apologetic for the co-ordination of plans which had evidently existed for months. The large-scale supply of French arms certainly pre-dated the nationalisation decree and was doubtless known by Nasser. Neither country concealed the mutually friendly relations they enjoyed. But with Britain the case was different. Her tight-rope Middle Eastern policy, with treaty obligations both towards Iraq and Jordan, precluded any overt show of sympathy towards Israel. France had little reason to conceal a joint operation which was partially designed to ensure the survival of a country convinced she was in danger of attack, and possibly of extinction. Neither the record nor present circumstances made it credible for Britain to advance similar reasons. The fact that until this day no official admission of collusion by Britain has been made indicates the sensitivity of subsequent Conservative administrations to charges of duplicity at the time.*

There is, however, sufficient attested evidence to suggest that discussions and preparations between France, Britain and Israel went back to a time prior to the expropriation of the Suez Canal Company. Both Britain and France had their own separate reasons for wishing to see Colonel Nasser overthrown, and just as the nationalisation decree provided the official excuse for intervention, so the Israeli plans for a Sinai campaign provided the military opportunity. There is no suggestion that Israel ever intended to occupy the Canal, which would have been sheer lunacy. Her pro-claimed objective was to destroy the Sinai bases and clear the Gaza Strip from which the Fedayeen sabotage squads were operating, and to capture the Sharm el-Sheik outpost overlooking the Tiran Straits in order to open the port of Eilat to Israeli shipping. In both these objectives she was successful.

* The articles published in *The Times* in May, 1967 by Anthony Nutting, relating to the Suez crisis and his own resignation as Minister of State at the Foreign Office, were hotly challenged by Conservative spokesmen. His book on the subject, *No End of a Lesson*, was published by Constable in July, 1967.

French and British motives were more complex. The official ones—the threats to trade and to oil supplies—were genuine, but others were not so openly expressed. France, by virtue of her historic associations with Egypt and her initiative in laying the foundations of the Canal in the nineteenth century, was particularly sensitive towards this threat to her power and prestige in the Mediterranean. No longer dominant in Syria and Lebanon, this additional blow to her pride in a traditional sphere of influence was hard to stomach. France was also deeply perturbed at developments in Algeria where Nasser's unconcealed policy of arming the rebels was seen as a deliberate provocation. Britain was mainly concerned at Nasser's growing influence among the Arabs of the Middle East, his obvious desire to see Nuri Said's administration in Iraq toppled, and his dangerous overtures to Jordan. The risk of Jordan being drawn into the Egyptian camp, especially after the dismissal of Glubb Pasha and other British officers, was very real.

Where Eden, Lloyd, Mollet and Pineau were in agreement was in regarding Nasser personally as the root of the trouble. Parallels with Mussolini and Hitler, memories of Munich, however unrealistic they may seem in retrospect, were frequently evoked and doubtless sincerely believed. Certainly, British and French statements following Nasser's coup suggest strongly that the element of personal vendetta was no small consideration in subsequent planning. Eden wired Eisenhower on July 27th, observing, "We are all agreed that we cannot afford to allow Nasser to seize control of the Canal in this way . . . My colleagues and I are convinced that we must be ready, in the last resort, to use force to bring Nasser to his senses."[*] And the leaflets dropped by British bombers bluntly proclaimed that the Egyptian people had brought retribution on themselves by committing the sin of placing their trust in Abdel Nasser.

It is probable that Eden was precipitated by the French into taking more rapid and drastic action then he had originally intended. In the event it was Britain who, despite claims of having achieved her objective, suffered the greatest loss, in moral if not military terms.[* *]

[*] Sir Anthony Eden, *Memoirs—Full Circle*, pp. 427-8.
[* *] The "collusion" issue is powerfully argued in Erskine Childers' *The Road to Suez*, Macgibbon & Kee, 1962, and, more objectively, by Terence Robertson in *Crisis: The Inside Story of the Suez Conspiracy* (Hutchinson, 1965). It was also the subject of one of the eight broadcasts in the Third Programme in 1966, devised by Peter Calvocoressi, and issued by the British Broadcasting Corporation in 1967 in book form, under the title *Suez Ten Years After*.

By mid-October the maritime traffic was still flowing smoothly through the Canal, thanks to continuing fine weather and the strenuous efforts of Younes and his expanding force of pilots. "It cannot be denied" wrote *The Times* Special Correspondent from Cairo on October 7th, "that the Egyptian Authority has succeeded beyond most expectations in keeping the Canal open." By October 24th Younes had 233 pilots from 17 nations, including the United States and Canada, of which about 100 were Egyptian. He announced that the crisis was over and that he had no need of further recruits. The training period had been reduced from three months to one, with two weeks in the Port Said roads and two on the Canal. Instead of learning the entire route they now concentrated either on the Port Said-Ismailia or the Ismailia-Suez stretch, and in only one direction. By curtailing the training period and working long hours of overtime the convoys were kept on the move. Between July 26th and October 23rd, 3,693 ships passed through the Canal, as against 3,585 in the same period of 1955, despite the increasing number of vessels being re-routed via the Cape. Only towards the end of the month, as the crisis flared up once more, did traffic dwindle almost to nothing, by which time the pilots were admittedly showing signs of severe strain. But the argument that Egypt could not keep the Canal open was proving patently false.

The general election in Jordan on October 21st turned out as Britain feared, with pro-Nasser elements victorious. Next day saw a further crucial meeting in Paris, at which Israeli leaders, including Prime Minister Ben-Gurion, were present. On October 28th Israel announced her mobilisation, but it was generally assumed that an attack, if it came, would be against Jordan. This would have placed Britain in a predicament, for she was bound by treaty to come to Jordan's aid in such an eventuality. The world at large, if not Britain and France, were therefore stunned when on October 29th Israeli forces crossed the Egyptian border and struck a double blow in the direction of Ismailia and Suez.

Britain and France now drew up a suspiciously hurried, and curiously worded, ultimatum, designed to separate the opposing forces. It called on both Egypt and Israel to withdraw their troops to ten miles on either side of the Suez Canal, failure to comply with which would result in Port Said, Ismailia and Suez being occupied by Anglo-French forces. This allowed for a further twelve-hour

Israeli advance, after which she accepted the ultimatum. Egypt, not unexpectedly, turned it down. A Security Council resolution, condemning the Anglo-French initiative, was promptly vetoed by both powers, and on the following day, October 31st, British and French planes bombed Egyptian airfields. By November 2nd Israel had sealed off the Gaza Strip and was mopping up the routed Egyptian forces in Sinai. The Egyptian air force was declared to have been destroyed and air attacks began on military installations around the Canal and Port Said.

In New York, again inspired by Lester Pearson, the Security Council frantically sought the means to put a stop to what threatened to become a major conflagration. The General Assembly called for a cease-fire, but by now, despite previous delays, the Anglo-French preparations for a landing were well advanced. It was reported that an Egyptian blockship, loaded with cement, scrap iron and other heavy rubbish, had been sunk, though it was not known whether it was in the Canal proper. But by November 3rd, with Britain and France playing for time, and Israel accepting a cease-fire provided the Egyptians did the same, it was confirmed that the Canal was indeed blocked by six or seven ships. The following day the Egyptians dynamited the supports of the El Ferdan railway bridge.

Matters were now confused and aggravated even more by the news of the Soviet Union's attack on Hungary. America's hands were still effectively tied because of the impending election on November 6th. On the 4th the Security Council demanded a halt to military operations by 5 a.m. the following morning. By then British and French paratroopers were landing at Port Fuad and Port Said. The former town was quickly captured but there was heavy fighting in Port Said which held out for seven hours, surrendered and then resumed fighting on instructions from Cairo. The Anglo-French sea-borne attack went into motion with both Britain and France agreeing to the cease-fire provided an international police force took over immediately. Meanwhile, Israel, her objectives achieved, accepted the cease-fire unconditionally.

On November 6th an Anglo-French force landed in the Port Said area and there was more bitter resistance by the Egyptians. Eventually the British and French broke out and headed south along the Canal for Ismailia. They had reached El Cap, 23 miles south of

Port Said, when orders were received announcing an immediate cease-fire.

The end had come suddenly and in military circles there was angry criticism of the politicians who had prevented the completion of an operation which was so close to success. But there had been overwhelming reasons for the abrupt stoppage. Russia had threatened to send "volunteers" and even to launch missiles on London and Paris; the Treasury was desperately concerned about the run on sterling and the fact that America refused to come to the rescue as long as fighting continued; there was increasing opposition at home, both in Government circles and among the public; and the fact that both Egyptians and Israelis had accepted a cease-fire now rendered the official reason for intervention unnecessary.

The immediate result was that some hundreds of Egyptian soldiers and civilians had been killed, though French and British casualties were comparatively light. Ironically, after three months of uninterrupted functioning, the Canal was now well and truly blocked by some forty assorted vessels. The devastating effect on British prestige and power in the Middle East, and the fact that Nasser now emerged morally victorious, with the Arab world united as never before, was to become evident later. "Fiasco" was not too exaggerated a term to use for the Anglo-French contribution to the operation; and the prospects for a permanent peace settlement in the Middle East became remoter than ever.

The British and French forces remained in Egypt for seven weeks. Total evacuation was agreed upon provided they were replaced by the United Nations Emergency Force. The last troops pulled out of Port Said on December 22nd. Two days later the citizens celebrated this second departure of foreign occupying forces by dynamiting the statue of de Lesseps and sinking the débris in the harbour.

CHAPTER XVIII

THE CANAL'S GOLDEN DECADE

POLITICAL repercussions apart, the blockage and closure of the Suez Canal threatened the major user nations with severe economic consequences. India, Ceylon and the Middle Eastern Arab States were hardest hit as a result of delays and re-routing of vital export commodities. Egypt herself had to bear the loss of Canal and harbour revenues and was compelled to borrow heavily from the International Monetary Fund. An austerity programme, including fuel rationing, was immediately introduced. Petrol rationing came into force both in Britain and France. Freight surcharges were imposed by all European maritime countries as shipping was diverted round the Cape. It was reliably estimated that three months at least would be required to clear the Canal.

British and French salvage teams set to work immediately after the cease-fire to clear the Port Said area. When the military and political dust settled, surveys revealed that some fifty obstacles were blocking the Canal at six points. They included blockships, tugs, a dredger, a tank-landing craft, a salvage vessel, floating cranes and a miscellany of smaller vessels. Two bridges, including the El Ferdan railway bridge, were also down. In and around Port Said there were thirteen obstacles visible above the surface and another seven submerged. One of the ships barring the entrance to the Canal was the world's largest dredger, the 3,500 ton *Paul Solente*. Another twenty-nine obstacles were thought to be blocking the channel between El Cap and Suez. In addition, fourteen foreign vessels were trapped in the Canal, twelve of them southbound, two northbound. They included the 38,000 ton Liberian tanker *Statue of Liberty*, and cargo ships flying the Dutch, Italian, Norwegian, Swedish and Panamanian flags. Damage to Canal and harbour installations was estimated at over half a million dollars.

Clearing operations were delayed by Nasser's insistence that all foreign troops—French, British and Israeli—should be withdrawn before the commencement of salvage work. In fact, British and

French operations were well advanced by the time their last troops pulled out three days before Christmas. By then an unobstructed 30-foot channel had already been opened through Port Said by a salvage fleet of thirty-five vessels. In the meantime, Egypt had approached the United Nations for financial and technical assistance in clearing the Canal, and Secretary General Dag Hammarskjold had agreed to shoulder the cost and assemble a U.N. salvage force. Lt.-General R. E. Wheeler, of the United States Army Engineer Corps was put in command of the U.N. operation. Ten nations agreed to advance a loan of 10.8 million dollars to help meet the cost of clearance. This proved more than enough for the final cost was approximately eight and a half million dollars, far less than had originally been feared. A temporary three per cent surcharge on tolls was also proposed and eventually approved by the General Assembly of the United Nations.

Independent British and French salvage work now ceased, and there were further delays as the role of Anglo-French vessels and crews in the United Nations clearance programme was disputed. Nasser too refused to provide any assistance until the Israelis had withdrawn from Sinai and Gaza. Under strong pressure both from the Security Council and her erstwhile allies, Israel pulled out of Sinai in the third week of January. On March 7th her troops left the Gaza Strip and Sharm el-Sheikh and were replaced by the hastily summoned United Nations Emergency Force.

In the northern section of the Canal work had progressed slowly since the beginning of the year. The *Paul Solente* was raised and removed, and thirteen of the trapped vessels sailed into the Mediterranean on January 8th. A German lifting craft raised and shifted the western span of the El Ferdan bridge and smaller vessels in the southern portion of the Canal were also removed. By February only three major obstacles remained—the cement-filled *Akka*, between Lake Timsah and the Bitter Lakes, the tug *Edgar Bonnet* at Ismailia, and the frigate *Abukir* at Suez.

The *Akka* was lifted and towed into the Great Bitter Lake on February 14th, and three days later the Egyptian freighter *Ramses* was the first vessel to traverse the whole length of the Canal. But Egypt still withheld permission to start work on the *Edgar Bonnet*, which was reported to be filled with explosives. A month passed and it was finally revealed that there were no explosives on board.

On March 25th the *Edgar Bonnet* was removed to Lake Timsah. Four days later a nine-ship convoy sailed north from Suez and after a temporary stoppage due to a sandstorm progressed to Port Said. On April 8th the *Abukir* was removed from the Canal's southern entrance and General Wheeler was able to announce completion of the salvage work. The Egyptian Government issued a statement that normal traffic would immediately be resumed for vessels of maximum 33 ft. draught, 2 ft. below the previous maximum, and convoys began moving through the Canal from both ends.

The Anglo-Egyptian Agreement of 1954 had been terminated by Nasser on January 1st, 1957, and was followed by a policy of "Egyptianisation" designed to reduce foreign commercial and financial influence. British banks, insurance companies and industrial concerns were among the first to be affected in a nationalisation programme which, within five years, embraced every sector of private enterprise in Egypt. At the same time Nasser took steps to re-establish normal diplomatic relations with the West, whilst increasing his economic dependence on trade with the Soviet Union and Eastern Europe. He also set about healing the rifts between Egypt and other Arab League nations, the first concrete result being the treaty with Syria, signed on February 1st, 1958, under which the two countries were linked as the United Arab Republic.

The reopening of the Canal involved all the user nations in major policy decisions. Britain, France, the United States and several other European countries announced their intention of boycotting the Canal for the time being, the main bone of contention being the payment of tolls. The SCUA had been stillborn. The fact that Egypt would henceforth collect all Canal traffic dues was generally accepted, but her insistence on being paid in hard currency aroused widespread protest. A compromise was eventually reached and each nation in turn cancelled the boycott. By mid-May traffic was building up to thirty or forty ships each day. On June 18th a record total of 51 ships passed through the Canal, on November 23rd 64, on December 21st 69. By the end of the year the maximum permissible draught was increased to 34 ft and four convoys were using the Canal daily.

The new Authority, under the direction of Mahmoud Younes, was quick to show how efficiently and profitably it could handle an increasing volume of Canal traffic. The period from April 1957 to June 1967, when the Canal was again blocked, was a decade of steady progress, confounding the gloomy predictions which accompanied the nationalisation decree. The figures speak for themselves. In 1955, the last full year of operation by the Suez Canal Company, 14,666 ships used the Canal, totalling 115¾ million net tons and yielding a revenue of £E32 million. In 1966, the number of vessels, at 21,250, showed a fifty per cent increase, tonnage was more than doubled at 274⅓ million, and—most important from Egypt's point of view—receipts were trebled at £E95 million. This steady improvement in revenues was achieved without any increase in tolls until 1964, when three successive annual increases of one per cent were enforced. Furthermore, Nasser had kept his pledge to put aside 25 per cent of Canal revenues for maintenance and improvements. Only in his impetuous promise to build the Aswan Dam out of Canal revenues was he proved wrong. It was soon clear that the Russians would have to shoulder the financial burden and provide the technical assistance for this ambitious project.

The unbroken smooth handling of Canal shipping for ten years was due partly to the genius of Younes himself and partly to the tremendous efforts of his force of pilots. They worked long hours, for comparatively low salaries, and this resulted in the gradual defection of many of the foreigners recruited at the time of nationalisation. When Younes was promoted in October 1965 and replaced by Mashour Ahmed Mashour, more than two-thirds of the pilots were Egyptian. When he handed over his duties the Canal was bringing in over £E85 million annually, 55 shjps were using it every day and more than £E38 million had been spent on improvements. *The Times*, in an article on July 26th, 1966, wrote: "The record of Egyptian management in the Suez Canal has been excellent. It stands in striking contrast to the muddle which has enveloped the rest of the economy."

In the early part of 1958 negotiations took place between the former Suez Canal Company and the Egyptian Government on compensation to shareholders for expropriation, with delegates from the World Bank acting as mediators. Agreement was reached on July 13th in Rome, whereby the Egyptian Government undertook to compensate shareholders to the extent of £E28,300,000, payable in six annual instalments. Egypt discharged the debt faithfully, completing it one year in advance. The agreement heralded the unfreezing of Egyptian assets in Paris, London and Washington.

Only in one respect did Egypt not observe the spirit of the 1888 Convention. Nasser steadfastly refused to open the Canal to Israeli ships and cargoes, in defiance of international opinion, The most highly publicised of several test cases was the Egyptian seizure, in May 1959, of the Danish cargo ship *Inge Toft*, bound for Haifa. The ship was not freed until the following February after unloading her cargo. The Greek vessel *Astypalea* was similarly detained in December 1959. After the release of the *Inge Toft* Nasser repeated his intention of retaining the blockade indefinitely. Israeli complaints to the Security Council were unavailing and the running sore of the dispute became ever more inflamed over the years. Freedom of navigation in the Canal and the Gulf of Akaba was to develop into a *casus belli* in June 1967, with even more serious consequences for Nasser and the Egyptian economy than in 1956.

While the Canal was blocked two feet of sand had formed on the bottom and constant dredging had been necessary to restore it to its former depth. But in order to cope with the growing volume of maritime traffic and the increasing size of tankers it was obvious that far-reaching improvement schemes would have to be launched, as recommended and planned by the Suez Canal Company. Work on a modified form of the Company's Eighth improvement plan began in 1958. It was a short-term two-year project, undertaken by three American firms, at a cost of between fifteen and twenty million dollars. It was designed to widen the Canal by almost 100 feet, and deepen it to allow the passage of 45,000 ton vessels, increasing the maximum draught from 35 ft. (as from August 31st, 1958) to 37 ft. By the end of 1960 this objective had been achieved.

Much more ambitious in scope, however, was the so-called Nasser Plan, a long-term project for which a World Bank loan of 56.5 million dollars was obtained in December 1959, repayable at 6 per cent over fifteen years. The first stage envisaged widening and deepening sufficiently to handle laden tankers of 70,000 tons with a maximum 45 ft. draught. The Canal's width would be doubled along its entire length, and an ambitious construction programme would modernise harbour facilities and workshops, build new roads and bridges, establish a network of radio, radar and television communications, expand the dredging fleet and attract new industry to the three main Canal zone cities. Although there was criticism of the World Bank decision at the time, there were few nations who did not, in the ensuing years, express a desire to be financially or practically involved in the improvement schemes. In Western eyes the Canal was considered to be a sounder economic proposition than the High Dam. Whether this will be borne out by events remains to be seen.

In April 1962 Krupps of Essen won the contract to build a new El Ferdan railway bridge, 900 ft. long, 30 ft. wide and capable of being opened electronically in seven minutes. Port Said, Ismailia and Suez were growing in prosperity and attracting a huge influx of labour from the countryside. The Canal continued to symbolise Egypt's revolutionary struggle despite the glaring weaknesses of the national economy at large.

The federation which had called into being the United Arab Republic had by now collapsed. The end came in the autumn of 1961, with Egypt alone retaining for herself the title U.A.R. It had been caused to some extent by the unpopular July Decrees, which extended the nationalisation programme, increased taxation to unprecedented levels and called for renewed revolutionary activity. In Egypt the Decrees were to lead to considerable discontent among the lower and middle classes, faced with continually rising costs and a fresh barrage of restrictions. Poor cotton crops, a perennial shortage of foreign exchange and the increased spending on defence resulted in regular budget deficits. In the teeth of difficulties both at home and abroad, the Suez Canal and the Aswan Dam were understandably given the fullest publicity. The Canal was an important source of revenue and the Dam, begun, under Russian direction, in January 1960, was proceeding according to schedule.

The work on the Dam had followed the signing of a Nile Waters Agreement by Egypt and the Sudan on November 8th, 1959. The Sudan was allocated 14,500 million and Egypt 7,500 million cubic metres of the additional available water. This brought the Sudan's total share to 18,500 million and Egypt's to 55,500 million cubic metres. The Sudan was also to be compensated suitably for flooded territory.

By the end of 1963 60,000 ton vessels, with maximum 38 ft draught, were using the Canal and both oil and dry goods traffic were recording their highest levels ever. The story of the next three

A dramatic aerial picture of the burning Nasr Oil Refinery at
Suez after shelling by Israeli guns. The Canal is seen lower right

Israeli soldiers alongside the Canal at Kantara, shortly after the Six-Day War

Two small vessels stranded in the Canal after the Six-Day War

years was one of unimpeded progress, despite troubles at home and abroad. On the military front the presence of United Nations troops in the Gaza Strip prevented the outbreak of hostilities on a large scale but warlike preparations continued on both sides. Nasser's intervention in the civil war in the Yemen was costly both in manpower and money, and damaging in the eyes of world opinion. Not until August 1965 was he able to disentangle himself from this expensive and ill-advised venture, his aims significantly unfulfilled.

By 1966 the new El Ferdan bridge was completed, as was a new shipyard at Port Fuad. Port Said's harbour capacity was being increased by the removal of six islets in the bay. A number of supertankers were already using the Canal, though not fully laden. There were clear indications of possible difficulties as giant waves thrown out by these ships battered and breached the retaining walls of the Canal and forced large quantities of sand down to the bed.

In July 1966 Mashour Ahmed Mashour announced a new six-year programme, as part of the Nasser Plan, designed to allow the navigation of 110,000 ton loaded tankers and 125,000 ton partially loaded vessels by 1972. Work on this stage of the plan began in February 1967. Beyond it beckoned the glittering prospect of a Canal which by 1980 would carry ships of 200,000 tons, with a permissible maximum draught of 60 ft. Significantly, in September 1966, Japan launched her 209,000 ton tanker *Idemitsu Maru*, an unmistakable symbol of things to come.

Such was the situation when the Six-Day War broke out in June 1967, putting an abrupt stop to all these ambitious improvement schemes and placing in jeopardy the whole future of the Suez Canal.

M

CHAPTER XIX

DOES THE WORLD NEED THE CANAL?

FOR nine years after the Suez crisis of 1956 Israel and her Arab neighbours observed a truce. But it was a fragile, uneasy truce, interrupted by border incidents, which, though held in check by United Nations observer teams, reflected the true tensions of a situation likely at any moment to explode and threaten the stability of the whole Middle East. The tragic plight of the Arab refugees was manipulated and exploited cynically by those who saw no profit in a peaceful settlement of the problem. Egypt still smarted from her Sinai humiliation, Israel was convinced her enemies were only awaiting an opportunity to deal a death blow. Nasser, claiming a state of war still existed between the two countries, continued to ban Israeli shipping from the Canal. The major powers poured in the modern weapons which, all agreed, were only to be used for defensive purposes. Below the deceptively calm surface smouldered the old suspicions and resentments—fuel for the conflagration which, by the spring of 1967, became inevitable.

It will take historians many years to establish conclusively whether the Six-Day War of June 1967 came about by design or miscalculation. But from the beginning of 1965, with the first Al Fatah terrorist attacks, inspired by Syria and launched from Jordan, the pattern of unofficial hostilities unfolded and gained momentum. Raids were followed by large-scale reprisals. The Security Council would be convened and issue an ineffectual condemnation of one or both sides. Arab propaganda against Israel reached new peaks of virulence. Military preparations continued, with political leaders under pressure from popular opinion, compelled by demands for action to take steps which admitted no turning back. Fear of attack, fear of reprisal, fear of losing face, fear of revolution, fear of extermination—a muddled and tragic progression of events.

The crucial occurrence in that tense month of May 1967 was the abrupt departure, at Nasser's request, of the United Nations Emergency Force from Egypt. Nasser was undoubtedly as surprised as anyone when U Thant ordered U.N. troops out of Gaza and Sharm el-Sheikh on May 19th, without any prior consultation of the Security Council. But Nasser was quick to take advantage of the situation. On May 22nd he proclaimed the blockade of the Gulf of Akaba and the sealing off of the Israeli port of Eilat. Reservists in Egypt and Israel were called up as armoured divisions moved into the Sinai peninsula. Jordan, thus far uncommitted, joined Egypt in a five-year defence pact and allowed Iraqi troops to enter the country. King Hussein flew back from Cairo to Amman with Ahmed Shukairy, the bellicose leader of the unofficial Palestine Liberation Organisation. In Jerusalem, Moshe Dayan, architect of Israel's Sinai victory in 1956, was appointed Minister of Defence.

Then came the erroneous report, circulated by Russia, that Israel was concentrating her troops for an imminent attack on Syria. For the Arabs, with their vastly superior weight of military strength and numbers, the moment had come. Egypt alone had assembled seven divisions—100,000 men and 1,000 tanks in Sinai. On paper Israel appeared hopelessly outnumbered by the encircling Arab armies. But Nasser miscalculated badly. He allowed Israel to get in the first vital blow. On the morning of Monday, June 5th, just before 8.00 a.m., local time, Israel's fighter force struck a series of devastating blows at the Egyptian air force, destroying 300 planes —280 of them on the ground—in three hours. The air supremacy thus achieved proved decisive in the days that followed as Israeli armoured columns and infantry swept deep into Sinai in a three-pronged attack.

By June 7th the Egyptian forces were in full retreat and by the 8th all objectives were achieved—capture of the Gaza Strip, occupation of Sharm el-Sheikh and command of the two main roads linking central Sinai with the Suez Canal. After a massive destruction of Egyptian armour and transport in the Mitla Pass it was all over. Israeli troops reached the Canal and deployed along the entire east bank, cutting off the escape routes across the bridges at Kantara, Ismailia and Suez. Then they dug in on the high ground dominating the Canal approaches, some twenty miles to the east. On Nasser's own admission Egypt had lost 10,000 troops, 1,500 officers and 40 pilots. Four of his seven armoured divisions had been wiped out, the other three paralysed. Three-quarters of his air force had been destroyed. His airfields and oil installations in Sinai were in

Israeli hands. And the Suez Canal, officially closed on June 6th, was blocked for the second time in ten years.

Once again the world's shipping faced crisis. Freight and passenger vessels were diverted round the Cape and immediate surcharges imposed. The initial confident predictions of a short period of closure were dispelled as each side adopted a stance of rigid intransigence. Nasser's brief resignation was followed by a return to power, at popular demand, and a massive army purge. Israel was determined this time not to give up any conquered territories until peace talks guaranteed them the recognition and full navigational rights she had insisted upon for twenty years. On June 11th the Israeli ship *Dolphin* sailed through the Straits of Tiran.

In the Suez Canal a dozen obstacles, including dredgers, freighters and floating docks, blocked the main channel. Trapped in the Great Bitter Lake were fourteen ships, four British, two West German, two Swedish, two Polish, and one each from France, United States, Bulgaria and Czechoslovakia. Another American tanker lay crippled with engine trouble in Lake Timsah. Though negotiations got quickly under way to release the ships the talks broke down at the end of July, after Israel threatened to send vessels through the Canal and Egypt promised retaliation. Several Egyptian patrol vessels were fired upon by the Israelis. In August both sides agreed to a cessation of navigation in the Canal. All maintenance work stopped. Sand began to fill the channel bed. The once-thriving towns on the west bank, battered by Israeli artillery, were almost at a standstill. As the Egyptians concentrated tanks and artillery on their side of the Canal Israeli gunners kept up their vigil from behind the dunes opposite. Occasionally the cease-fire was broken by sniper fire and artillery exchanges. The sinking of the Israeli destroyer *Eilat* off Port Said on October 21st brought reprisal three days later when Israeli guns shelled the Suez oil refineries, destroying one, damaging another and reducing their capacity by fifty per cent.

Throughout 1968 the dreary stalemate continued, Israel refusing to withdraw an inch and Nasser using the Canal as a bargaining weapon to persuade the major powers to enforce a withdrawal. Tentative clearance work was resumed on January 27th but abandoned a few days later when Israel again refused to permit a survey of the Canal prior to the release of the trapped vessels. This was because Israel had agreed that the southern end could be cleared to release the ships, but when Egyptian boats turned into the northern section above Lake Timsah, the Israelis opened fire and the Egyptians then refused to continue operations. Israel did not wish the whole Canal to be cleared unless she was guaranteed passage for her own ships. Apart from supplies for the crews of these ships no traffic was allowed. On the anniversary of their blocked passage all fourteen ships steamed round the Lake, blowing sirens in protest; but there they remained as the second year of their imprisonment drew to a close, their cargoes long since written off by the insurance companies, symbols of international impotence.

After a century of service to world shipping, commercial prospects for the future are none too bright. The world's maritime nations are reconciled to the fact that it may be several years before it is reopened. The question is—how vital is the Canal in terms of world trade? Certainly the temporary loss of Canal facilities is nothing like so serious to the user nations as it was in 1956. As the 1967 crisis approached shipping companies were making plans to divert their fleets round the Cape and already thinking in terms of years rather than weeks and months.

Chief sufferer is obviously Egypt herself, with £E100 million annually lost from Canal revenues, the Nasser Plan at a standstill, some two-thirds of her oil-producing capacity gone, her tourist trade severely curtailed. It is true that Russia is helping to bolster the economy, has already more than replaced the guns, tanks and planes lost in the Six-Day War, and that the rich Arab oil states are compensating her to the tune of 266 million dollars a year. Moreover, Egyptian exports have risen in ten years from £E166 million to £E279 million, with significant increases in non-traditional commodities such as petroleum products, textiles, cotton yarns and rice. The improved figures for rice are due to the increasing acreage irrigated by waters from the Aswan Dam. Nevertheless, unemployment is high and the austerity measures have not been relaxed. *Pravda* itself, in a recent article, revealed that Egypt's losses arising from the war amounted to some 500 million dollars, of which 310 million could be attributed to closure of the Suez Canal.

Russia herself derives no benefit from the protracted closure of the Canal as she becomes increasingly involved in Middle East affairs. The short sea route from Odessa down to the Red Sea, the

Persian Gulf, the Indian Ocean and the Far East is now more than ever important. The 1966 figures for Canal traffic showed Russia as easily the leading exporter of oil products southwards bound—totalling 5,618,000 tons, with 3.7 per cent of the Canal's traffic (1,469 vessels, net weight over 10 million tons). Russia already stands in seventh place as a Canal user and is rapidly overhauling Greece, Italy and France. It is therefore likely that she will exert strong pressure, in her own interests, to get the Suez waterway reopened to shipping in the near future.

America stands virtually where she did in 1956, less dependent than ever on the Canal, well down on the user list in 1966 with only 2.4 per cent of total traffic. But it is in Europe that the most striking change has taken place in the course of a decade. Britain, France and other Western European nations who have relied traditionally on the Canal for their imports of oil from the Middle East are now finding alternative sources of supply, especially in Libya and Algeria. Britain, who took 60 per cent of her oil supplies through the Canal in 1956 was by 1966—before the new crisis erupted—importing only 25 per cent of her oil requirements via Suez. France, her total traffic through the Canal decreasing year by year, was bringing in little more—39 per cent of her oil imports came by the Suez route in 1966. Furthermore, Britain, still the Canal's main user—apart from Liberia—will be less dependent strategically on the Canal as her cutdown of armed forces east of Suez continues, an operation which will be completed by 1971.

Egypt, of course, still relies predominantly on revenues from oil traffic in both directions. In 1966 oil products accounted for 175,671,000 out of a total of 241,893,000 tons of cargo—the other main commodities being cereals, fertilisers and manufactured metals. But, as Egypt realised very well when she first took over the sole operation of the Canal, the future of her oil business is itself in jeopardy. The expensive improvement plans were designed to cope with the problem of supertankers, but even if the Nasser Plan were today proceeding according to schedule it is doubtful whether the Canal would by 1972 be capable of handling half of the world's tanker fleet. Only some 13 per cent of the tankers under construction are below 80,000 tons and two-thirds of them are over 150,000 tons. And today, according to an article in *The New Middle East* (January 1969), a 200,000 ton tanker taking the Cape route can cut 9/- per ton off the price of a 75,000 ton tanker on the Suez run.

Moreover, as the same article points out, there is no reason why dry goods should not also be transported in vessels of this size, utilising the container method already common on the U.K.-Australia run. Container shipping, with its rapid loading and unloading procedure, enabling a medium-sized vessel to be turned round on a single tide, is likely to revolutionise maritime trade in the latter part of this century. Although relatively small vessels are now in operation, economy will inevitably dictate the use of larger ships as the years pass.

As for passenger traffic through the Suez Canal, this will become negligible as air travel becomes ever cheaper and faster. In 1966 mail ships through the Canal totalled only 778, as against 934 in 1965, recording a tonnage of only 7,242,000 out of the total 274 million.

Looming over the whole situation, however, and quite separate from the sphere of tonnages and draughts and costs, is the bleak international outlook in the area. So precarious and unpredictable is the pattern of events in the Middle East that few nations will be prepared, if and when the Canal reopens to traffic, to risk a similar major disruption two, five or ten years hence. Whilst the overall economic effect of this second closure has been less severe, the psychological damage has been extensive. There seems little doubt that the Canal has seen its greatest days.

Yet it should be emphasised that de Lesseps' vision of a great waterway serving the interests of mankind still has tremendous relevance to us in this troubled age. The Canal, after all, is part of a permanent pattern of communication, whether it be over land, over water, or even under water. It was, and still is, a potential bridge between men and nations. We should not see it merely in terms of commerce and economics. Its human and psychological impact on our thinking and attitudes is considerable. For this reason alone the world needs the Suez Canal.

TEXT OF FIRMAN OF CONCESSION

Granted by the Khedive Mohammed Pasha al-Said to Ferdinand de Lesseps*

Our friend Mons. Ferdinand de Lesseps, having called our attention to the advantages which would result to Egypt from the junction of the Mediterranean and Red Seas, by a navigable passage for large vessels, and having given us to understand the possibility of forming a company for this purpose composed of capitalists of all nations ; we have accepted the arrangements which he has submitted to us, and by these presents grant him exclusive power for the establishment and direction of a Universal Company, for cutting through the Isthmus of Suez, and the construction of a canal between the two Seas, with authority to undertake or cause to be undertaken all the necessary works and erections, on condition that the Company shall previously indemnify all private persons in case of dispossession for the public benefit. And all within limits, upon the conditions and under the responsibilities, settled in the following Articles.

ARTICLE I

Mons. Ferdinand de Lesseps shall form a company, the direction of which we confide to him, under the name of the **UNIVERSAL SUEZ MARITIME CANAL COMPANY**, for cutting through the Isthmus of Suez, the construction of a passage suitable for extensive navigation, the foundation of appropriation of two sufficient entrances, one from the Mediterranean and the other from the Red Sea, and the establishment of one or two ports.

ARTICLE II

The Director of the Company shall be always appointed by the Egyptian Government, and selected, as far as practicable, from the shareholders most interested in the undertaking.

ARTICLE III

The term of the grant is ninety-nine years, commencing from the day of the opening of the Canal of the two Seas.

*This Act of Concession was replaced, with several alterations and modifications, by the Act of Concession of 1856. (See Appendix B.) Later, in 1863, two Conventions between the Egyptian Government and the Company were attached to it. This text is therefore mainly of historical interest as expressing the intentions of the parties at the time.

ARTICLE IV

The works shall be executed at the sole cost of the Company, and all the necessary land not belonging to private persons shall be granted to it free of cost. The fortifications which the Government shall think proper to establish shall not be at the cost of the Company.

ARTICLE V

The Egyptian Government shall receive from the Company annually fifteen per cent of the net profits shown by the balance sheet, without prejudice to the interest and dividends accruing from the shares which the Government reserves the right of taking upon its own account at their issue, and without any guarantee on its part either for the execution of the works or for the operations of the Company; the remainder of the net profits shall be divided as follows: Seventy-five per cent to the benefit of the Company; ten per cent to the benefit of the members instrumental in its foundation.

ARTICLE VI

The tariffs of dues for the passage of the Canal of Suez, to be agreed upon between the Company and the Viceroy of Egypt, and collected by the Company's agents, shall be always equal for all nations; no particular advantage can ever be stipulated for the exclusive benefit of any one country.

ARTICLE VII

In case the Company should consider it necessary to connect the Nile by a navigable cut with the direct passage of the Isthmus, and in case the Maritime Canal should follow an indirect course, the Egyptian Government will give up to the Company the uncultivated lands belonging to the public domain, which shall be irrigated and cultivated at the expense of the Company, or by its instrumentality.

The Company shall enjoy the said lands for ten years free of taxes, commencing from the day of the opening of the canal; during the remaining eighty-nine years of the grant, the Company shall pay tithes to the Egyptian Government, after which period it cannot continue in possession of the lands above mentioned without paying to the said Government an impost equal to that appointed for lands of the same description.

ARTICLE VIII

To avoid all difficulty on the subject of the lands which are to be given up to the Company, a plan drawn by M. Linant *Bey,* our

Engineer Commissioner attached to the Company, shall indicate the lands granted both for the line and the establishments of the Maritime Canal and for the alimentary Canal from the Nile, as well as for the purpose of cultivation, conformably to the stipulations of Article VII.

It is moreover understood, that all speculation is forbidden from the present time, upon the lands to be granted from the public domain, and that the lands previously belonging to private persons and which the proprietors may hereafter wish to have irrigated by the waters of the alimentary Canal, made at the cost of the Company, shall pay a rent of.........per *feddan* cultivated (or a rent amicably settled between the Government and the Company).

ARTICLE IX

The Company is further allowed to extract from the mines and quarries belonging to the public domain, any materials necessary for the works of the canal and the erections connected therewith, without paying dues ; it shall also enjoy the right of free entry for all machines and materials which it shall import from abroad for the purposes of carrying out this grant.

ARTICLE X

At the expiration of the Concession the Egyptian Government will take the place of the Company, and enjoy all its rights without reservation, the said Government will enter into full possession of the Canal of the two Seas, and of all the establishments connected therewith. The indemnity to be allowed the Company for the relinquishment of its plant and moveables, shall be arranged by amicable agreement or by arbitration.

ARTICLE XI

The statutes of the Society shall be moreover submitted to us by the Director of the Company, and must have the sanction of our approbation. Any modifications that may be hereafter introduced must previously receive our sanction. The said statutes shall set forth the names of the founders, the list of whom we reserve to ourselves the right of approving. This list shall include those persons who labours, studies, exertions or capital have previously contributed to the execution of the grand undertaking of the Canal of Suez.

ARTICLE XII

Finally, we promise our true and hearty co-operation, and that of all the functionaries of Egypt in facilitating the execution and carrying out of the present powers.

To my attached friend

FERDINAND DE LESSEPS

of high birth and elevated rank.

Cairo, 30th November, 1854.

The grant made to the Company having to be ratified by his Imperial Majesty the Sultan, I send you this copy that you may keep it in your possession. With regard to the works connected with the excavation of the Canal of Suez, they are not to be commenced until after they are authorised by the Sublime Porte.

3 Ramadan, 1271.

(The Viceroy's Seal.)

A true translation of the Turkish text.

KOENIG BEY,
Secretary of Mandates to
His Highness the Viceroy.

Alexandria, May 19th, 1855.

CHARTER OF CONCESSION AND BOOK OF CHARGES

for the Construction and Working of

THE SUEZ GRAND MARITIME CANAL AND DEPENDENCIES

We Mohammed-Said Pasha, Viceroy of Egypt, considering our charter bearing date the 30th November, 1854, by which we have granted to our friend M. Ferdinand de Lesseps exclusive power to constitute and direct a *Universal Company* for cutting the Isthmus of Suez, opening a passage suitable for large vessels, forming or adapting two sufficient entrances, one on the Mediterranean, the other on the Red Sea, and establishing one or two ports, as the case may be:

M. Ferdinand de Lesseps, having represented to us that in order to constitute a company as above described under the forms and conditions generally adopted for companies of that nature, it is expedient to stipulate beforehand by a fuller and more specific document, the burthens, obligations, and services to which that company will be subjected on the one part, and the concessions, immunities, and advantages to which it will be entitled, as also the facilities which will be accorded to it for its administration, on the other part:

Have decreed as follows the conditions of the concession which is the subject matter of these presents.

I. CHARGES

ARTICLE 1

The Company founded by our friend M. Ferdinand de Lesseps in virtue of our charter of the 30th November, 1854, shall execute at its own cost, risk, and damage all the necessary works and constructions for the establishment of:

> 1st A canal navigable by large vessels between Suez on the Red Sea, and the Gulf of Pelusium on the Mediterranean ;
> 2nd A canal of irrigation adapted to the river traffic of the Nile, joining that river to the above-mentioned Maritime Canal ;

3rd Two branches for irrigation and supply, striking out of the preceding canal, and in the direction respectively of Suez and Pelusium.

The works shall be completed within the period of six years, unavoidable hindrances and delays excepted.

ARTICLE II

The Company shall have the right to execute the works they have undertaken, themselves and under their own management, or to cause them to be executed by contractors by means of public tender or private contract under penalties. In all cases, four-fifths of the workmen employed upon these works shall be Egyptians.

ARTICLE III

The Canal navigable by large vessels shall be constructed of the depth and width fixed by the scheme of the International Scientific Commission.

Conformably with this scheme, it will commence at the port of Suez ; it will pass through the basin of the Bitter Lakes and Lake Timsah, and will debouche into the Mediterranean at whatever point in the Gulf of Pelusium may be determined in the final plans to be prepared by the engineers of the Company.

ARTICLE IV

The Canal of Irrigation adapted to the river traffic, according to the terms of the said scheme, shall commence in the vicinity of the city of Cairo, follow the Wadi Tumilat (ancient land of Goshen), and will fall into the Grand Maritime Canal at Lake Timsah.

ARTICLE V

The branches from the above Canal shall strike out from it above the debouchure into Lake Timsah, from which point they shall proceed, on one side to Suez, and on the other to Pelusium, parallel to the Grand Maritime Canal.

ARTICLE VI

Lake Timsah shall be converted into an inland harbour capable of receiving vessels of the highest tonnage.

The Company shall moreover be bound, if necessary:

1st To construct a harbour of refuge at the entrance of the Maritime Canal into the Gulf of Pelusium ;

2nd To improve the port and roadstead of Suez so that it shall equally afford a shelter to vessels.

ARTICLE VII

The Maritime Canal, the ports connected therewith, as also the Junction Canal of the Nile and the branch Canals, shall be permanently maintained in good condition by the Company and at their expense.

ARTICLE VIII

The owners of contiguous lands desirous of irrigating their property by means of water-courses from the Company's canals shall obtain permission so to do in consideration of the payment of an indemnity or rent, the amount whereof shall be fixed according to Article 17 hereinafter recited.

ARTICLE IX

We reserve the right of appointing at the official headquarters of the Company a special commissioner, whose salary they shall pay and who shall represent at the Board of Direction the rights and interests of the Egyptian Government in the execution of these presents.

If the principal office of the Company be established elsewhere than in Egypt, the Company shall be represented at Alexandria by a superior agent furnished with all necessary powers for securing the proper management of the concern and the relations of the Company with our Government.

II. CONCESSIONS

ARTICLE X

For the construction of the Canals and their dependencies mentioned in the foregoing articles, the Egyptian Government grants to the Company, free of impost or rent, the use and enjoyment of all lands not the property of individuals which may be found necessary.

It likewise grants to the Company the use and enjoyment of all uncultivated lands not the property of individuals which shall have been irrigated and cultivated by their care and at their expense, with these provisos:

    1st That lands comprised under the latter head shall be free of impost during ten years only, to date from their being put in a productive condition;

    2nd That after that period, they shall be subject for the remainder of the term of concession, to the same obligations and imposts to which are subjected under like circumstances, the lands in other provinces of Egypt;

3rd That the Company shall afterwards, themselves or through their agents, continue in the use and enjoyment of these lands and the water-courses necessary to their fertilisation, subject to payment to the Egyptian Government of the imposts assessed upon lands under like conditions.

ARTICLE XI

For determining the area and boundaries of the lands conceded to the Company under Article X, reference is made to the plans hereunto annexed, in which plans the lands conceded for the construction of the Canals and their dependencies free of impost or rent, conformably to Clause 1 is coloured black, and the land conceded for the purpose of cultivation, on paying certain duties conformably with Clause 2 is coloured blue.

All acts and deeds done subsequently to our charter of the 30th November, 1854, the effect of which would be to give to individuals as against the Company either claims to compensation which were not then vested in the ownership of the lands, or claims to compensation more considerable than those which the owners could then justly advance, shall be considered void.

ARTICLE XII

The Egyptian Government will deliver to the Company, should the case arise, all lands the property of private individuals, whereof possession should be necessary for the execution of the works and the carrying into effect of the concession, subject to the payment of just compensation to the parties concerned.

Compensation for temporary occupation or definitive appropriation shall as far as possible be determined amicably ; in case of disagreement the terms shall be fixed by a court of arbitration deciding summarily and composed of :

1st An arbitrator chosen by the Company ;

2nd An arbitrator chosen by the interested parties ;

3rd A third arbitrator appointed by us.

The decisions of the court of arbitration shall be executed without further process, and subject to no appeal.

ARTICLE XIII

The Egyptian Government grants to the leasing Company, for the whole period of the concession, the privilege of drawing from the mines and quarries belonging to the public domain, without paying duty, impost, or compensation, all necessary materials for the construction and maintenance of the works and buildings of the undertaking. It moreover exempts the Company from all duties of customs, entrance dues and others, on the importation into Egypt of all machinery and materials whatsoever which they shall bring from foreign countries for employment in the construction of the works or working the undertaking.

ARTICLE XIV

We solemnly declare for our part and that of our successors, subject to the ratification of His Imperial Majesty the Sultan, that the Grand Maritime Canal from Suez to Pelusium and the ports appertaining thereto, shall always remain open as a neutral passage to every merchant ship crossing from one sea to another, without any distinction, exclusion, or preference of persons or nationalities, on payment of the dues and observance of the regulations established by the *Universal Company* lessee for the use of the said Canal and its dependencies.

ARTICLE XV

In pursuance of the principle laid down in the foregoing Article, the *Universal Company* can in no case grant to any vessel, company, or individual, any advantage or favour not accorded to all other vessels, companies, or individuals on the same conditions.

ARTICLE XVI

The term of the Company's existence is fixed at 99 years reckoning from the completion of the works and the opening of the Maritime Canal to large vessels.

At the expiration of the said term, the Egyptian Government shall enter into possession of the Maritime Canal constructed by the Company, upon condition, in that event, of taking all the working stock and appliances and stores employed and provided for the naval department of the enterprise, and paying to the Company such amount for the same as shall be determined either amicably or by the decision of sworn appraisers.

Nevertheless, if the Company should retain the concession for a succession of terms of 99 years, the amount stipulated to be paid to the Egyptian Government by Article XVIII, hereinafter recited, shall be raised for the second term to 20 per cent, for the third term to 25 per cent, and so on augmenting at the rate of 5 per cent for each term, but so as never to exceed on the whole 35 per cent of the net proceeds of the undertaking.

ARTICLE XVII

To indemnify the Company for the expenses of construction, maintenance and working, charged upon them by these presents, we authorise the Company henceforth, and during the whole term of their lease, as determined by Clauses 1 and 3 of the preceding Article, to levy and receive for passage through and entrance into the canals and ports thereunto appertaining, tolls and charges for navigation, pilotage, towage or harbour dues, according to tariffs which they shall be at liberty to modify at all times, upon the following express conditions :

1st That these dues be collected, without exception or favour, from all ships under like conditions ;

2nd That the tariffs be published three months before they come into force, in the capitals and principal commercial ports of all nations whom it may concern ;

3rd That for the simple right of passage through the Canal, the maximum toll shall be ten francs per measurement ton on ships and per head on passengers, and that the same shall never be exceeded.

The Company may also, for granting the privilege of establishing water-courses, upon the request of individuals by virtue of Article VIII, receive dues, according to tariffs to be hereafter settled, proportionable to the quantity of water diverted and the extent of the lands irrigated.

ARTICLE XVIII

Nevertheless in consideration of the concessions of land and other advantages accorded to the Company by the preceding Articles, we reserve on behalf of the Egyptian Government a claim of 15 per cent on the net profits of each year, accord to the dividend settled and declared by the General Meeting of Shareholders.

ARTICLE XIX

The list of Foundation Members who have contributed by their exertions, professional labours, and capital to the realisation of the undertaking before the establishment of the Company, shall be settled by us.

After the said payment to the Egyptian Government, according to Article XVIII above recited, there shall be divided out of the net annual profits of the undertaking, one share of 10 per cent among the Foundation Members or their heirs or assigns.

ARTICLE XX

Independently of the time necessary for the execution of the works, our friend and authorised agent, M. Ferdinand de Lesseps, shall preside over and direct the Company, as original founder, during ten years from the first day on which the term of concession for 99 years shall begin to run, by the terms of Article XVI above contained.

o

ARTICLE XXI

The Articles of Association hereunto annexed of the Company, established under the title of THE SUEZ MARITIME CANAL UNIVERSAL COMPANY, are hereby approved, and the present approval shall have force as an authority for its constitution in the form of *Sociétés Anonymes,* to date from the day when the entire capital of the Company shall be completely subscribed.

ARTICLE XXII

In witness of the interest which we feel in the success of the undertaking, we promise to the Company the loyal co-operation of the Egyptian Government ; and we expressly, by these presents, call upon the functionaries and agents of all our administrative departments to give aid and protection at all times to the Company.

Our engineers, Linant-Bey and Mougel-Bey, whose services we place at the disposal of the Company for the direction and conduct of the works ordered by the said Company, shall have the superintendence of the workmen, and shall be charged with the enforcing of regulations respecting the execution of the works.

ARTICLE XXIII

All provisions of our Charter of the 30th November, 1854, and others which are inconsistent with the clauses and conditions of the present book of charges, which alone shall constitute the law in respect of the concession to which it applies, are hereby revoked.

Done at Alexandria, 5th January, 1856.

To my devoted friend of high birth and elevated rank,

Mons. Ferdinand De Lesseps

The concession accorded to the Suez Canal Universal Company, requiring the ratification of His Imperial Majesty the Sultan, I remit you this authentic copy in order that you may constitute the said Financial Company. As regards the works for cutting the Isthmus, the Company may execute them as soon as the authorisation of the Sublime Porte has been accorded to me.

Alexandria, the 26 Rebi-al-akher, 1272 (5th Jan., 1856)

(*The Viceroy's Seal.*)

Translated according to the original in the Turkish language, deposited in the Archives of the Cabinet.

Koenig Bey,
Secretary of Mandates to
His Highness the Viceroy.

TEXT OF CONVENTION*

Between Great Britain, Germany, Austria-Hungary, Spain, France, Italy, The Netherlands, Russia, and Turkey, respecting the free navigation of the Suez Maritime Canal. Signed at Constantinople, October 29, 1888.

ARTICLE I

The Suez Maritime Canal shall always be free and open, in time of war as in time of peace, to every vessel of commerce or of war, without distinction of flag.

Consequently, the High Contracting Parties agree not in any way to interfere with the free use of the Canal, in time of war as in time of peace.

The Canal shall never be subjected to the exercise of the right of blockade.

ARTICLE II

The High Contracting Parties, recognising that the Fresh Water Canal is indispensable to the Maritime Canal, take note of the engagements of His Highness the Khedive towards the Universal Suez Canal Company as regards the Fresh Water Canal ; which engagements are stipulated in a Convention bearing the date of 18th March, 1863, containing an *exposé* and four Articles.

They undertake not to interfere in any way with the security of that Canal and its branches, the working of which shall not be exposed to any attempt at obstruction.

ARTICLE III

The High Contracting Parties likewise undertake to respect the plant, establishments, buildings, and works of the Maritime Canal and of the Fresh Water Canal.

ARTICLE IV

The Maritime Canal remaining open in time of war as a free passage, even to ships of war of belligerents, according to the terms

*The text is complete apart from the preamble, which has been omitted as being of little interest or importance

of Article I of the present Treaty, the High Contracting Parties agree that no right of war, no act of hostility, nor any act having for its object to obstruct the free navigation of the Canal, shall be committed in the Canal and its ports of access, as well as within a radius of three marine miles from those ports, even though the Ottoman Empire should be one of the belligerent Powers.

Vessels of war of belligerents shall not revictual or take in stores in the Canal and its ports of access, except in so far as may be strictly necessary. The transit of the aforesaid vessels through the Canal shall be effected with the least possible delay, in accordance with the Regulations in force, and without any other intermission than that resulting from the necessities of the service.

Their stay at Port Said and in the roadstead of Suez shall not exceed twenty-four hours, except in case of distress. In such case they shall be bound to leave as soon as possible. An interval of twenty-four hours shall always elapse between the sailing of a belligerent ship from one of the ports of access and the departure of a ship belonging to the hostile Power.

ARTICLE V

In time of war belligerent Powers shall not disembark nor embark within the Canal and its ports of access either troops, munitions, or materials of war. But in case of an accidental hindrance in the Canal, men may be embarked or disembarked at the ports of access by detachments not exceeding 1,000 men, with a corresponding amount of war material.

ARTICLE VI

Prizes shall be subjected, in all respects, to the same rules as the vessels of war of belligerents.

ARTICLE VII

The Powers shall not keep any vessel of war in the waters of the Canal (including Lake Timsah and the Bitter Lakes).

Nevertheless, they may station vessels of war in the ports of access of Port Said and Suez, the number of which shall not exceed two for each Power.

This right shall not be exercised by belligerents.

ARTICLE VIII

The Agents in Egypt of the Signatory Powers of the present Treaty shall be charged to watch over its execution. In case of any event threatening the security or the free passage of the Canal, they shall meet on the summons of three of their number under the presidency of their Doyen, in order to proceed to the necessary verifications. They shall inform the Khedival Government of the danger which they may have perceived, in order that that Government may take proper steps to insure the protection and the free use of the Canal. Under any circumstances, they shall meet once a year to take note of the due execution of the Treaty.

The last-mentioned meetings shall take place under the presidency of a Special Commissioner nominated for that purpose by the Imperial Ottoman Government. A Commissioner of the Khedive may also take part in the meeting, and may preside over it in case of the absence of the Ottoman Commissioner.

They shall especially demand the suppression of any work or the dispersion of any assemblage on either bank of the Canal, the object or effect of which might be to interfere with the liberty and the entire security of the navigation.

ARTICLE IX

The Egyptian Government shall, within the limits of its powers resulting from the Firmans, and under the conditions provided for in the present Treaty, take the necessary measures for insuring the execution of the said Treaty.

In case the Egyptian Government shall not have sufficient means at its disposal, it shall call upon the Imperial Ottoman Government, which shall take the necessary measures to respond to such appeal ; shall give notice thereof to the Signatory Powers of the Declaration of London of the 17th March, 1885 ; and shall, if necessary, concert with them on the subject.

The provisions of Articles IV, V, VII, and VIII shall not interfere with the measures which shall be taken in virtue of the present Article.

ARTICLE X

Similarly, the provisions of Articles IV, V, VII, and VIII, shall not interfere with the measures which His Majesty the Sultan and His Highness the Khedive, in the name of His Imperial Majesty, and within the limits of the Firmans granted, might find it necessary to take for securing by their own forces the defence of Egypt and the maintenance of public order.

In case His Imperial Majesty the Sultan, or His Highness the Khedive, should find it necessary to avail themselves of the exceptions for which this Article provides, the Signatory Powers of the Declaration of London shall be notified thereof by the Imperial Ottoman Government.

It is likewise understood that the provisions of the four Articles aforesaid shall in no case occasion any obstacle to the measures which the Imperial Ottoman Government may think it necessary to take in order to insure by its own forces the defence of its other possessions situated on the eastern coast of the Red Sea.

ARTICLE XI

The measures which shall be taken in the cases provided for by Articles IX and X of the present Treaty shall not interfere with the free use of the Canal. In the same cases, the erection of permanent fortifications contrary to the provisions of Article VIII is prohibited.

ARTICLE XII

The High Contracting Parties, by application of the principle of equality as regards the free use of the Canal, a principle which forms one of the bases of the present Treaty, agree that none of them shall endeavour to obtain with respect to the Canal territorial or commercial advantages or privileges in any international arrangements which may be concluded. Moreover, the rights of Turkey as the territorial Power are reserved.

ARTICLE XIII

With the exception of the obligations expressly provided by the clauses of the present Treaty, the sovereign rights of His Imperial Majesty the Sultan and the rights and immunities of His Highness the Khedive, resulting from the Firmans, are in no way affected.

ARTICLE XIV

The High Contracting Parties agree that the engagements resulting from the present Treaty shall not be limited by the duration of the Acts of Concession of the Universal Suez Canal Company.

ARTICLE XV

The stipulations of the present Treaty shall not interfere with the sanitary measures in force in Egypt.

ARTICLE XVI

The High Contracting Parties undertake to bring the present Treaty to the knowledge of the States which have not signed it, inviting them to accede to it.

ARTICLE XVII

The present Treaty shall be ratified, and the ratifications shall be exchanged at Constantinople, within the space of one month, or sooner, if possible.

In faith of which the respective Plenipotentiaries have signed the present Treaty, and have affixed to it the seal of their arms.

*Done at Constantinople,
the 29th day of the month of October,
in the year 1888.*

NOTE: Great Britain, though she respected this Convention, did not formally adhere to it until the signature of the Anglo-French Agreement of April 8th, 1904, and then on the condition that paragraphs (i) and (ii) of Article VIII should remain in abeyance. After the Great War the "enemy" Powers who had signed the Convention agreed to the replacing of Turkey by Great Britain in the Treaty. By Article 152 of the Versailles Treaty, "Germany consents in so far as she is concerned, to the transfer to His Britannic Majesty's Government of the powers conferred on His Imperial Majesty the Sultan by the Convention. . . ." Declarations to the same effect were signed by Austria (Article 107, Treaty of St. Germain), by Hungary (Article 91, Treaty of Trianon) and by Turkey (Article 109, Treaty of Sèvres and Article 99, Treaty of Lausanne).

THE ANGLO-EGYPTIAN TREATY OF ALLIANCE OF 1936

Article VIII and Annex

ARTICLE VIII

In view of the fact that the Suez Canal, whilst being an integral part of Egypt, is a universal means of communication between the different parts of the British Empire, His Majesty the King of Egypt, until such time as the High Contracting Parties agree that the Egyptian Army is in a position to ensure by its own resources the liberty and entire security of navigation of the Canal, authorises His Majesty the King and Emperor to station forces in Egyptian territory in the vicinity of the Canal, in the zone specified in the Annex to this Article, with a view to ensuring in co-operation with the Egyptian forces the defence of the Canal. The detailed arrangements for the carrying into effect of this Article are contained in the Annex hereto. The presence of these forces shall not constitute in any manner any occupation and will in no way prejudice the sovereign rights of Egypt.

It is understood that at the end of the period of twenty years specified in Article 16 the question whether the presence of British forces is no longer necessary owing to the fact that the Egyptian Army is in a position to ensure by its own resources the liberty and entire security of navigation of the Canal, may, if the High Contracting Parties do not agree thereon, be submitted to the Council of the League of Nations for decision in accordance with the provisions of the Covenant in force at the time of signature of the present treaty or to such other procedure as the High Contracting Parties may agree.

ANNEX TO ARTICLE VIII

1. Without prejudice to the provisions of Article 7, the numbers of the forces of His Majesty the King and Emperor to be maintained in the vicinity of the Canal shall not exceed, of the land forces, 10,000, and of the air forces, 400 pilots, together with the necessary ancillary personnel for administrative and technical duties. These numbers do not include civilian personnel, e.g., clerks, artisans, and labourers.

2. The British forces to be maintained in the vicinity of the Canal will be distributed (a) as regards the land forces, in Moascar and the Geneifa area on the south-west side of the Great Bitter Lake, and (b) as regards the air forces, within five miles of the Port Said-Suez railway from Kantara in the north to the junction of the railway Suez-Cairo and Suez-Ismailia in the South, together with an extension along the Ismailia-Cairo railway to include the Royal Air Force Station at Abu Sueir and its satellite landing grounds ; together with areas suitable for air firing and bombing ranges, which may have to be placed east of the Canal.

3. In the localities specified above there shall be provided for the British land and air forces of the numbers specified in paragraph 1 above, including 4,000 civilian personnel (but less 2,000 of the land forces, 700 of the air forces, and 450 civilian personnel for whom accommodation already exists), the necessary lands and durable barrack and technical accommodation, including an emergency water supply. The lands, accommodation, and water supply shall be suitable according to modern standards. In addition amenities such as are reasonable, having regard to the character of these localities, will be provided by the planting of trees and the provision of gardens, playing fields, etc., for the troops, and a site for the erection of a convalescent camp on the Mediterranean coast.

4. The Egyptian Government will make available the lands and construct the accommodation, water supplies, amenities, and convalescent camp, referred to in the preceding paragraph as being necessary over and above the accommodation already existing in these localities, at its own expense, but His Majesty's Government in the United Kingdom will contribute (1) the actual sum spent by the Egyptian Government before 1914 on the construction of new barracks as alternative accommodation to the Kasr-el-Nil Barracks in Cairo, and (2) the cost of one-fourth of the barracks and technical accommodation for the land forces. The first of these sums shall be paid at the time specified in paragraph 8 below for the withdrawal of the British forces from Cairo and the second at the time of the withdrawal of the British forces from Alexandria under paragraph 18 below. The Egyptian Government may charge a fair rental for the residence accommodation provided for the civilian personnel. The amount of the rent will be agreed between His Majesty's Government in the United Kingdom and the Egyptian Government.

5. The two Governments will each appoint, immediately the present treaty comes into force, two or more persons who shall together form a committee to whom all questions relating to the execution of these works from the time of their commencement to the time of their completion shall be entrusted. Proposals for, or outlines of, plans and specifications put forward by the representatives of His Majesty's Government in the United Kingdom will

191

be accepted, provided they are reasonable and do not fall outside the scope of the obligations of the Egyptian Government under paragraph 4. The plans and specifications of each of the works to be undertaken by the Egyptian Government shall be approved by the representatives of both Governments on this committee before the work is begun. Any member of this committee, as well as the Commanders of the British forces or their representatives, shall have the right to examine the works at all stages of their construction, and the United Kingdom members shall also have the right to make at any time, while the work is in progress, proposals for modifications or alterations in the plans and specifications. Effect shall be given to suggestions and proposals by the United Kingdom members, subject to the condition that they are reasonable and do not fall outside the scope of the obligations of the Egyptian Government under paragraph 4. In the case of machinery and other stores, where standardisation of type is important, it is agreed that stores of the standard type in general use by the British forces will be obtained and installed. It is, of course, understood that His Majesty's Government in the United Kingdom may, when the barracks and accommodation are being used by the British forces, make at their own expense improvements or alterations thereto and construct new buildings in the areas specified in paragraph 2 above.

6. In pursuance of their programme for the development of road and railway communications in Egypt, and in order to bring the means of communications in Egypt up to modern strategic requirements, the Egyptian Government will construct and maintain the following roads, bridges, and railways . . .

[*Details follow of roads (para. A) and railways (para.B).*]

7. In addition to the roads specified in paragraph 6 (A) above, and for the same purposes, the Egyptian Government will construct and maintain the following roads:

    (i) Cairo south along the Nile to Kena and Kus ;
    (ii) Kus to Kosseir ;
    (iii) Kena to Hurghada.

These roads and the bridges thereon will be constructed to satisfy the same standards as those specified in paragraph 6 above.

It may not be possible for the construction of the roads referred to in this paragraph to be undertaken at the same time as the roads referred to in paragraph 6, but they will be constructed as soon as possible.

8. When, to the satisfaction of both the High Contracting Parties, the accommodation referred to in paragraph 4 is ready (accommodation for the forces retained temporarily at Alexandria in accordance with paragraph 18 below not being included) and the

works referred to in paragraph 6 above (other than the railways referred to in (ii) and (iii) of part (B) of that paragraph) have been completed, then the British forces in parts of Egypt other than the areas in the Canal Zone specified in paragraph 2 above and except for those maintained temporarily at Alexandria, will withdraw and the lands, barracks, aircraft landing grounds, seaplane anchorages, and accommodation occupied by them will be vacated and, save in so far as they may belong to private persons, be handed over to the Egyptian Government.

9. Any difference of opinion between the two Governments relating to the execution of paragraphs 3, 4, 5, 6, 7, and 8 above will be submitted to the decision of an Arbitral Board, composed of three members, the two Governments nominating each a member and the third being nominated by the two Governments in common agreement. The decision of the Board shall be final.

10. In order to ensure the proper training of British troops, it is agreed that the area defined below will be available for the training of British forces: (a) and (b) at all times of the year, and (c) during February and March for annual manœuvres:

(a) West of the Canal: From Kantara in the north to the Suez-Cairo railway (inclusive) in the south and as far as longitude 31 degrees 30 minutes east, exclusive of all cultivation ;

(b) East of the Canal as required ;

(c) A continuation of (a) as far south as latitude 29 degrees 52 minutes north, thence south-east to the junction of latitude 29 degrees 30 minutes north and longitude 31 degrees 44 minutes east and from that point eastwards along latitude 29 degrees 30 minutes north.

The areas of the localities referred to above are included in the map (scale 1 : 500,000) which is annexed to the present treaty.

11. Unless the two Governments agree to the contrary, the Egyptian Government will prohibit the passage of aircraft over the territories situated on either side of the Suez Canal and within 20 kilometres of it, except for the purpose of passage from east to west or vice-versa, by means of a corridor 10 kilometres wide at Kantara. This prohibition will not, however, apply to the forces of the High Contracting Parties or to genuinely Egyptian air organisations or to air organisations genuinely belonging to any part of the British Commonwealth of Nations operating under the authority of the Egyptian Government.

12. The Egyptian Government will provide when necessary reasonable means of communication and access to and from the localities where the British forces are situated, and will also accord facilities at Port Said and Suez for the landing and storage of

material and supplies for the British forces, including the maintenance of a small detachment of the British forces in these ports to
handle and guard this material and these supplies in transit.

13. In view of the fact that the speed and range of modern aircraft necessitate the use of wide areas for the efficient training of
air forces, the Egyptian Government will accord permission to the
British air forces to fly wherever they consider it necessary for the
purpose of training. Reciprocal treatment will be accorded to
Egyptian air forces in British territories.

14. In view of the fact that the safety of flying is dependent upon
provision of a large number of places where aircraft can alight, the
Egyptian Government will secure the maintenance and constant
availability of adequate landing grounds and seaplane anchorages in
Egyptian territory and waters. The Egyptian Government will
accede to any request from the British air forces for such additional
landing grounds and seaplane anchorages as experience may show
to be necessary to make the number adequate for allied requirements.

15. The Egyptian Government will accord permission for the
British air forces to use the said landing grounds and seaplane
anchorages, and in the case of certain of them to send stocks of fuel
and stores thereto, to be kept in sheds to be erected thereon for this
purpose, and in case of urgency to undertake such work as may be
necessary for the safety of aircraft.

16. The Egyptian Government will give all necessary facilities for
the passage of the personnel of the British forces, aircraft and stores
to and from the said landing grounds and seaplane anchorages.
Similar facilities will be afforded to the personnel, aircraft, and
stores of the Egyptian forces at the air bases of the British forces.

17. The British military authorities shall be at liberty to request
permission from the Egyptian Government to send parties of
officers in civilian clothes to the Western Desert to study the ground
and draw up tactical schemes. This permission shall not be
unreasonably withheld.

18. His Majesty the King of Egypt authorises His Majesty the
King and Emperor to maintain units of his forces at or near
Alexandria for a period not exceeding eight years from the date of
the coming into force of the present treaty, this being the approxi-
mate period considered necessary by the two High Contracting
Parties:

(a) For the final completion of the barrack accommodation in
the Canal Zone;

(b) For the improvement of the roads:
   (i) Cairo-Suez;
   (ii) Cairo-Alexandria via Giza and the desert;
   (iii) Alexandria-Mersa Matruh;

so as to bring them up to the standard specified in part (A) of paragraph 6 ;

(c) The improvement of the railway facilities between Ismailia and Alexandria, and Alexandria and Mersa Matruh referred to in (ii) and (iii) of part (B) of paragraph 6.

The Egyptian Government will complete the work specified in (a), (b), and (c) above before the expiry of the period of eight years aforesaid. The roads and railway facilities mentioned above will, of course, be maintained by the Egyptian Government.

19. The British forces in or near Cairo shall, until the time for withdrawal under paragraph 8 above, and the British forces in or near Alexandria until the expiry of the time specified in paragraph 18 above, continue to enjoy the same facilities as at present.

AGREEMENT
BETWEEN SUEZ CANAL COMPANY AND EGYPTIAN GOVERNMENT, MARCH 7th, 1949

The principal clauses of this Agreement are as follows:

1. The number of Egyptian Directors will gradually be increased from two to seven. To this end two Egyptian Directors will be appointed to the Board on ratification of the Agreement, and they will fill two seats at present vacant in the French Directors' quota. An Egyptian Director will be allotted the first seat to become vacant from the quota of non-Government British Directors, and two more Egyptian Directors will be appointed, one in 1959 and the other in 1964*

2. Yearly on the 1st July, the Suez Canal Company will pay the Egyptian Government an allowance amounting to seven per cent of the gross profits of the preceding financial year, with a guaranteed minimum of £E350,000. This allowance, however, shall not exceed the total of the gross profit should this fall below the figure of £E350,000.

3. Exemption from Canal dues will be granted to transiting vessels of less than 300 tons gross Suez measurement without discrimination as to nationality or cargo.

4. As from 1949, the Suez Canal Company will engage its staff working in Egypt on the scale of four Egyptians for every five vacancies on the technical staff and nine Egyptians for every ten vacancies on the administrative staff.

   Further, the Company will recruit during the next few months a certain number of Egyptian officials to occupy intermediate positions of the Staff, but such appointments shall not entail the premature retirement or affect the promotion prospects of the present personnel.

5. Twenty Egyptian pilots will be granted priority of engagement to fill forthcoming vacancies subject to the candidates possessing the professional qualifications normally required of Canal pilots.

   Subsequently, one appointment in every two vacancies will be reserved for an Egyptian pilot.

6. The Company renounces its right to the remainder of the sums due to the town of Port Said in reimbursement of development carried out in the past.

* The effect of this clause was to reduce the quota of French Directors to sixteen, and of non-Government British Directors to six.

7. In Ismailia the Egyptian Government will establish a municipality which will henceforth be responsible for all development and maintenance expenses in this town.

8. The Company will hand over to the Egyptian Government the Ismailia-Port Said fresh water canal, the Government assuming responsibility for its upkeep and for providing the Canal Company's waterworks in Port Said with the water necessary for the requirements of the town and shipping generally.

9. The Company will create a basin for the fishing fleet at Port Said.

10. In order to allow the Company to cut the twelve kilometre by-pass Canal, which the increase in Canal traffic has rendered necessary and which will allow convoys to pass with speed and safety in the northern part of the Canal, the required tract of land will be conceded to the Company in exchange for double the surface of land elsewhere, not indispensable for the running of the Canal.

11. The Concession for the exploitation of the Attaka Quarries providing stone required by the Canal Company will be renewed and extended up to the end of the Company's Concession.

THE ANGLO-EGYPTIAN AGREEMENT OF 1954 REGARDING THE SUEZ CANAL BASE

The Government of the United Kingdom of Great Britain and Northern Ireland and the Government of the Republic of Egypt, desiring to establish Anglo-Egyptian relations on a new basis of mutual understanding and firm friendship, have agreed as follows:

ARTICLE I

H.M. forces shall be completely withdrawn from Egyptian territory in accordance with the schedule set forth in Part A of Annex I* within a period of 20 months from the date of signature of the present agreement.

ARTICLE II

The Government of the United Kingdom declare that the Treaty of Alliance signed in London on August 26th, 1936, with the agreed minute, exchanged notes, convention concerning the immunities and privileges enjoyed by the British forces in Egypt and all other subsidiary agreements, is terminated.

ARTICLE III

Parts of the present Suez Canal Base, which are listed in Appendix A to Annex II**, shall be kept in efficient working order and capable of immediate use in accordance with the provisions of Article IV of the present agreement. To this end they shall be organised in accordance with the provisions of Annex II.

---

* Lays down the phases for withdrawal. 22 per cent of troops within four months from date of signature; 35 per cent within eight months; 54 per cent within twelve months; 75 per cent within sixteen months; and 100 per cent within twenty months, i.e. by June 19th, 1956.

** Installations including, among others, the base workshops, ordnance depots, vehicle depot and power station at Tel el Kebir; the base ammunition depot and power station at Abu Sultan; the engineer stores base depot, base workshops, spare parts depot, and power station at Fayid and Fanara; a number of petrol and oil installations, storage tankers and pumping stations at Agrud, Fanara, Nefisha, and Suez.

ARTICLE IV

In the event of an armed attack by an outside Power on any country which at the date of signature of the present agreement is a party to the Treaty of Joint Defence between Arab League States, signed in Cairo on April 13th, 1950, or on Turkey, Egypt shall afford to the United Kingdom such facilities as may be necessary to place the base on a war footing and to operate it effectively. These facilities shall include the use of Egyptian ports within the limits of what is strictly indispensable for the above-mentioned purposes.

ARTICLE V

In the event of the return of British forces to the Suez Canal base area in accordance with the provisions of Article IV, these forces shall withdraw immediately upon the cessation of the hostilities referred to in that Article.

ARTICLE VI

In the event of a threat of an armed attack by an outside Power on any country which at the date of signature of the present agreement is a party to the Treaty of Joint Defence between Arab League States or on Turkey, there shall be immediate consultation between Egypt and the United Kingdom.

ARTICLE VII

The Government of the Republic of Egypt shall afford over-flying, landing and servicing facilities for notified flights of aircraft under Royal Air Force control. For the clearance of any flights of such aircraft, the Government of the Republic of Egypt shall accord treatment no less favourable than that accorded to the aircraft of any other foreign country with the exception of states parties to the Treaty of Joint Defence between Arab League States. The landing and servicing facilities mentioned above shall be afforded at Egyptian airfields in the Suez Canal base area.

ARTICLE VIII

The two contracting Governments recognise that the Suez maritime canal, which is an integral part of Egypt, is a waterway economically, commercially, and strategically of international importance, and express the determination to uphold the convention guaranteeing the freedom of navigation of the canal signed at Constantinople on October 29th, 1888.

N

ARTICLE IX

(a) The United Kingdom is accorded the right to move any British equipment into or out of the base at its discretion.

(b) There shall be no increase above the level of supplies as agreed upon in Part C of Annex II*** without the consent of the Government of the Republic of Egypt.

ARTICLE X

The present agreement does not affect and shall not be interpreted as affecting in any way the rights and obligations of the parties under the Charter of the United Nations.

ARTICLE XI

The annexes and appendices to the present agreement shall be considered as an integral part of it.

ARTICLE XII

(a) The present agreement shall remain in force for the period of seven years from the date of its signature.

(b) During the last twelve months of that period the two contracting Governments shall consult together to decide on such arrangements as may be necessary upon the termination of the agreement.

(c) Unless both the contracting Governments agree upon any extension of the agreement it shall terminate seven years after the date of signature and the Government of the United Kingdom shall take away or dispose of their property then remaining in the base.

ARTICLE XIII

The present agreement shall have effect as though it had come into force on the date of signature. Instruments of ratification shall be exchanged in Cairo as soon as possible.

In witness whereof the undersigned, being duly authorised thereto, have signed the present agreement and have affixed thereto their seals.

Done at Cairo,
this nineteenth day of October, 1954,
in duplicate, in the English and Arabic
languages, both texts being equally
authentic.

*** Include 50,000 tons of ammunition, 300,000 tons of ordnance and engineering equipment, 2,000 vehicles, 30 locomotives, 100 railway wagons, 80,000 tons of air and ground fuels, 1,300,000 jerricans as petrol and water containers, etc.

SUEZ CANAL COMPANY NATIONALISATION LAW, JULY 26th, 1956*

In the Name of the Nation,
The President of the Republic,
Considering.

Firmans dated November 30th, 1854, and January 5th, 1856, relative to the concession for the working of the Suez Canal waterway and the establishment of an Egyptian limited company to operate it,

Law No. 129 of 1947, relative to monopoly of public utility enterprises,

Law No. 317 of 1952, relative to unilateral contract,

Law No. 26 of 1954, relative to private companies, joint stock companies and limited liabilities companies, and

The opinion of the State Council,

Decree as follows:

ARTICLE I

The Suez Maritime Canal Company, S.A.E. is nationalised. All money, rights and obligations of the company are transferred to the State. All organisations and committees now operating the company are dissolved.

Shareholders and holders of constituent shares shall be compensated in accordance with the value of the shares on the Paris Stock Market on the day preceding the enforcement of this law.

Payment of compensation shall take place immediately the State receives all the assets and property of the nationalised company.

ARTICLE II

The management of the Suez Canal traffic utility will be in the hands of an independent body enjoying juristic personality and attached to the Ministry of Commerce. The formation of said body

* Egypt, Ministry for Foreign Affairs, *White Paper on the Nationalisation of the Suez Maritime Canal Company* (Government Press, Cairo, 1956).

and the amount of compensation to be paid to its members shall be determined by order of the President of the Republic. The body will be invested with all the powers necessary for the proper management of the utility.

Without prejudice to the control of the Audit Department over the balance sheet, said body shall have an independent budget whose preparation shall be in accordance with commercial principles. The budget shall commence on July 1st and end on June 30th of every year. The budget and balance sheet shall be sanctioned by a decree of the President of the Republic. The first budget shall commence on the date this law comes into operation and end on June 30th, 1957.

Said board can delegate one or more of its members to execute its decisions or perform any duty assigned to him.

It is also permissible to form from among its members the technical committees to help carry out research work as well as undertake the study of major issues.

Said board shall be represented before the courts, the government and other authorities by its Chairman.

ARTICLE III

The money and property of the nationalised company in Egypt and abroad are frozen. Banks, organisations and individuals are prohibited from disposing of same in any manner except by order of board mentioned in Article II.

ARTICLE IV

Said board shall retain all the employees and workers of the nationalised company. They will continue performing their duties and none can leave his work or give it up in any manner or for any reason except with the permission of the Authority mentioned in Article III.

ARTICLE V

Any contravention of Article III is punishable with imprisonment and a fine equal to three times the value of the money in question. Every contravention of Article IV shall be punishable with imprisonment in addition to denying the person concerned any right to compensation, pension or end of service gratuity.

ARTICLE VI

This decree shall be published in the Official Gazette, and will have the force of law from the day it is published. The Minister of Commerce is empowered to issue the necessary executory orders.

This decree shall bear the seal of the State and be executed as one of its laws.

SUEZ CANAL TRAFFIC, 1869-1966
Total Transits and Tonnage

Year	Total Number of Transits	Net Suez Tonnage	Number of British Transits	Net Suez Tonnage of British Ships
1869	10	11,280		
1870	486	436,609	314	289,234
1871	765	761,467	502	546,453
1872	1,082	1,160,744	761	854,037
1873	1,173	1,367,768	813	994,131
1874	1,264	1,631,650	898	1,200,222
1875	1,494	2,009,984	1,061	1,476,775
1876	1,457	2,096,772	1,090	1,576,711
1877	1,663	2,355,448	1,303	1,839,338
1878	1,593	2,269,678	1,268	1,809,597
1879	1,477	2,263,332	1,144	1,751,390
1880	2,026	3,057,422	1,592	2,433,441
1881	2,727	4,136,780	2,251	3,429,800
1882	3,198	5,074,809	2,565	4,126,253
1883	3,307	5,775,862	2,537	4,406,088
1884	3,284	5,871,501	2,474	4,466,930
1885	3,624	6,335,753	2,734	4,864,049
1886	3,100	5,767,656	2,331	4,436,688
1887	3,137	5,903,024	2,330	4,516,773
1888	3,440	6,640,834	2,625	5,223,255
1889	3,425	6,783,187	2,611	5,352,886
1890	3,389	6,890,094	2,522	5,331,095
1891	4,207	8,698,777	3,217	6,837,665
1892	3,559	7,712,029	2,581	5,826,862
1893	3,341	7,659,060	2,405	5,752,934
1894	3,352	8,039,173	2,386	5,996,796
1895	3,434	8,448,383	2,318	6,062,587
1896	3,409	8,560,284	2,162	5,817,769
1897	2,986	7,899,374	1,905	5,319,136
1898	3,503	9,238,603	2,295	6,297,743
1899	3,607	9,895,630	2,310	6,586,311
1900	3,441	9,738,152	1,935	5,605,421
1901	3,699	10,823,840	2,075	6,252,819
1902	3,708	11,248,413	2,165	6,772,911
1903	3,761	11,907,288	2,278	7,403,553
1904	4,237	13,401,835	2,679	8,833,929
1905	4,116	13,134,105	2,484	8,356,940
1906	3,975	13,445,504	2,333	8,299,931
1907	4,267	14,728,434	2,651	9,495,868
1908	3,795	13,633,283	2,233	8,302,802
1909	4,239	15,407,527	2,561	9,592,387
1910	4,533	16,581,898	2,778	10,423,610
1911	4,969	18,324,794	3,089	11,715,947
1912	5,373	20,275,120	3,335	12,847,621
1913	5,085	20,033,884	2,951	12,052,484
1914	4,802	19,409,495	3,078	12,910,278
1915	3,708	15,266,155	2,736	11,656,038
1916	3,110	12,325,347	2,388	9,788,190
1917	2,353	8,368,918	1,647	6,164,201

Year	Total Number of Transits	Net Suez Tonnage	Number of British Transits	Net Suez Tonnage of British Ships
1918	2,522	9,251,601	1,862	7,356,371
1919	3,986	16,013,802	2,679	11,355,067
1920	4,009	17,574,657	2,359	10,838,842
1921	3,975	18,118,999	2,418	11,397,019
1922	4,345	20,743,245	2,736	13,382,710
1923	4,621	22,730,162	2,839	14,264,214
1924	5,122	25,109,882	2,973	14,994,681
1925	5,337	26,761,935	3,099	16,016,439
1926	4,980	26,060,377	2,744	14,968,938
1927	5,545	28,962,048	3,085	16,534,445
1928	6,084	31,905,902	3,393	18,124,074
1929	6,274	33,466,014	3,517	18,114,282
1930	5,761	31,668,759	3,125	17,600,483
1931	5,366	30,027,966	2,976	16,624,352
1932	5,032	28,340,290	2,787	15,721,294
1933	5,423	30,676,672	2,974	16,733,484
1934	5,663	31,750,802	3,071	17,238,128
1935	5,992	32,810,968	2,775	15,734,818
1936	5,877	32,378,883	2,690	15,052,138
1937	6,635	36,491,332	3,073	17,254,182
1938	6,171	34,418,187	3,028	17,357,743
1939	5,277	29,573,394	2,627	15,208,712
1940	2,589	13,535,712	1,354*	7,449,913*
1941	1,804	8,262,841	1,173*	5,632,544*
1942	1,646	7,027,763	1,057*	4,578,441*
1943	2,262	11,273,802	1,350*	6,711,511*
1944	3,320	18,124,952	1,830*	10,344,856*
1945	4,206	25,064,966	2,686*	15,149,927*
1946	5,057	32,731,631	3,087	20,485,786
1947	5,972	36,576,581	2,813	17,276,262
1948	8,686	55,081,056	3,394	20,726,246
1949	10,420	68,861,548	3,952	24,883,987
1950	11,751	81,795,523	4,098	26,557,386
1951	11,694	80,356,338	4,091	26,900,063
1952	11,694	26,643,186	4,212	86,137,037
1953	12,731	92,905,439	4,446	31,262,257
1954	13,215	102,493,851	4,493	32,909,191
1955	14,666	115,756,398	4,358	32,789,874
1956**	13,291	107,006,000	3,586	27,104,000
1957***	10,958	89,911,000	2,279	18,342,000
1958	17,842	154,479,000	3,993	33,010,000
1959	17,731	163,386,000	3,955	35,352,000
1960	18,734	185,322,000	4,087	39,710,000
1961	18,148	187,059,000	4,005	41,059,000
1962	18,518	197,837,000	4,072	42,870,000
1963	19,146	210,498,000	3,965	44,009,000
1964	19,943	227,991,000	3,808	44,490,000
1965	20,289	246,817,000	3,524	41,494,000
1966	21,250	274,250,000	3,601	45,580,000

** Figures of net tonnages from 1956 onwards provided only to nearest thousand tons.
*** No traffic during first quarter.

SUEZ CANAL TRAFFI[

Year	British	French	Dutch	Italian	Austro-Hungarian
1870	289,234	84,657	313	5,795	19,382
1875	2,181,387	226,446	130,740	79,783	92,079
1880	3,446,431	271,598	174,485	104,567	103,030
	British	French	German	Dutch	Italian
1885	4,864,049	573,646	198,842	252,145	159,463
1890	5,331,095	365,904	490,587	248,512	143,721
1895	6,062,587	672,899	693,645	365,771	146,161
	British	German	French	Dutch	Austro-Hungarian
1900	5,605,421	1,466,392	751,759	506,976	341,327
1905	8,356,940	2,113,484	844,372	577,731	458,402
1910	10,423,610	2,563,749	833,099	854,561	642,826
1913	12,052,484	3,352,287	927,787	1,287,354	845,830
	British	Dutch	German	French	Italian
1920	10,838,842	1,425,808	14,777	774,784	605,564
1925	16,016,439	2,699,365	1,791,228	1,628,215	1,416,386
1930	17,600,483	3,312,531	3,388,842	2,001,837	1,502,559
	British	Italian	German	Dutch	French
1935	15,734,818	6,077,376	2,692,792	2,316,430	1,774,295
1936	15,052,138	6,544,745	2,883,072	2,255,105	1,650,168
1937	17,254,182	5,866,087	3,313,220	2,800,144	1,819,783
1938	17,357,743	4,625,818	3,134,597	3,028,324	1,747,825
	British	U.S.A.	Norwegian	Dutch	Panamanian
1946	20,485,786	5,944,126	1,716,618	1,984,210	161,661
1947	17,276,262	7,302,241	2,666,377	2,386,726	1,599,468
1948	20,238,844	8,302,295	5,143,861	3,196,556	5,153,166
	British	Norwegian	U.S.A.	Panamanian	French
1950	26,557,386	11,530,812	8,315,723	7,905,581	6,326,251
	British	U.S.A.	Panama	Netherlands	Denmark
1951	26,900,063	7,909,222	6,412,054	3,763,983	2,378,464
	British	French	U.S.A.	Netherlands	Swedish
1952	26,643,186	7,737,864	6,257,613	3,901,799	2,608,068
	British	Norwegian	French	Panamanian	Liberian
1953	31,262,257	13,926,235	8,425,534	7,943,845	5,016,656
	British	Norwegian	Liberian	French	Panamanian
1954	32,909,191	14,305,032	9,570,472	9,418,814	7,538,944

NST—Net Suez Tonnage.

ONNAGE BY FLAG

Spanish	German	Russian	Egpytian	Other Flags	Total
732	—	480	22,053	13,963	436,609 NRT
43,963	45,880	24,524	34,200	81,706	2,940,709 GRT
84,517	52,551	45,900	13,956	47,485	4,344,520 GRT
Austro-Hungarian 120,081	Spanish 59,988	Norwegian 38,497	Russian 47,364	22,678	6,335,753 NST
118,047	70,173	57,416	35,073	29,566	6,890,094 NST
166,427	95,623	108,686	87,101	49,483	8,448,383 NST
Russian 307,173	Japanese 245,679	Italian 158,565	Norwegian 68,187	286,673	9,738,152 NST
177,056	—	189,565	116,328	300,227	13,134,105 NST
288,165	350,937	218,322	46,109	360,520	16,581,898 NST
340,595	343,732	290,576	93,313	499,926	20,033,884 GRT
Japanese 1,601,468	U.S.A. 723,716	Norwegian 172,127	Danish 230,031	1,187,540	17,574,657 NST
1,066,941	811,803	371,630	359,918	600,010	26,761,935 NST
938,700	670,391	965,827	431,965	855,824	31,668,759 NST
Norwegian 1,389,362	Japanese 823,412	Greek 444,272	Danish 429,806	1,128,405	32,810,968 NST
1,275,003	834,747	593,929	421,970	868,006	32,378,883 NST
1,657,437	966,503	881,493	668,682	1,263,801	36,491,332 NST
1,484,312	674,746	789,741	488,300	1,086,781	34,418,187 NST
French 886,597	Italian 311,474	Swedish 410,461	Danish 280,968	549,730	32,731,631 NST
1,429,333	1,416,784	572,351	598,894	1,328,145	36,576,581 NST
2,464,455	4,040,950	1,335,344	973,224	3,232,171	55,080,866 NST
Italian 5,352,401	Dutch 4,507,422	Liberian 2,569,159	Swedish 2,156,710	6,581,028	81,795,523 NST
Norway 11,367,373	France 6,592,418	Italy 4,891,579	Liberia 2,567,605	Other Flags 7,573,577	Total 80,356,338 NST
Norway 13,547,914	Panama 6,804,377	Italy 4,654,807	Liberia 3,051,540	8,929,869	86,137,037 NST
Italian 4,991,152	Dutch 4,230,149	U.S.A. 4,123,498	Swedish 3,169,113	9,817,000	92,905,439 NST
Italian 6,912,440	Dutch 4,551,493	Swedish 3,557,403	U.S.A. 3,102,927	10,627,135	102,493,851 NST

SUEZ CANAL TRAFFIC

1955	British 32,789,874	Norwegian 15,594,949	Liberian 14,030,172	French 10,826,255	Italian 9,220,244
1956*	British 27,104,000	Norwegian 16,747,000	Liberian 12,918,000	French 10,017,000	Italian 7,496,000
1957**	British 18,342,000	Norwegian 14,153,000	Liberian 13,887,000	Italian 7,963,000	French 6,535,000
1958	British 33,010,000	Norwegian 24,479,000	Liberian 23,369,000	French 15,335,000	Italian 12,801,000
1959	British 35,352,000	Liberian 25,102,000	Norwegian 22,466,000	French 15,463,000	Italian 12,435,000
1960	British 39,710,000	Liberian 29,284,000	Norwegian 23,909,000	French 16,325,000	Italian 13,075,000
1961	British 41,059,000	Liberian 27,161,000	Norwegian 23,890,000	French 15,624,000	Italian 11,893,000
1962	British 42,870,000	Liberian 27,082,000	Norwegian 24,632,000	French 15,798,000	Italian 13,567,000
1963	British 44,009,000	Liberian 30,645,000	Norwegian 27,310,000	French 14,837,000	Italian 14,429,000
1964	British 44,490,000	Liberian 37,482,000	Norwegian 29,755,000	Italian 19,202,000	French 15,809,000
1965	Liberian 44,390,000	British 41,494,000	Norwegian 37,450,000	French 16,082,000	Italian 14,358,000
1966	Liberian 56,455,000	British 45,580,000	Norwegian 43,840,000	French 16,517,000	Italian 15,231,000

* Figures of net tonnages from 1956 onwards provided only to nearest thousand tons.
** No traffic during first quarter.

TONNAGE BY FLAG

				Other Flags	Total
Panamanian 8,074,498	Dutch 4,774,138	Swedish 3,822,236	U.S.A. 3,134,238	13,489,794	115,756,398 NST
Panamanian 6,897,000	Dutch 5,260,000	Swedish 3,288,000	U.S.A. 2,947,000	14,332,000	107,006,000 NST
Panamanian 5,084,000	Dutch 4,479,000	German 3,290,000	Swedish 2,922,000	13,256,000	89,911,000 NST
Panamanian 6,553,000	Dutch 6,408,000	Swedish 5,658,000	Danish 5,410,000	21,456,000	154,479,000 NST
Panamanian 6,844,000	Dutch 6,812,000	Swedish 6,645,000	German 6,172,000	26,075,000	163,386,000 NST
Dutch 7,984,000	German 7,754,000	Swedish 7,697,000	Greek 7,032,000	32,552,000	185,322,000 NST
Greek 9,637,000	Dutch 9,404,000	German 7,323,000	Swedish 7,266,000	33,802,000	187,059,000 NST
Dutch 10,823,000	Greek 10,478,000	German 8,035,000	Swedish 7,696,000	27,967,000	197,837,000 NST
Dutch 11,534,000	Greek 11,238,000	German 8,286,000	Swedish 7,582,000	40,428,000	210,498,000 NST
Greek 12,727,000	Dutch 11,407,000	German 8,389,000	U.S.A. 7,573,000	41,077,000	227,911,000 NST
Greek 12,673,000	Dutch 9,685,000	Russian 8,619,000	German 8,136,000	49,920,000	246,817,000 NST
Greek 12,554,000	Russian 10,156,000	Dutch 9,106,000	Swedish 8,196,000	56,615,000	274,250,000 NST

INDEX

A

Abbas Pasha, 19f., 22.
Abyssinia, 6, 55, 57, 88ff., 93, 108.
Adowa, 55, 58.
Ahmed Fuad II, 136.
Akaba, 169.
Al Fatah, 168.
Al-Mansour, Aben-Jafar, 5.
Albania, 91, 93f.
Alexander, General, 109.
Alexandria, 4, 6, 11, 15, 17, 20ff., 29f., 49f., 66, 94, 101, 117, 120f.
Algeria, 157.
Ali, El-Eudj, 6.
Ali, Mohammed, Pasha, 13f., 16ff., 20f.
Ali, Rashid, 107.
Amiens, Peace of 12.
Amru, 4f.
Anglo-Egyptian Agreements on Sudan 139, 163.
Anglo-Egyptian Agreements on Suez Canal base, 198-200.
Anglo-Egyptian Condominium (Sudan), 59, 76, 116ff., 140f.
Anglo-Egyptian Treaty, 77f., 81, 115ff., 120, 123, 126, 128, 130, 190-5.
Anglo-Iranian Oil Company, 130.
Anglo-Italian Agreement, 96.
Arab League, 141, 143-4, 163.
Arabi, Ahmed, 49ff.
Arsinoë, 4.
Aswan High Dam, 145, 147-8, 152, 164, 166, 171.

B

Bagdadbahn (see Berlin-Baghdad Railway).
Balbo, Italo, 79, 82.
Baldwin, George, 8.
Balfour Declaration, 72, 115.
Ballah, Lake, 41.
Bandung Conference, 144.
Baring, Major, 49.
Barrot, 18f.
Benghazi, 58, 80, 108.
Ben-Gurion, David 158.
Berkeley, Henry, 31.

Berlin-Baghdad Railway, 62f.
Bevin, Ernest, 115, 118f., 126f.
Bismarck, 55.
Bitter Lakes, 3, 41, 71, 105, 126, 128, 162, 170.
Britain, Interest in the India route, 9, 14f., 63.
  Invasion and salvage, 154-63.
  Purchase of Suez Canal Shares, 47ff., 78.
  Recognition of Nasser, 140.
  Withdrawal of troops, 136, 141-2, 146.
Burns, General, 144.

C

Cairo, 4, 6, 14f., 18, 20, 23, 94, 115f., 117, 120f., 135.
Canada, 151.
Canal of the Prince of the Faithful, 5.
Canal of the Pharaohs, 3f., 6, 11, 41.
Canal Zone, 77, 79, 101, 108, 111, 115f., 120f., 133, 135, 137, 139-40.
  Invasion of, 149, 155-160, 161-2, 168-9.
Capper, James, 9.
Ceylon, 151, 161.
Chamberlain, Neville, 96.
Charles-Roux, François, 141.
Chesney, F. R., 16.
China, 144, 147.
Churchill, Winston S., 106, 109, 111, 133, 144.
Ciano, Count, 96.
Clarendon, Earl of, 27, 44.
Clemenceau, 49.
Clysma, 3, 128.
Cobden, Richard, 24, 30.
Columbus, Christopher, 5, 43.
Communism, 144-5.
Compagnie Universelle du Canal Maritime de Suez (see Suez Canal Company).
Constantine I, 4.
Crete, Invasion of, 107.
Crispi, Francesco, 56, 58.
Cyprus, 141.
Cyrenaica, 55, 59f., 79f., 107, 109.
Czechoslovakia, 145-6.

211

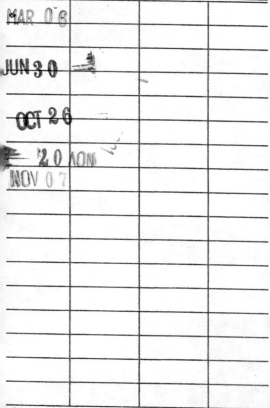